D1736951

To Roger –

Sailor on Ice: Tom Crean

With Scott in the Antarctic

thirteen years may not be enough, but you never know what may turn up.

David Hirzel

[signature] 9 7 15

for Alice Cochran, the light of my life
without whose constant and energetic encouragement
this book might never have come to print

First Edition 2011

Terra Nova Press, P. O. Box 1808, Pacifica CA 94044

650-757-6604

Printed in the United States of America

The Author may be contacted at info@terra-nova-press.com

Back cover photo: Author David Hirzel at the wheel of Crean's first Antarctic ship *Discovery*

Sailor on Ice: Tom Crean
With Scott's Last Antarctic Expedition

Table of Contents

Introduction 7

Prologue 15

Chapter One: Another Departure. 19

Map One: Track of the Terra Nova 20

Chapter Two: The Gale 51

Chapter Three: Landing at Cape Evans 73

Map Two: Ross Island 74

Chapter Four: Trial on the Sea Ice 89

Chapter Five: Roughing It — Life at Hut Point. . .111

Chapter Six: Winter Quarters at Cape Evans . . .129

Chapter Seven: The South Polar Trail. 153

Map Three: Route of the Last Supporting Party. . . .154

Chapter Eight: The Glacier 175

Chapter Nine: The Long Walk Home. 197

Chapter Ten: Another Winter 227

Chapter Eleven: The Search 245

Appendix One: Crew List 265

Appendix Two: Glossary 267

Appendix Three: Bibliography. 273

Author's note regarding the use of quotations in this book:

Every effort has been made to tell Tom Crean's story truthfully, but the present book is not to be taken for a work of *biography*. Spoken or written quotations attributed to individuals that can be sourced to published or unpublished accounts noted in the bibliography are shown in *"Italics between quotation marks."*

In the interest of a more immediate narrative, some spoken words are attributed to individuals that are entirely imagined, derived from the author's understanding of the men and the context involved. Spoken words that can *not* be sourced to published or unpublished accounts are shown in *--Italics between dashes--*.

This book does not attempt to tell Crean's story for him. Only he could do that, and it is well understood that he never talked much about his Antarctic adventures, certainly not to journalists. *Sailor on Ice* does, however, relish the language and diction of spoken English current in the early years of the twentieth century. The author hopes his words have captured some of the flavor of that bygone era where *science, duty,* and *honor* were the driving forces in an explorer's life.

Introduction

Some men are born for the sea. They run away to it early in life, and it shapes their adolescence and young manhood, their view of themselves and the world, and everything that follows. Tom Crean was such a man.

A sailor's world is defined by the boundaries set by the rail of his ship. Beyond that rail, at an indeterminate distance, he sees but cannot reach the endless circle of the horizon dividing the blue water below from the blue sky above. It appears the same wherever in the world his ship may be, afloat on the heaving swells of any one of the seven seas. The sky and water may not always be blue. They may be gray, white with driving foam and fog, obscured by night, defined by stars, the water calm and flat as a mirror glass or risen in waves beaten by ceaseless gales. It is always so--changeless and ever changing, the same and never the same.

This is in part the allure of the sea, this placement of man against nature--defined by nature, overwhelmed by nature. If he comes home to tell the tale, he finds himself in some small measure triumphant against forces far greater than his limited power.

The call of the ice is not so different from the call of the sea. The horizon is much the same, the sky above as blue while the ice below has taken the place of water as far as the eye can see. The ice can assume many colors other than the expected white; descriptions of it are full of words like azure, lemon, topaz, aquamarine. But its apparent end is still a horizon always out of reach, its undulations and sudden motions as treacherous as a rogue wave to the unwary traveler. Some men are born with a love of this.

The sound of brash ice scraping along the side of the ship with a sound like broken glass shaken in a box is a lullaby to their ears, a familiar song they know long before the first time the hear it. The ever present knowledge that their ship might be gored by a floe and sink without a trace only serves to heighten their desire. When he said *"What the ice gets, the ice keeps,"* Shackleton was referring to more than just the doomed *Endurance* splintering under the irresistible pressure of sea-ice in motion.

Sir Ernest Shackleton had known the siren call of the unbroken plain of the Barrier ice, of the slow-motion rapids of the glacier, the bleak white desert of the plateau, the coldest place on earth. A host of other explorers had also followed the call of the ice and come home with tales of wonder and suffering, as though the two experiences were somehow unalterably linked.

Tom Crean heard it too. He had chosen the path of the sea as a lad, and when a chance opportunity arose to follow it a little farther south, on a whim he took it. That decision changed his life forever. He was later seduced by the ice, as many before him had been, and many yet to come. One voyage to the Antarctic was not enough. A second ended in tragedy and the loss of two of his best and dearest friends, but even that was not enough to keep him away. The third finally released him, not through tragedy, but through triumph enough against all odds to last him till his final breath.

It may have been less a sense of triumph than a flood of weariness with the whole dance of it, the final resolution in his bones that whatever it was he sought there in the ice of the south, he had without quite knowing it got his fill. Other voices called him now--back to the place of his birth, to a new life with a wife and children and the quiet days of a sailor home from the sea, once and for all.

Tom Crean was a man whose life as an explorer shows, by his actions, what the finest measure of a man can be. If he knew fear, he never showed it; if he grew weary on the trail, it never slowed his step. If there was a difficult job to be done, he took it on. His story is told in the early years of the twentieth century before the age of radio communication and motor transport, when poorly understood concepts of survival doomed travelers in the bitterly cold and desolate landscape of the Antarctic to malnutrition, scurvy, and the very real possibility of death by exposure. In Edwardian Britain, many men were called by the strange lure of this forbidding life, by a romantic notion of heroism through suffering and the ultimate reward attached to the quixotic goal of being first to set foot at the earth's South Pole.

Crean joined the Royal Navy in 1893 at the age of fifteen, as a Boy 2nd Class. For a young man of his background and station, scion of Ireland's rocky Atlantic coast, it was the best opportunity that had yet appeared to make something of his life. The storm-tossed seas he'd chosen swept away the ties that might have bound him to the land or kept him a fisherman along the stony cliffs of the Dingle. He'd yielded to a different calling, one of the few open to an Irish lad of otherwise dim prospects. His stock was not invested in the land or the meager rewards of the fishing-life, but in the wide blue sea he'd come to live on, the gray-blue sea he'd chosen, the restless changeful sward of the sea he'd come to plough.

He was a sailor in the Queen's Navy in late 1901, a seaman on board a gunboat in the Pacific Squadron, when an opportunity arose to try something a little different. The sailing ship *Discovery* was in New Zealand, looking for a few good men. She was going south on the largest, most thoroughly equipped polar expedition that had ever been mounted. Crean volunteered, was accepted, and changed his life forever. The Navy gave him a job, the ship gave him a sailor's true home on the sea, but the ice gave him a destiny.

He was a man who was quick to volunteer for almost anything. When the very first party ventured over the Great Ice Barrier for an overnight and a record for "farthest South", he was in it. Whenever a hand was needed to row ashore or unload a ship or set out on the first push into the wilderness of ice, he was there. At the end of his two years' service with the *Discovery*, he'd so impressed his commanding officer that Captain Robert F. Scott kept him close for years as his personal aide, his "Captain's Coxswain." In this position he was already chosen in 1910 to go south again with Scott in the *Terra Nova* to complete the unfinished work of the *Discovery* expedition.

Crean distinguished himself, not by leadership, but by steadfast endurance in the face of the most impossible trials that would have drained away the strength and broken the spirit of a lesser man. When he and his shipmates find themselves adrift on broken ice and floating out to sea, it is Crean who leaps from floe to floe, ignoring killer whales and certain death, to find help to save them all. He is the man who, after a journey of 1,300 miles on foot, finds the strength to march the last thirty-five--alone, without stopping, to get the help that saves his companions. When Ernest

Shackleton bought the sailing ship *Endurance* and determined to make his Antarctic crossing in 1914, he knew Crean would be indispensable. He was right. Crean proved himself the man to pull through against the most unbearable odds. Here again he was one of three, upon whom the survival of all would depend.

Tom Crean was not the most famous or the most renowned of the explorers during the so-called "heroic era" of Antarctic exploration. For that, the palms go to Shackleton, Amundsen, and Scott, with the names of other leaders not far behind. Other men, better educated and connected, would write the stories of these expeditions in the stately measured diction of the era. Crean's name is occasionally mentioned in these works, as it should be; his was a distinguished career of service, not as a leader, but as a seaman. His story is not one of trial and privation leading to a tragic end, because without one man's endurance and unflinching resolve in the face of hopeless adversity, there would be no survivors. There would be no story.

When the *Discovery* expedition left for the Antarctic in 1901, nearly everything known about the place had been derived from James Clark Ross's voyages in 1840-1842 seeking the magnetic pole that was known to exist somewhere in the far south. Nothing was known of the Antarctic save that it was girdled with impenetrable ice that would crush any wooden ship that came within its grip. Ross had led the expedition from his ship *Erebus*; Francis Crozier, his Irish second-in-command, was captain of the *Terror*. With nothing more than sail-power fearless determination and the seamanship of their true British tars, the two ships pushed right into the frozen pack that barred the way south.

Some of the sailors on that voyage might have had tattooed on the backs of their fingers the letters H O L D   F A S T. This common admonition was directed as much to the Almighty who directed the course of all events as to the sailor aloft whose hands--one for the ship and one for himself--must never relinquish their hold, whatever trial might test his grip. It spoke also of a tradition of that quality of Royal Navy seamen which so impressed Nelson's Spanish opponents at Cape St. Vincent. Each man knows his comrades will be driven by the same principles, the sacred law of mutual support, and knows with absolute certainty that in no matter how fearful the crisis of the moment, he will not be deserted.

Sailing south into the midnight sun, Ross's two ships discovered and explored an ironbound unknown coast. Calling it Victoria Land after their queen, they applied names to its salient points as they went along: Cape Adare, Mount Sabine, Coulman Island, Cape Washington. Watching their magnetic instruments with the greatest of care, they located the elusive South Magnetic Pole in the highlands beyond. Cruising south, they found a smoking volcano and named it *Erebus*. No one could say what lay ahead, none could know whether any ships would ever return once locked in the icy grip. Still, no one doubted for one second that if any ship on earth could unlock these last secrets of the earth, it would be an English ship.

The view of this strange new world unfolding before them revealed an extravagantly compelling beauty that not for the first time would challenge the capacities of the English language.

". . .the sun never setting, among huge bergs, the water and sky, as blue or rather more intensely blue than I have ever seen in the tropics, and all the coast one mass of beautiful peaks of snow, and when the sun gets low they reflect the most brilliant tints of gold and yellow and scarlet; it is a

sight far exceeding anything I could imagine and which is very much heightened by the idea that we have penetrated far farther than was once thought practicable, and there is a sort of awe that steals over us all in considering our total insignificance and helplessness."

There is something about this newness, this isolation and desolation, this hardship bending only to the most determined ambition, which infects some men's souls and calls them back again and again. The work gives an inexpressible meaning to their lives, a bond with those who have shared the hardships, a story to tell to those who can only imagine. Its subtle grasp takes hold and many a man once in its grip is so seduced as to give all his livelihood over to it, to find in it his life's work. So it was with Tom Crean.

He went south on a whim, a chance opportunity to visit some part of the world that most men never get to see, to satisfy this yearning that calls some men away from the land, sure and known, to the sea. He knew no more than that he would find there something new, something to tell the folks at home. That whim, that chance, would change his life forever. He would spend the next sixteen years in the Antarctic, or heavily involved in planning a return there, or hanging on by the merest thread to his chances to escape it.

More than once he would find himself one of three, and then the only one, upon whose determination in the face of the most appallingly insurmountable obstacles, the fate of his companions would ultimately rest. He was a man who, as long as he had strength to place one foot before the other and ground to put it on, never stopped moving. Never. Without that singular endurance, he and all of those whose very survival bore upon that abiding perseverance would have all succumbed to the bitter snows and breathed no more.

Some men are lured deeper and deeper into the white desert, past the limits of their endurance. Others make it out alive, but barely. Many times, they return--again, again. Some of the names are familiar: Franklin, Ross, Scott, Shackleton, Amundsen. Others are not: Frank Wild, Ernest Joyce, Taff Evans, Bill Lashly, Tom Crean.

The familiar names belong to those who claimed to lead, but those who lead are nothing without those who come a few steps behind, hauling the gear, pitching the camp, walking the long walk. Steadfast, enduring. Without them, there would be no leaders. There would be no survivors, and no story to be told.

Prologue

The Great Ice Barrier.   *February 18, 1911*

Although it was risky for Crean to set out alone on this last thirty miles, his odds were better than the certain death that would come to the three men had they all remained in camp.   Two companions waited in the tent pitched on the Barrier ice fifteen miles back.   They had walked with Crean the whole long way almost to the South Pole and back until, bereft of strength after three months on the trail, they had reached the limit of their common endurance.   Barely a crumb of food remained for them, and only the merest glimmer of oil for the lamp.   Of the three, one was almost dead from scurvy, unable to walk another inch.   Left alone in the tent, he would surely, and quickly, die.   The other two were almost equal in the last remnants of their waning strength.   Together they might have made it in, but neither would agree to leave the third behind to die alone.

The Hut was only thirty miles farther on.   Someone might be waiting there, ready with the dog teams to come out to meet them, to help them in.   Just as likely, the Hut might be empty.   At last report the Polar parties had been going strong, and would need no help to make it home under their own steam.

The reports were wrong.   Out on the Barrier, the Last Supporting

Party in their diminishing marches knew the truth of the matter—the whole long walk, thirteen hundred miles of it to the Pole and back, was more than any man could bear.

Now, of the three, one man must go forward to get what help there may be, or die trying. For Crean and Lashly, it had mattered little who drew the short straw and who the long—who died on the trail and who in the tent with Lieutenant Evans. Thirty more miles to the hut required more strength than either of them could muster. One man would go forward, thirty miles over the windswept icy plain, and bring back aid or die in the attempt.

Crean drew the short straw. He made his farewells—they might well have been his last—to Bill Lashly the stouthearted stoker and Lieutenant Evans, too sick to come to the tent's door to wave good-bye. Two sticks of chocolate and two biscuits in his pocket, that was all he took. Whether or not it was enough he would find out, but it mattered little. There was not another ounce of food to be taken for the journey. Nothing to shelter himself from the blizzard but his windproofs and jacket, the jumper next to his skin and his scapular's two strips of stained and faded linen hung like sails before and aft his neck to steady his course. The priest said long as he wore this, his brown scapular, he need not fear death. Not that he ever had.

He stopped, as he supposed, at the halfway point. Fifteen miles on, fifteen more to go. The chocolate in his outer pocket was frozen hard as a brick, broke up like sand in his parched mouth. It was the last food in his pocket, the last thing he might ever eat. He sat down on the snow to rest his legs.

Funny the thoughts that enter unbidden into a man's head, like the

words of a trollop shouted in passing. *--Come love, let's lie down awhile.--*
--No, I don't believe I will. I've business to attend to.--   *--Come, lie down. No one would know.--*   --I won't.--   *--It would be easy. I've a warm place for you.--*

It *would* be easy for him to throw it all over, to lie down and rest. It's been a long time now, since he let himself feel the comfort of a downy bed, since dreams of any kind but hunger's nightmares had softened a night's passing. But *easy* has no place here, it makes no sense, has no allure. He stood, looked back at the long straight line of his shadowed footsteps leading back to the tent, and forward at the empty snow-covered plain ahead. The well marked road on the level ice ahead had at its end the *Discovery* Hut and in it the promise of survival, almost within reach.

If he weakened and fell short on this final stretch, if he stopped to rest a moment and fell asleep, if a blizzard closed over him and blotted out the light one final fatal time, then so be it. Who was he to challenge God's will? But it was Crean's will now, and it was one foot in front of the other with only another fifteen miles left to go. What were they to the thirteen hundred out-and-back that lay behind?

No one walked beside him, but he was not alone. Two companions waited in the tent pitched on the Barrier ice fifteen miles back.

Chapter One

Another Departure

London. May 1910

" 'Ware open hatchways!"

Tom Crean had his hands full squiring lower-tier dignitaries about the ship, all of them sweating freely in their black tweed suits. King Edward VII had just died, and no one who was anyone would be seen abroad clad in anything but mourning dress, no matter how hot the sun, how stifling the late May air of the waterfront. Crean, mindful of the impressions to be left upon his charges, led them politely around the cluttered decks of the polar expedition ship *Terra Nova* loading for departure.

By sheer coincidence his two stout wooden ice-ships lay within shouting distance of each other in East London's Victoria Dock. His first, *Discovery*, was looking a little weather-worn ten years on. Although that ship had left the Antarctic-exploration business, she was still pursuing her icy destiny, now loading a season's supplies for the fur trade in northern Canada. Crean's own present billet was aboard the venerable Dundee whaling barque *Terra Nova* now abustle with the urgent comings and goings of agents, stevedores, dignitaries, the press, well-meaning individuals whose presence only added to the confusion.

Ever since he'd signed on with Captain Scott, his daily routine had

Approximate Track of the *Terra Nova* across the
Southern Hemisphere 1910

been one of unending toil. He didn't mind it much. Any sailor can get bored with the excess of time the Royal Navy seems to want to give each man for every little chore. Scott's newest expedition was a private affair, to be conducted with too little money on too tight a schedule. It was enough to drive a good man to show what he was made of, and what he hoped to gain.

Captain Robert Falcon Scott had made a name for himself in 1901 as the leader of the *Discovery*'s successful foray into the then-unknown wastes of the Antarctic continent. In his seaman's manner, so had Crean. His name had not found fame in the larger world, but he had impressed his captain enough to land a good berth in the new expedition. A wise leader knows he'll get nowhere at all without good men behind him every step of the way. Scott was lucky—he had the support of stouthearted bluejackets like Crean and Taff Evans and Bill Lashly in the *Discovery*, and he was wise enough to return their loyalty and ask them to join him now in the *Terra Nova.*

Tom Crean had been his "Captain's Coxswain" for three years. There was not much extra money in the job, but there was honor in heading the oarsmen on the captain's barge, and in serving as his personal attaché, steward, bodyguard. In all that time spent in company, bound by a sort of professional intimacy, Crean and Captain Scott had shared remarkably little in the way of conversation. They were separated by rank and class, and each man knew by birth and training his place and its limits. More to the point, they had come to know each other's strengths and faults and facility of expression so well, that there was almost no need of idle talk. The details of naval administration were neither the interest nor concern of the seaman. A discerning aide-de-camp, he knew which of his captain's words he was not intended to hear, and quite reliably failed to hear them. Seldom did a word between the two men transcend the ordinary business of the day. In some ways Crean came to know the man better than his own wife did. She would not have seen him under the duress of command or shared with him the life of the sailor, the code of the sea.

The work on board came to a standstill when the day's most distinguished visitors--the royal family--made their way up the gangway for a formal review of the proceedings. The officers stood stiffly at attention by the main hatch while the Queen consort spoke to some of the men. Crean was not given to introspection, to self-examination. A man of the earth does not indulge such luxuries. And having never really asked of himself the question, he stumbled for a moment when Queen Alexandra asked of him: *--Why are you going south?--* An Irish lad of humble birth, he was not acquainted with the proper way to address a queen, except to do so with his hat in his hand. *--Oh I don't know, Mum--* he replied. In truth, he didn't. *"I s'pose we ought to go back and finish the job we started."* The answer would do, for the Lady and for himself. Could there be more, than to finish the job he'd started?

* * * * *

The work of that first *Discovery* expedition between the years 1901 and 1904 was not yet complete. It had done much of great value in science and discovery—located and named coasts and mountain ranges, determined the elevation and nature of the high plateau of solid ice on which the South Pole must surely be located. But the Pole itself had never been reached. Shackleton himself had tried in 1907 and fallen short. Now Scott felt it was his own destiny to unlock this the last great secret of the natural world, and claim the honor of it for Britain. Scott would be the man, the *Terra Nova* his ship, and the best of the *Discovery*s his crew.

If the barque was not purpose-built for exploration as the *Discovery* had been, she was the nearest thing to it to be had on the open market. She had a stout, sturdy look about her, a trifle weather-beaten after twenty-five years in the whaling trade. At her launch in 1884 the *Terra Nova* was the biggest whaler of her day and a beauty in her own right, a working vessel with every line and spar directed toward a lean efficiency of strength and volume. She was in her heyday the latest of a longish line of Dundee-built steam whalers from Stephens' yard. As such she was built already ice-strengthened with stout oak frames closely spaced and double-sheathing below the waterline, with an iron forefoot bolted to the ice-cleaving axe of her overhanging prow. Though her engine was not the latest-design triple expansion engine, as *Discovery*'s had been, it would answer today's purpose--not with speed, but with short powerful bursts for charging the floe.

Today she sported taut rigging newly set up. Patchwork and fresh paint filled in all but the deepest of her scars. Gloss black, though hardly mourning, gleamed from her newly painted sides. A gold stripe accented the foc's'le-head and quarterdeck rails, and another ran along the waist her entire length. The funnel and deckhouses were clad in a fashionable buff, and new varnish gleamed wherever the woodwork showed. All the brightwork glistened with a high polish amid the disorder and confusion of the growing deckload.

She'd had a thorough scrubbing below decks as well. She'd needed it. These Dundee whalers didn't try out the oil at sea the way the spermers and Yankee whalers did. Instead they flensed the whales alongside, packing the raw blubber into casks for the duration of their short summer voyages in the Greenland seas, to be brought back and processed ashore for the jute trade. Raw as it was, the oozing blubber did not keep well. Over the years the fat seeped from leaking casks, saturated the wooden floors and ceilings with rancid oil until the old girl positively stank. None but a whaling man could stand her now, not before she was freshened with a thorough scrubbing and the buttery smell of new white lead paint.

Those whitewashed spaces were now being filled to bursting with the stores and gear required to sustain the most ambitious, most complete polar expedition of modern times. The demands of scientific work were greater now than they had been in the old days, the necessary instruments and their housings more numerous and sophisticated. The new scheme for transport over the ice called for dogs and ponies and newly engineered motor-tractors, and each would be wanting its own allotted space from the overburdened whaler.

Her new crew had been assembling for weeks out of the leading candidates from the naval depots at Chatham and Portsmouth, coming together at the quarterdeck on May 30 to sign their names to the articles. Crean was among old friends again. Catching up, as old friends do, on what has gone before, and looking to the future. And relishing the plots and turns of their lives that have led them, each in his own way, back to this same place—a wooden ship in a frenzy of preparation for a departure to the remotest places on earth. To the Pole. This time to bring it home.

Aye, there is glory enough in that to overwhelm the faded memories of cruel hardship on the trail when the frozen fingers burned as they thawed and the demanding hunger swept away every other sense and thought but the neverending wonder of *new land*. So here they are all gathered together again, the leaders and the led, on the baking wood deck of a wooden ship in the muggy swill of London's dockside summer.

Scott—Captain Scott—was his old agitated self, at once the genteel host of a wide array of dignitaries on board to look over his ship and men, and the ill-tempered dispenser of countermanding orders to those same men of whom he claims such pride. The men all knew it--the ones come back for more--and let the harsher of his words fly over the rail with the breeze. His other words—they were orders. A seaman in the Royal Navy understands his job: to follow orders.

Thousands had wanted to join; only a few were admitted. Once again Scott was relying on the naval men's innate sense of order and discipline to help lead them through the trying times to come. The cream of the lot, in Crean's eyes, were the old hands from *Discovery* ready for another go at the Pole. Bill Lashly from the black gang was coming, now Chief Stoker in the *Terra Nova*, and his old messmate Taff Evans. Crean and Evans were petty officers now, as high as men their age--thirty-five--were likely to get. They fell right into the old ways, taking up where they had left off as though they had never parted.

Taff was, like any Welshman, full of stories, some of them grounded in truth. He'd had an experience, an intimacy with an officer—not any officer, but Scott himself, leader of two expeditions, captain of His Majesty's most powerful capital ships. Lashly had enjoyed the same intimacy, but was far less inclined to talk about, or enlarge upon it.

In 1903 those two had been five weeks on the plateau alone with Scott, facing the bitter wind and the likely failure of the navigation that was the only means to guide the three men homeward. Five weeks in a tent together, the three of them exposed in the closest contact to each other's doubts and fears, with only the small jokes and hopes and tales of life at home to relieve those doubts. These weeks joined them into one thinking, striving machine with all eyes on the horizon and all hopes bent on a return. This experience shaped these men and helped to shape the men who heard them talking of it afterward--of how when it comes down to it, men are men and rank has almost no meaning or importance at all.

The best men are complicated beyond all understanding. They mostly heed their own rules while outwardly honoring those of their employers, and inwardly the spark of independence and self-interest burns brightly. Taff Evans was like this—tall and large, athletic and boisterous, skilled in the arts of the sea, garrulous and inclined to the drink. Such words describe many men, many seamen, and yet with this one they fall short.

Taff had gone and surrendered himself to the bonds of holy matrimony and now had a pretty young bride. He must have charmed her with his bluster and bravado, the way he had Scott on the first trip south, and let her find out later how those qualities translated when lubricated by an excess of gin. No doubt she was happy to see him off—a little adventure ought to calm the big boy down, and with any luck he'd come home with a Polar medal to garnish a promotion. As for the three little ones who call him Daddy, they'll be standing at attention on the dockside, all of them a foot taller than when he'd seen them last, to welcome home their triumphant explorer.

That was the plan he'd instilled into the receptive minds of his little family, and the goal he'd set himself. He'd won over Scott, if not quite Wilson, in the *Discovery*, and there was no doubt Taff would be one of the leading men all the way to the South Pole. Whatever might happen after that could only add more luster to the polish of his star.

Tom Crean's own aspirations were more in keeping with his quieter, simpler approach to things. The Pole--unlikely, but certainly a solid role in the taking of it. No seaman aboard besides Taff and Lashly could match him for days and miles spent on the ice, or strength in the shoulder and hip to haul the sledges wherever they were bound. The Pole--perhaps, but Hannah seemed to care for who he was at home in Kerry, not who he might become in the frozen wasteland of the Antarctic. This parting, these oceans that would now lay between them, made but a temporary separation. A friend at home would arrange everything with her father for the two of them, and a wedding on Tom's return. A handful of her letters, safe in the bottom of his sea-chest would have to keep him until that day.

Scott stayed behind in London on business and left the ship in the hands of Lt. Teddy Evans—*Mr*. Evans to Crean--to make her way down the Channel and around to Portsmouth and then Cardiff for her final departure. Until the captain rejoined the *Terra Nova* at Cape Town to run her easting down to Melbourne, Mr. Evans would be master of the ship. It was early in the game to know just what to make of him. Until the moment Scott stepped ashore, the lieutenant had never been in full command of any ship. As an officer, he was outgoing and friendly, perhaps a bit too friendly for the men, who liked their skippers to maintain a distance and a sense of rigid discipline.

The new third officer was another unknown quantity. Lt. Henry Bowers enlisted from the Royal Indian Marine, coming from Bombay by steamer to join the ship when she put in at Portsmouth. He hadn't much of a seamanlike appearance—short stumpy legs, a huge beaklike nose that quickly earned him the nickname "Birdie," a high-pitched nasal voice that didn't seem to carry orders well. In time it would become clear that he was overflowing in his enthusiasm for everything he did, but here at the dock it just seemed like he was trying to be everywhere and attending to all things at once. When he moved about it was with the impatient hopping moves of his namesake birds. Unlike them however, he could not fly and when his toe tripped over the hatch coaming while his eyes were cast upward, he fell. Not to the deck, but right through the gaping hatch, down seven feet to the orlop deck below, where he landed with a thud.

--Lieutenant Bowers!-- A handful of men on the busy deck saw him tumble in and ran to the open hatch. He lay like a broken doll on the floor below, motionless. Before any of them could scramble down the gangway to reach him, he stirred and stretched like a man waking from a deep sleep, and then sat up. He stood unsteadily and brushed the sawdust off his clothing, wagged his head back and forth as though to clear away any cloudy thoughts.

*--I'll be all right--*he said, shaking off the loose hold his shipmates had taken.

And that was Lt. Bowers, the way he would always be. Always hard at work no matter what the circumstance, plugging on where an ordinary man must stand by and gather his strength. *--I'll be all right.—*

* * * * *

Just before departure Scott called all hands aft to thank them for the work they'd just completed. By five o'clock on June 1, 1910, the *Terra Nova* was secured to the tug. The great hawsers tightened against the heavy steel bitts, creaking under the tension. She slipped her mooring and eased into the Thames. A tug had charge of the ship now, and for the first time in weeks there were no urgent details or visitors wanting immediate attention. Leaning against the high wooden rail in the waist, Crean felt in his pocket for the pipe and tobacco that were his sustenance and reward after a long job well done. The match sizzled into flame and a first welcome puff of fragrant blue smoke leapt from the glowing bowl. His new home was an old ship, the kind he liked best, with wood for rails and wood for deck and nothing but wood between man and the sea. Overhead, the heavy yards in their slings and the webbed tracery of idle rigging wove a familiar pattern against the sky, a map of the whaling barque's airy realm. The canvas was still gasketed tight in a good harbor stow, waiting, like Crean, to be filled with the clean fresh blast of a first good gale.

Alongside, the gray and gritty warehouses of London's east side parted to show the long green sward of Greenwich and the observatory on the hill. Flocks of small boats were on the river punting and sailing as the the steam launches shrilly whistled a noisy farewell. The schoolship *Worcester*, forever anchored at the bank, still had yards to be manned in a final, fitting salute to those of her graduates now on the way to the South Pole.

The sendoff from Portsmouth was another noisy affair. The *Terra Nova*, dwarfed by the enormous bulk of the dreadnoughts at anchor, passed between these latter-day ships of the line, receiving and returning the cheers of the Navy for the undoubted courage of their own about to take the Pole. Crean's old shipmates from the *Essex* and *Victorious* would be envious of him now, to see him freed of the grey gunmetal boredom of a battleship for an adventure few would ever know.

The City of Cardiff was the last scheduled stop before leaving Great Britain for good. A new officer joined the ship there, a soldier—a cavalryman at that. From his manner he seemed like a farmer, common enough to be one of the men. Crean sized him up: *"We never for a moment thought that he was a officer, they were usually so smart. We made up our minds he was a farmer, he was so nice and friendly, like one of ourselves, but oh! he was a gentleman, quite a gentleman, and always a gentleman."* Farmer he might seem to be now, but the services of Captain L. E. G. Oates, late of the Inskilling Dragoons, would be needed later on. It was his cavalry experience--along with his joining the expedition without pay--that won him the post as superintendent of the expedition horses to be boarded in New Zealand. He didn't say much at first, showing himself to be taciturn to an extreme met only by the biologist Dr. Atkinson. How any man could get along without saying ten words in as many minutes was a mystery to Crean. The two of them could have each other, and they did, forming on the spot a lasting friendship founded on a shared desire to avoid conversation at all costs.

Dr. Wilson, well-known to Crean from *Discovery* days, also joined the ship at Cardiff as Chief of Scientific Staff. Bill Wilson stood apart from all the men. Not above, nor aloof, but still apart. Though he didn't talk about it much, or preach about it at all, the strength of his faith stood him upright like a tall oak to weather every storm that sought to topple him. Dr. Wilson did not boast either. Even so a man could tell where he stood always, and had an idea of the foundation from which he would not be shaken. Lieutenant Bowers was the same, and Crean. Of all the men, these three carried on no matter how heavy the work, no matter how daunting the circumstances. They would always, without fail, pull through. Scott, Taff, Lt. Evans, Lashly—the other men all read their parts, and that was good enough. Wilson, Bowers, Crean—they lived them.

Among the many volunteers applying for a berth, those who could afford to help with the expedition's finances received special attention. Apsley Cherry-Garrard was one of them. Although only ten years separated them in age, it was hard for Crean to think of Cherry as anything other than a youth. He was smallish of build and tight-skinned about the face like one who has had little exposure to the sun or hard work, but it was the unvarnished innocence and vigor of his demeanor that carried the glow of this impression. The boy—for at first who couldn't help thinking of him as such—looked up to every one of the Antarctic veterans with unabashed respect, as though each of them carried the secret wisdom of the ages—or at least a wealth of practical knowledge born of hard experience.

To the seamen he was always Mr. Garrard. He came from wealth that might have made the seamen envious, and bought his way into the expedition with a thousand pounds—fifteen years' wages for the likes of Taff and Crean. The money didn't put him above them, though. Many of them were quite charmed by his total disregard of the nominal strictures and definitions of class and rank that would have been expected to color the perceptions of a young man of his station. And as he took all men, even the seamen of the lower deck, at face value, so he was taken in turn by each of them.

So it was that he and Crean became friends in a way that would never have happened on board any other ship than the *Terra Nova*. In another time and place, their paths might have crossed with at best a cursory introduction, and each man gone on about his business within the confines of an established social stratum. But here on board a discovery ship, each is taken for the weight he pulls.

There was another young fellow who, no matter how he tried, could not quite figure where he belonged in the circumscribed community of the expedition. Tryggve Gran was the youngest of the lot and so junior to everyone--nominally of the afterguard, but too much of a babe in years to wield any authority. He had been brought along to instruct the shore party in the art of the ski. Better educated than all the sailors, he could never find a place among them, even if he were not the only Norwegian amid this British society. This accident of birth was not his fault, but it defined him.

❋ ❋ ❋ ❋ ❋

The City of Cardiff, the expedition's final point of departure, had prepared its own gaudy sendoff. It was Taff's home port, and the whole countryside would be coming down to celebrate their own native son, already famous in his own right for the part he'd played in Scott's *Discovery* expedition. Further honors and festivities ashore awaited, a farewell banquet for the officers and men. Taff Evans, never one to shirk the limelight, had a place on the dais with the town's councilmen and the ship's officers, and when the calls of *--Speech! Speech!--* got loud enough, he answered:

"Every man in this Expedition is heart and soul in the business, and it

has got to be a success this time –every man will do his best. . . .No one else would have induced me to go there again, but if there is a man in the world who will bring this to a successful issue, Captain Scott is the man!"

He went on to drink more than was good for him, slurring and stumbling over his words. The bare electric lights hung like too-bright stars over his head, deepening the shadows of his puffy cheeks. He was always so much better a man when someone held his liquor for him. The seamen were embarrassed—a man who let himself go drunk in the spotlight just confirmed the public's worst expectations. Still, on the morning of June 15, the good people of Cardiff turned out in droves to cheer him off. His own wife Lois came with their three young children to say goodbye for the last time. Crean made them a promise—*I'll bring your man home in one piece*--wishing there were someone with a reason to do the same for him.

This sendoff for the Cape was, if anything, noisier here than any of those Crean had yet experienced. His ship was gaily decorated for the occasion, with the signal halyards aflutter with every brightly colored flag at hand. Tugs and steamers whooped madly, a noisy roar rose from the crowds on the quay at the sight of their own Red Dragon flying from the masthead. Along Bristol Channel the blufftops and beaches were packed with admiring spectators raising cheer after cheer across the water to spur the expedition on to the greater glory of the empire. It all could go to a man's head, were there not so everlastingly much work to be done.

He would be glad when his ship was clear of all this ruckus and could let loose the canvas, shut down the boilers, and run as she ought. She had to be a better sailer than the *Discovery*—it wouldn't take much.

This one at least was a whale chaser, with some notion for speed that's lacking in Scott's first old tub back then. She might be dryer, but these wooden boats, they all leak. And the men all pump. With more hands aboard, and most of them idlers, he could hope the scientific officers of the afterguard would take a turn at the cranks. They'd need to raise some blisters, just to prove they're real men. If not real sailors, then real men will have to do.

To lighten their pulling at the halyards, the new men learned the timeless work-songs of the sea. "Away Rio" was the reigning favorite for departures, with the hauling synchronized to the rhythm of the hearty chorus.

>*Oh, the anchor is* weighed *and the sails they are* set
> *A—way—*Rio!
>*The* maids *that we're leaving we'll never for*get
>*For we're* bound *for the Rio* Grande
> *And a—way—*Rio!
> *Aye—*Rio!
>*Sing fare ye* well, *my bonny young* girl,
>*And we're* bound *for the Rio* Grande.

Captain Scott was not aboard to hear his men singing, or feel the joy of the admiring crowds. There was business to attend to. After Cardiff he'd gone back to London to oversee further details of the expedition, leaving Mr. Evans in charge. A stiff breeze picked up out of the north, broad across the sweeping Irish Sea.--*Hands aloft to loose the sails!*--No further orders would be needed. The ratlines joggled to the fall of many feet; freed at last of the restraining gaskets, the canvas fell from each yard and bellied to the wind. The shores of old Cornwall slipped along the port quarter, falling faraway behind with every passing mile.

All hands cast one longing backward glance as the bare spire of Bishop Rock dipped beneath the horizon, wondering as sailors will when they should see their home again, and what adventures may befall.

Eight days out they made first landfall at Madeira. It was warm and sunny on the island, the air spiced with the perfume of lemons and oranges, the scent of onions, the odor of decay. There was enough time here for a quick game of football between the *Terra Nova*s and the men of the Telegraph Company, but after this brief stop the real voyage began in earnest. Out on the open sea the Aberdeen barque *Inverclyde* passed, a beautiful sight bowling along under a full cloud of canvas with her signal flags speaking pleasantries across a widening gulf of lonely ocean. Dolphin and bonito played about, dashing through the wave beneath the bowsprit. Flying fish landed with a slap on the baking deck and sizzled in the cook's big black frying pan shortly after. The freshwater allowance of a half-gallon a day was barely enough to replace the streams of sweat pouring from the men, and not at all enough to wash away the stink that saltwater soap left behind.

* * * * *

Lieutenant Evans was showing himself to be an interesting mix of officer and overgrown boy. The boy part of him seemed to find something to like, and nothing to criticize, about every man and circumstance around him. When the officer was in charge, one never knew what jokes and games might be afoot during the watch, frivolities that would never be allowed when the captain was on board. A man could relax, stop minding his every word and action with the precision that was expected when the Owner was on deck. He had an easy way about him and it was easy to take his orders knowing that if the job weren't done this instant, as long as it were done soon there'd be no fireworks from the bridge. That's not to say he wasn't physically tough as nails when the weather got dirty and the work got hard.

Mr. Evans reveled in whatever adversity the elements might throw his way. The harder the unalterable circumstances of wind and wave at sea, of ice and cold ashore, the happier he seemed to grow, as though through sheer willpower he could master them. He could drive himself without stopping past any obstacle that nature put in his path, and never recognize what personal cost might be entailed.

These are admirable traits in any seaman. It is to Lt. Evans' lasting credit that by example he instilled them into his afterguard during the voyage to Cape Town. He took this random selection of men from all walks of life, many of them city-bred and Oxford educated, and melded them into one cheerful, dependable, hard-working crew of explorers. His seamen needed no such handling.

Early in the morning of July 5, far at sea, a sharp-eyed seaman glimpsed a tuft of smoke coming through a split in the main hatch cover. He knew in an instant what it must be. The ship was alight! --*Fire stations!*--

Navy drill has its uses; by instinct the seamen snapped shut every porthole, skylight, door and hatchway. Never mind who was inside, or below. The extinguishers slipped readily from their brackets; an acrid cloud of chemical mist spouted forth, shot to the base of the bonfire. Good luck and better timing stopped the orange flames just short of the straw packing of the wine shipped at Madeira. One spark in that tinder and the ship would have surely gone up and doomed the expedition and everyone on board. Another ship gone missing in the Atlantic and that would have been the end of it all. Davies, the carpenter, was well and brutally scolded for his carelessness for leaving a lamp alight in the hold to be upset by the ship's roll. Only the motorman Hooper's timely discovery saved the expedition. This time.

*   *   *   *   *

With the oppressive heat of the tropics came the clear certainty that frequent turns at the pumps would become the order of the day. For whatever reason, Scott was showing himself to be the chooser of leakers. *Terra Nova* gained about a foot-and-a-half of water a day. It was not unexpected for an older wooden ship, certainly manageable, but still it meant a turn at the cranks for the afterguard each morning to clear the well to ten inches. Good—let them pump! The seamen taught them a chantey to help time and ease their hours at the cranks, then stood by to listen from the tops.

> *The sweetest flower in the valley,*
> *Aye, aye, roll an' go*
> *Is my dear girl, my pretty Sally,*
> *Spent my money on Sally Brown.*

Many of these same gentlemen were about to find themselves unwilling players in the curious initiation required of all deepwater seamen. The naval men, jack tars all, had themselves been tried and castigated by Neptune's minions on board other ships at their own first crossing of the equator. Each of them carried safe in his sea-chest the certificate of induction. The pollywogs on board, crossing the line without proof of prior passage, would be found out--tried, convicted, and subjected to the rough punishment of tradition. No one was exempt. Those with an inkling of what was about to befall would be better served to go along and consider the whole charade a bit of good-natured roughhousing designed to cement the crew together. Those who objected would find themselves the target of yet harsher treatment until, battered into seeing the point, they joined the fun.

As the ship drew near the equator, the sun's overhead passage through the long hot and nearly windless days seared the drying planks of the decks. It was too hot to run barefoot now, too hot to sleep in the hammock below. A long wake remained behind her on the heaving oily swell. On a calm July evening Evans called down--*Slow ahead!*--to the engine room. Forward on the foc'sle head a strange apparition appeared, a robed bearded figure climbing over the rail. Two sailors in blue greeted him, crowned him with a gleaming tin diadem, and turned to another, stranger figure just then climbing aboard. The four marched in solemn dignity toward the break of the poop. A well-known voice with a Kerry brogue to it called out--*You men of the barque* Terra Nova—*I give you the King!*--

Neptune had come aboard to greet his subjects. A long beard of oakum hung down to his knees; beneath it a flowing robe of sailcloth trailed onto the deck. Beside the king stood his queen Amphitrite, her bosom a pair of enamel serving bowls from the galley, her hair a flowing cascade of spunyarn. Rapping the heel of his trident on the foredeck, the king demanded the presence of those aboard who had never yet declared their obedience to him. The rest of his retinue, his Doctor and Barber, his Policemen and Bears stood by the sail-cloth bath built and filled with seawater in the night. They all, if one looked close, might be taken for various of the seamen in not-so-deep disguise.

Dressed in the makeshift uniforms of policemen, Crean and Williamson took a special delight in hauling before the bench new victims—most of them of the afterguard--to face the rough treatment of Neptune's justice. This initiation rite is a time-honored tradition of the sea, visited upon every English sailor of whatever stripe. Crean, Taff, Lt. Evans—the whole crowd—had all run this gauntlet once themselves and would damned well see to it that no new man was missed.

The sea-king's court is held on the quarterdeck. There is no escaping the trial. Each new conscript is seated upon the stool with his back to the rail and the bath six feet below. *--Have ye crossed my line before, sailor, have ye entered my realm?--* Talk is no defense here; either a man has his certificate--his proof of prior initiation--in hand, or he is about to be charged, examined, shaved, and convicted. No man is admitted to Neptune's kingdom unless he's passed as clean, sound and healthy by the doctor. It was no surprise that *all* the first-timers were found to be in need of a dose of medicine in the shape of a large pill, a ball of soap and tallow to be swallowed with a draft of vinegar laced with cayenne. Once so cured each man was stripped to a gantline and found to be in need of a shave. Alf Cheatham was the Barber, stropping an enormous wooden razor against the seat of his pants ready to scrape away the soot-and-whitewash lather and as much skin as he could find beneath it. Each new man saw what has happened to those who went before. The wiser of them took note how a struggle gets a man nothing but a stiffer sentence executed without pity or delay.

Blindfolded and subdued, his stool tipped backwards, he tumbled over into the saltwater bath. Rough hands kept his head under until the soap and tallow were rinsed from his gums and the whitewash and ashes from his cheeks. Those who protested got even harsher treatment from their mates. The Norwegian Gran fought back and carried the Doctor into the bath with him. In all no tempers were too sorely lost. Whatever wounded spirits were salved with a splice of the main brace and a sing-song on the foc's'le head under the calm blessing of a flaming gold and scarlet tropic sunset. A man could get used to this kind of seafaring, a life on the high seas shared with a band of like-minded jolly roving tars bearing the work of a noble cause as gaily as its pleasures.

*   *   *   *   *

Eastbound after a brief call at the lonely island of South Trinidad, they picked up their first long swell. The *Terra Nova* could match or better the *Discovery* for the extremes of her rolls--35 degrees each way--her yardarms nearly dipping into the sea with the passing of every wave across the beam. The first real gale of the voyage brought the first of many green seas over the rail. Lieutenant Bowers thought the ship exceptionally seaworthy and dry as a cork, as though a finer sea-boat had never sailed, but then he of all men saw the brightest side of every circumstance.

The truth was, with a following sea the poop was almost always awash. Water continually found its way through the ship's gaping deck seams to dampen the beds, if not the spirits, of the seamen below. Forty gallons of heavy Colsa oil went adrift and found its way into the bilges where it congealed with coal-dust from the bunkers into greasy balls and clogged the pumps periodically until they could be cleared by hand. Pumping now assumed for the gentlemen an arduous aspect it had not previously held. The true sailors stayed well out of sight, or otherwise employed in some seemingly important deck-work. Cold weather had set in, and the gray woolen Shetland foul-weather gear made its appearance.

The unmistakable flatiron headland of Table Mountain showed through the flying scud of alternating squalls as the *Terra Nova* rolled into the bay August 15, nearly a fortnight overdue. She snugged into her berth at the naval dockyard at Simon's Bay twenty-two miles away from Cape Town. The officers took off to spend their time socializing at the Cape, leaving Crean and the men to work with the naval fatigue parties sent aboard the ship to help fit her out for the next leg of the passage. The men at work daydreamed of picnics and celebratory dinners ashore, of the gay smiles and delightful laughter of the fair sex all during the days and days of shifting stores in the saturating rain.

Captain Scott arrived at last, having come down by steamer to join the ship and take back the role of captain. Dr. Wilson left it to escort the wives — his own Oriana, and Scott's and Mr. Evans' --to Melbourne. The seamen were in fact quietly relieved when Captain Scott took command of the ship to run her easting on down to Australia.   He planned to use the occasion to really know his men, all of them, to try them out and figure who should remain in the ship and who would winter over in the Antarctic in the shore party.   Only the best of them would figure in the run for the Pole.

Two weeks of shore life at the Cape was plenty.   The dinners and honors were enough to try the patience of any man of modest aspirations.   The adventure of polar expedition was its own reward, earned in the doing and not in the anticipation.   An explorer's life was on the breaking trail in an unknown land, a sailor's on the sea.   Once the ship set off again no time was wasted in putting that sailor's life to the test.   A Force 10 gale — "*two hoops*"--rose up out of the east, driving the old girl along like an aging racehorse with her lee rail under water.   When that wind dies and the sky clears, the big prevailing swell out of the west, the long unbroken wave that sweeps unimpeded around the globe shows its true power.

These swells might be a mile from crest to crest.   Each wave sweeping up to the ship seemed to threaten her very existence, to lift her to heights unimaginable from which she must surely be overwhelmed, swamped, and sent to the bottom.   But this was an illusion.   The crests of these waves, rounded hills smooth as glass or sometimes curling over with just a trace of creamy froth, and the gentleness of the sloping valleys between, were so mild they posed no danger and no discomfort.   She rose to each summit and slid down the backside quiet as you please, sailing onward uninterrupted until the next swell came along to lift her keel again.

Running her easting down. The phrase carries more than a hint of power, of romance, of hard efficient sailing to the remotest ports on the globe. The passage belonged to the big windships, to the last of the windjammers whose very existence was now doomed. The quest for speed under sail had reached its zenith and been surpassed. Steam power had taken over the world's commerce with short direct routes sustained and linked by coal depots and canals. But the *Terra Nova* was not engaged in commerce and there was no money to buy coal; her sails would suffice. With coal in diminishing supply and the leak in full feather, the afterguard manned the cranks and took up a hearty pumping chantey:

> *In Amsterdam there lived a maid,*
> *Mark well what I do say,*
> *In Amsterdam there lived a maid,*
> *And she was mistress of her trade,*
> *I'll go no more a-roving with you, fair maid!*
> *A-roving, a-roving, since roving's been my ru-i-in*
> *I'll go no more a-roving with you, fair maid.*

Crean and his ship had both in their separate lives been far south. The *Terra Nova* had been a companion relief ship to the *Morning* in the *Discovery* days, but neither ship nor sailor had in their careers run this easting down. Now both had rounded the

African continent like old Vasco De Gama, and cleared for distant lands.   The ship renewed her rolling—50, 55 degrees each way—in the unimpeded sea, giving rise to a saying, *"a moderate roll rings the bell and a big roll brings out the cook."*   The old whaler began to show her true colors — two hundred miles a day steaming in a gale, more like a hundred and fifty under sail alone.

The wind freshened and for the first time the faint glow of the Aurora Australis colored the night sky in the south.   With all sail set the old "Terra Push" was making nearly eight knots, a good clip for her and enough to give the lie to the soldier Oates' complaint that she had but two speeds—slow and dead slow.   As the wind continued to rise she wore her topgallants well, gathering in every breath she could, but when a squall hit the morning of October 9th, it was more than she could handle.

--Let go t'gallant yards.--   The fore dropped readily, the sail collapsed and was quickly gathered in, but the main jammed halfway down.   The canvas bellied forward in a great balloon, whipping round the yard, fouling the gear.   The heavy yard was swung crazily from side to side at a deadly tilt, every swing ending with a great boom like a cannon shot.   The ship's old timbers shook to the keelson with each blow.   A few more of these and the mast would shatter into matchwood and bring the whole tophamper crashing down onto the deck.

One man stepped forward to take control.   All that was needed was a knife to cut the sail free from the galloping yard before the real damage was done, and a stout hand to wield it. Crean would go it alone.

Permission was refused. The watch stood by at the ratlines. No man would be allowed to go aloft until the fury of the wind abated. In the end the damage amounted to no more than a strained mast and a split sail, with a new one bent on in the morning. From that morning forward she ran before the gale, making Melbourne harbor in the dark night of October 12.

There was a telegram waiting for Scott. It was from the Norwegian explorer Amundsen, announcing a change of plans. The communication was private, but it contents quickly leaked out, and in minutes word of it spread through the ship like a fire. *"Beg leave to inform you Fram proceeding Antarctic."* It looked as though Scott's designs for science and exploration were to be turned into a race. If that was to be the case, may the best man win.

There was to be no run ashore here in Australia. Although time was growing short, Admiral Poore came aboard to look things over. He took special note of the tiny hammock, two feet long, that Crean had stitched for the ship's cat, complete with all regulation lashings, and a blanket and pillow to suit. It was slung from the ceiling like a seaman's, with the cat in it, head on pillow, and--off-watch--taking no notice of his superior's presence. The admiral asked Crean how he liked going back south. *"Oh, I don't know sir; I thought I'd like to see the end of it."* The South Pole, for all

Shackleton's efforts in 1907, was still unconquered. This time the Royal Navy, despite Amundsen's threat, would take the prize. There was no doubt of that.

Dr. Wilson came aboard again at Melbourne, heartily tired of the constant company of three wives, even if one of them was his own. Scott went ashore again to turn his attention to business matters, leaving the ship again under the command of Lt. Evans for the passage to New Zealand. The ship departed after a brief stay, too brief even to load much in the way of fresh meat and vegetables. Time enough for that during the last sojourn in Christchurch before heading south. Her departure between the lines of warships assembled in the harbor would do her present master and the seamen at his command proud. Evans knew how to handle a windship in a tight corner. A lucky slant of wind filled her sails and gave her headway enough to thread the narrow course with all canvas billowing, her yards manned and returning cheer for cheer to the crews of the ponderous steel men-of-war.

She sailed in through Lyttleton Heads on October 28; final departure was slated for one month later. It wouldn't do to depart for the Antarctic any sooner than November 27, 1910. The ice would not allow a passage before the first of December in any year. Ten years had passed since Crean had walked these piers on shore leave from his former berth on the steel gunboat *Ringarooma*. In December 1901 he had watched the bustle and flow of activity surrounding the *Discovery* wishing for the opportunity to join. He'd leapt at the chance when it came and never once regretted the decision. From thence he'd been south toward the Pole, whirled round the world in the years since to come ashore here again and retrace his ice-bound path. It would begin as it had before, in a nearly unbroken round of work for weeks on end, preparing for another two years in the Antarctic.

The month ahead turned out to be--no surprise--a busy one. In a grim reflection of the *Discovery*'s troubles, the *Terra Nova* had proven herself a bad leaker on the way out, and the leak must be found out and made good. This meant emptying the forehold and building a cofferdam across and flooding it. Sloppy workmanship among the builders had set a long through-bolt in a hole double the required size. That was one leak, at any rate, that once fixed allowed the pumps to clear the bilges in a quarter hour twice a day.

After the repair, the stores were restowed and augmented with new goods. With a generous supply of cheese and butter, meat and jam, all the local produce of New Zealand, it was clear no one would starve during the coming season in the South. Then the real loading for the expedition began--two years' supplies for the shore party, and everything for the Pole. The two huts, in numbered pieces brought out in the ship, were set up ashore for practice, then dismantled and wedged back into place. There was the homely furniture of shore life to be considered--tables and chairs, spring mattresses, a galley stove along with the cook's associated gear, scientific instruments and bundles of furs to be sewn into bags for the trail, bunker coal for the passage and patent fuel for the shore base. Seven more men had arrived in New Zealand to join the afterguard. The seamen volunteered to give up their foc's'le to become the stable for the ponies, and slung their hammocks in the forehold below it. In the crowded quarters there, they shared the space, with one watch turning out as the next turned in.

Here the ponies and dogs came aboard, declared healthy following their sojourn on quarantine island. Cecil Meares had scoured the livestock markets of Manchuria and Siberia on behalf of the expedition for the best of the hardy little beasts of burden. Somehow horses had never seemed quite right for the barren fields of the Antarctic, even though Shackleton had done rather well with them. Slow and steady, they'd gotten their loads south for him, and that was all that was expected. Meares knew his dogs, but as was soon found out, his ponies not so well. On board, berths and stalls were to be found for them all, as well as room for the tons of forage and dog biscuit. The three motor sledges, still in their huge crates, were swung aboard and chained into place, one by the foremast and two just aft of the ice-house, where their bulk created a hangar for the dogs. Coal in sacks, too much for the bunkers, along with square tins of petrol two to a case, laid a second deck above the real one. In the end, the *Terra Nova's* own gaping deck-boards were all but invisible from stem to stern. All the same, there was nothing loaded aboard that could in any way be spared.

Ever since their shared march of discovery across the high frozen plateau in 1903, Taff Evans had enjoyed the undiluted respect of his captain and was held as an example to all the seamen. There almost nothing the sailor could do to damage this respect, but on the eve of departure from Lyttleton he fell from this grace. In fact, he fell overboard, coming back drunk as a lord to the *Terra Nova* after a last wild night on the town. No seaman facing a year or more of enforced isolation on an empty continent would be blamed for making the most of a night ashore. But this seaman, in this state, was a public humiliation that even Scott could not overlook. Evans was summarily dismissed from the expedition. In this Scott was obstinate; he'd had enough. There would be no mending of it this time. The ship would go south without him.

--How could he do it! His last night ashore! Damn him!-- Taff's behavior was a disgrace to the shared reputation of all the seamen on board. Worse, his absence would be keenly felt. Now it would be up to Crean to take all these fledgling explorers in tow and teach them the ropes. They might be good pupils, but there was a devilish lot of them in the afterguard for one man to teach every little trick of the trade that makes it all possible. The afterguard would need all the help they could get from the men,

whose number was now diminished by one of the best. Worse than that, the messdeck's star football player was taken away.

More hullabaloo accompanied the ship out of Lyttleton. Departure had been advertised for weeks in advance. The workers of the port had been given the day off and the bishop came aboard to deliver the farewell address. As the doughty whaler passed, the big guns of the harbor fired off a thunderous salute. The novelty of it all had, after three such departures already since June, worn thin.

While the ship sailed down the coast of New Zealand, a few members of the expedition remained ashore and took the train south to the final jumping-off place at Dunedin. Taff –always a silver-tongued devil--managed to talk his way into that party, and showed up unannounced at the ship to beg his captain's forgiveness. Whatever words and promises he used must have made a fine impression. He was, if not immediately forgiven, restored to his old berth in the messdeck. To everyone's relief the expedition left for the southern continent whole again.

Tuesday November 29, brought even more fanfare, albeit of the smaller scale to be found in this remote port. The wives—Scott's, Lt. Evans' and Wilson's—remained aboard until the ship was well clear of the mainland, then rode the steam tug back to shore. None could tell how long this parting might be. In the evening, the last blinkings of Cape Saunders light vanished from view. Now for the south, the frozen wasteland, where circumstances unlike any other on the globe might challenge a man and find him equal, or better.

Chapter Two

The Gale

The Southern Ocean, 52 degrees 05' South Latitude.

November 30, 1910.

Tom Crean, Antarctic explorer, was on his way south again. He'd gotten his fill of the hubbub and hero-worship of the shorebound folk of the empire, of tight-fitting clothes and fancy-dress balls and well-meant speeches in crowded rooms too full of the trappings of civilized life. He was off to sea again—off to cross desolate storm-tossed waters toward still more desolate and icebound shores, where a man's true strength might be found out, the mettle of his spirit tested. To sea again, where *life* and *work* melded into one undivided state of affairs: let the newspapermen and the poets find the romance in it.

The last day of November 1910 dawned as fine a morning as the late austral spring could offer. A fresh breeze swung out of the north to fill the spread of canvas and drive the ship easily toward her distant goal. She was heavily overburdened, though not nearly so much as Shackleton's little *Nimrod* had been with her paltry three feet of freeboard. True, there was a lot of gear on the *Terra Nova*'s deck, but it was cleverly stowed. Her deck planks were almost nowhere visible. They had been buried under layers of auxiliary deckload: the timbers of the shore huts laid and lashed flat, cases of petrol in big five-gallon cans packed in side by side like cobblestones until they made a second tier above the decks where the sailors walked. Coal in hundredweight sacks was piled on top of this false deck, and bales of pony-fodder, all lashed as securely as such an ungainly load could be. Two of the motor-tractors in their enormous crates were butted up against the ice-house with a space between, to make an unroofed shelter for the dogs. Tom Crean in his watch on deck was happy to have a call to go aloft and get clear of the noise and confusion and the odor arising from the close confinement of thirty-three dogs and nineteen ponies.

But the *Terra Nova* was a whaler, not a cargo ship, and she was running two feet down by the stern. She wallowed uneasily under the burden, pitching heavily about in the southwesterly swell. A few of the green hands were proving themselves just that, fresh recruits to the afterguard just now finding their sea-legs and heaving their breakfasts over the rail.

During the second day the wind gradually increased, giving the old girl eight, nine, nine-and-a-half knots. The sea was still calm enough to show her wake streaming along behind, but by next morning the ship was pushing fitfully into a confused chop. Heavy seas were breaking over the weather bulwarks, making it a wet excursion for anyone who ventured into the waist. Under the fo'c'sle head the ponies penned in their narrow stalls swayed to the motion of the ship. Water was finding its way through the deck-seams, bearing with it the pungent odor of dog and pony urine into the bilge, where the steam pumps sucked it away.

The men ran out on the swinging yards, taking in canvas in a gale to ease the ship. When it wasn't raining such work was sometimes almost a lark, especially when contrasted with the grimy make-work chores available on the Navy's dull grey gunboats. The stiff sailcloth billowed in the wind, flapping and booming madly, pulling itself free of the men's grip like an unruly child before yielding to their control. Here on the wooden barque a full watch of nine seamen made light work of jobs like furling. It would not be so simple for the shorthanded crew left to bring her home when the ship returned from the Antarctic shore. True, by then she'd be relieved of her burden, but also of Crean and some of the best of her men to the shore party.

The weather started to turn ugly in the afternoon watch. The wind rose sharply, and in short order the rest of the canvas was brought in, all but the staysails, jibs, and topsails. On deck, the afterguard hauled at the clews and buntlines, closing the sails tight to the yards before they thrashed themselves to shreds in the coming fury. Up in the rigging it was not such a simple task, hauling in the courses to the yards; blood from torn fingers mingled with the vilest and most intense language, to be spun away out over the foaming ocean.

This was a treacherous job. Crean felt the breath squeezed out of his lungs by the force of the gale flattening him against the yard, pressing the knotted cords of his brown scapular sharply into the flesh over his heart. Its leaves, one forward and one abaft and each emblazoned with a verse from the Holy Bible, had lain long hidden beneath the layers of his jumpers and windproofs, bathed there in his sweat. He'd worn it daily ever since he first went to sea, a gift of his mother blessed by the priest, a reminder of the peculiar faith that they share: *"Those who die wearing this scapular shall not suffer eternal fire."* Not that he had any intention of dying right now.

The whipping canvas ripped from his grasp could easily reach and sweep him right out of the footropes and into the sea at any moment. Overhead the mastheads swayed wildly back and forth against the sullen sky. *--Hold Fast!--* He did; sometimes it was two hands for the ship and none for himself, if she was to survive this thrashing.

The abrupt jerkings of the ship brought out the afterguard again to work the deckload, grunt labor heaving coal from the sacks through the manholes into the now-emptied bunkers. It all helped her trim, but did not save the ship from plunging ever more heavily into the surging seas. She began to wallow like a drunken sot, falling off into the deep troughs and never quite coming back, her bulwarks dipping under the water on either side to flood the decks with every roll. Anyone caught in the waist found the inside of the rail was as wet as the outside. The outlook, should the gale continue for any length of time, was decidedly uncomfortable. The stout old *Terra Nova* had weathered many such a gale, but never under such a heavy load as this.

The breaking waves did more than soak the dogs and hamper the men working in the waist. *Hamper* is hardly the word for it. At times they were all entirely submerged. It was less a matter of water coming on board than that of the ship herself seeming to settle into the water, unable to drain it away before the next wave came breaking on. Green seas coming over the lee rail began to get under the floor of petrol cases laid out on the deck, lifting them and starting every lashing that had seemed so secure in port. Even Dr. Wilson, himself so unflappable and calm in the most adverse of circumstances, was appalled at this vision of the ship beginning to go to pieces. Jute sacks full of coal began careering about like battering rams, smashing into gear and men and loosening yet more of the deckload. Valuable as coal was to the success of the expedition, the time had come to throw it overboard before it could do more damage. This was one loss that could in some measure be remedied once ashore; other gear, and dogs, and ponies, and men, could not be easily replaced. *--One, two, three—heave!--* and another sack went over the side, the splash of it lost to the screaming gale. Thus lightened, the old ship ought to stick it out.

The gale pounded away with ever-mounting fury, rising from Force 6 in the forenoon to Force 9 by midnight. This was truly alarming. All the canvas was in, save the jibs and lower topsails to give her a little way, but the time had come to bring in the rest and trust to the bare poles. Given the choice, Crean would rather risk his neck in a fall from the yard fighting the wind-whipped topsails than wallow in the havoc on deck. Hauling in and furling the last of the jibs out on the bowsprit was another matter.

Lieutenant Bowers took personal charge of that operation and would ask no man to do what he would not do himself. The bowsprit was plunging deep into the water with each advancing wave, then rising toward heaven as though in momentary supplication. Any man who ventured out there would come back on deck half drowned, if he came back at all. Bowers called for volunteers, four of the stoutest hands to follow him out onto the diving jibboom to save themselves and the ship. It was one hand to the canvas, one hand to the gasket, and just before the boom drove deep into the freezing water, one hand for himself. At one moment the bowsprit pointed skyward like the hand of Adam reaching out to his God, and the next it dove toward the bottom of the sea. Each man was left to his own grip and inner strength. There were no lifelines, but to the sailors that was a small matter. Each could look out for himself, but if the ship could not be eased, there would be no survivors. Their duty was clear. Each time the heaving ship plunged them into the freezing water, each time the boom rose free, the five men were all still hanging on for dear life and dearer ship. Wetter, each swore, than he'd ever yet been.

The view from the masthead was no more encouraging. As far as the eye could see to windward, rows of huge wall-faced seas—no end to them in sight--charged down on the laboring ship. They swept the deck entirely, at times buried the ship completely until all that could be seen from above was a heaving sea with three poles sticking up out of it, and the roofs of deckhouses awash in the surging water. *This must be what it is like to watch your ship sink beneath you.* From a vantage on the pitching bridge the waves could be seen rising thirty-five feet from crest-to-trough, racing down on the ship like toppling cliffs in a wicked and relentless procession.

The din of it all defied description. The hurricane wind tore at every vibrating line, pulsed its pitch to a banshee wail. Each marauding wave breaking aboard pounded the ship like a Frenchman's broadside, as though it would render her into pieces before she could sink. Hundredweight sacks of coal and heavy tins of oil, now sliding around the deck in utter abandon, smashed into deckhouse and motor-crate with the boom of a cannon shot. A long stretch of the starboard rail went by the board, and the water roamed the waist more freely than ever, washing away anything within reach.

Earlier there had been much shouting back and forth, but the ship was out of control now and there was nothing much to be done. The captain and his deck officer paced the bridge, the men on watch huddled in whatever lee they could find, ready for orders. There was no need to go aloft; the sails were secure in their gaskets, the yards triced up a snug as possible. If anything got loose now it will be beyond the power of man to rein it in.

Every wave lifted that false deck and everything on it. Body-and-soul lashings to the oilskins meant nothing here. Every wave aboard meant another full-immersion baptism, so the soul at least might be accounted-for. As for the body, a man's grip on stay or ratline would have to serve. Each man in the waist had to look out for himself, and grab onto any part of the ship within reach as another wave came aboard to bury him to his shoulders. The false floor lifting beneath his feet seemed out to pitch him over the side; once overboard, there would be no rescue in this weather.

Momentarily idle hands were commandeered by Oates and Atkinson to help with the ponies. These poor creatures had been walled into their stalls for the duration of the passage, nailed into confined slots that gave them no room to lay or turn about. Despite the awful noise and violent motion, they seemed at times to fall asleep on their feet, forgetting all until their legs gave out and down they went. Once collapsed in their stalls from the pitching of the ship, it was the very devil to get them back up. The luckiest of them managed to keep their footing. Others, upended, screamed and fought and bit at their benefactors struggling to lift them to their feet. Two, Davy and Jones, struggled mightily until their hearts gave out. The dogs suffered nearly as much, tossed about like

57

rubbish, their necks snapping to the ends of their chains with every boarding wave. One of them, Osman, his collar broken by the force of the wave, was swept overboard. The next wave passing swept him back aboard again. Lucky dog! Such miracles inspired a welcome bit of hope when it most needed.

The ship fought bravely on, steaming into the tumult. Her sides and timbers held strong. The real problem was not a leaking hull, but leaking decks. Age, drying, the shrinking heat of the tropics, the overwhelming deckload all combined to open the deck seams to the coursing water. There was not a dry place anywhere on board. Rain fell in torrents from above; the bridge and foc'sle head were swept by boarding waves at either hand. The waist submerged entirely at times with the swaying bare pole of the main sticking up out of the water like a lone tree in a flooded valley. The ship was leaking like a basket, water sluicing through the open seams above in a thousand cascades and pooling on the floor of the 'tweendeck before running down into the bilges. Everything was saturated--bedding, books and clothing reduced to a sodden pulp redolent of pony urine washed down from the stables just above. Nothing was spared the deluge. Worst of all, there was no dry tobacco and no dry match to light it.

Beneath the deck plates in the engine-room, the water in the bilge was beginning to rise. The capacity of the steam pumps to keep up with the flow was starting to fail. An old problem with the intakes in the depths of the bilge, first noticed while the ship was making her easting down, had returned and the implications of it were distinctly unpleasant. Coal-dust from the bunkers, rinsed down by the flood from above, had made its way to the bilges, mixing there with lubricating oil from the engine-room. The two substances had a natural affinity for each other, combining into balls of a sticky black paste. These, drawn by the suctions, choked the intakes and stopped the flow of water.

Under ordinary conditions, routine maintenance took care of the problem. Once cleared, the steam pumps drew freely and the water flowed again out of the spigots on deck. Normally the ship suffered no danger and the deck-watch were spared their turn at the hand-pumps. But now, in the heart of the storm, the pumps were working beyond their ordinary measure. Beneath the floor-plates in the stokehold, Bill Lashly was up to his neck in the bilgewater, but the steam pumps were clogging faster than he could clear them. The water beneath the engines was on the rise.

By the morning watch Friday the water in the sump was four feet deep. The clogged pumps had stopped working hours before. The water in the bilge is rose steadily, and when it became clear that the level must inevitably reach the boilers, the fires were doused and the metal allowed to cool. The water was now inches deep *above* the floorplates and flowing in a slow wave from side to side.

The afterguard flailed away manfully at the hand-cranks on deck but the outflow slowed to a trickle as though to mock their best efforts. The intakes for these pumps, now thoroughly choked, were located at the bottom of the well under the main hatch just abaft the mainmast. There was only one access to the bottom of the well, and that was through that hatch itself, then through the bunkers in the 'tween-decks and the main hold to the sump in the very bottom of the ship just above the keel. This sump was also by now quite full of water, and these were no ordinary conditions. With water coming aboard by the ton with every passing wave, taking the cover off that main hatch would bring the immediate foundering of the ship. She would fill in minutes, settle into the water, and overloaded as she was, quickly sink beneath the waves. No open boat would long survive. As it was now, she was filling by the hour and unless the pumps could be cleared, her fate would be the same. Even Dr. Wilson was starting to doubt the *Terra Nova*'s chances of survival. *"It looked to everyone who knew what was going on that we must go to the bottom."* Crean had no room in his mind for any such cheerless thoughts. If a man gave credence to the worst that could happen, then most assuredly it would.

All the same, there was no denying the situation was becoming more desperate by the hour. With no working pumps it was only a matter of time, and not much at that, before the *Terra Nova* would fill and founder. And when she did, she would take them all--ponies, dogs, tractors, seamen and scientists alike--to the bottom, with no trace left afloat to tell to the world their sad tale. The ship would not even be reported missing for nearly a year. The men would not let her sink, not without a fight. *Do the best you can with what you've got.*

Lieutenant Evans led the charge. It would take some doing, but there *was* a way to get into the hold without removing the hatch. It involved climbing with a hammer and chisel to the top of the boiler to cut a manhole through the half-inch sheet-iron lining of the bulkhead there. Once through that curtain of metal, a man could burrow down through the coal in the bunkers and with a little pluck dive into the bilgewater beside the keelson and clear the suctions to the hand-pumps. Then it just might be possible to pump the ship enough to stay afloat until the gale blew itself out. If not, then not. This was the one chance.

Cutting a hole large enough for a man to climb through, by hand through solid iron, was not something easily or quickly accomplished. With hand-drills and chisels it would take hours at best, hours while the *Terra Nova* was steadily filling. Bowers, back on deck from the bowsprit adventure, joined the mate on the bridge. The ship took a roll, slow and sluggish, over until the lee coamings of the main hatch were under water. Even more slowly, she righted herself. *"She won't do that often"*. When a ship goes over that far, she goes down.

Above the din rose the one sound a human voice can make louder than the screaming gale, the shout that every sailor dreads: *"Ship afire!"* Smoke was seen to be rising through the seams of the planking. The patent fuel in the afterhold had not been ventilated since the storm had overtaken the ship. Everyone knew that explosive gases were accumulating there. A fire now would do as well as any to spell the end. The only possible way to deal with it would be to open the hatch and flood the hold. And sink the ship. Panic ran in a flash like a seared nerve through the ship, but the smoke turned out to be nothing more than steam rising from the seawater in contact with the still-hot coals of the fireboxes. It would not be fire that would sink the expedition.

If there was to be any saving of the ship at all, it was to be through bailing. Impossible though the task might seem, there was nothing for it but to get the water out of the bilge by any means available. Given the utter failure of every other system the ship could offer, then bailing it would be. There were men, strong and willing, desperate for their very lives, and buckets. The afterguard formed themselves into two watches, ranged themselves up and down the series of iron ladders that led from the depths of the stokehold making the bucket-brigade that became the last chance to save the ship. Forty-eight hours into the gale, it had come to this last-ditch effort. Failure would spell the end of hope, of the dreams of Antarctic glory, and of life itself. The ship was cold and powerless, and she was filling with water. With every roll to leeward she seemed to lie over longer, as if beaten. She had not many more such rolls in her, before she would fail to come up again.

The scene was something out of Dante's *Inferno*: sweating bodies glistening in the dim lamplight, whipped by their desperation to a task, dripping with oil and slime, driven by fear and desperation. Each bucket swinging upward slopped the filthy water onto the man below, and back into the bilge. The water was warm from the still-hot boilers, the stokehold filled not with steam but with the oppressive humid fug of a tropic night with no breeze to stir the still air inside. Sweat poured off the bodies of the men. Some chose to go naked, for what was the point of modesty when one's life might so soon be ended. The watches spelled each other and new men came below. Up above and behind the boiler, Evans, Bowers, and Lashly whaled away at the iron bulkhead, measuring slight progress with each passing minute.

All day and Friday night the bailing gangs labored without letup. Their efforts relieved the ship of five tons of water while the engineers worked at the bulkhead behind the boiler. The minutes grew to hours. Overhead, the gale roared without letup, the seas as high as ever. Crean had long since learned to know the racket of a fresh whitecap sweeping clear the waist, and to reach up and grab the highest line at hand and haul himself clear of the coming surge. He knew beyond all doubt the ship would survive the storm and safely make the Antarctic shore. Crean hadn't been born to be drowned.

The gale had battered the ship for two days now and in all that time the sun's light has been swept from the sky, until this very moment. A break on the far horizon sent a few bright rays beneath the layer of black clouds, spreading like the fingers of a golden hand reaching across a stretch of the sea through a squall to leeward. Beyond, in the east, the bright arc of a rainbow reached up from the heaving sea. The colors, iridescent with their own light, showed for just half a minute. The sight of it sent a chill through him, a glimmer of hope, a promise of better times to come. The sigh of the wind through the bare poles ceased, a moment's unearthly silence before the rainbow vanished beneath the scudding storm-clouds. It might be taken for a sign that all will be well, but the gap in the cloud closed over. The gale picked up with renewed fury. The sun disappeared, taking with it the rainbow, but one moment's passing hope sustains. Within the hour the wind speed fell, and the hole through the iron bulkhead was broken through.

Lieutenant Evans, scuttling through the new-made manhole, took it on himself to clear the suctions. It meant climbing into the bilges and ducking head under—from nine to midnight—to reach his arm up into the intakes. Twenty buckets of black tarballs went up through the engine-room and pitched into the sea. On deck all free hands rushed to the hand-cranks on deck. After a momentary gurgling the black water of the bilge spilled out of the spigots and over the deck. A great cheer rose from those on hand to see the miracle. No one was too weary to stand his trick at the pumps now.

In three hours the ship was cleared, only half as full of water as she called normal. In these last desperate hours, the gale had begun to blow itself out. At 12:30 p.m. on Saturday, Crean went up to set the main t'gallant; then came the fore, then the inner jib. The ship was beginning to sail again. She had been blown twenty-three miles to leeward. Ten tons of coal, sixty-five gallons of petrol, and two dogs had gone overboard. Two ponies, Davy and Jones, had died. Their carcasses, slung from the foremast, were hauled out through the foc's'le skylight. Everything was wet through. The messdeck reeked. The storm had left behind these reminders, but still it was over, passed along now to harry some other ship abroad on the wild southern ocean, running her own easting down.

Sunday the ship went peacefully along on her way south under sail and easy steam while the men busied themselves in the waist making good the damage wrought by the storm. The weary afterguard lay about the quarterdeck, all piled together and sunning themselves like so many seals, dozing and writing up their diaries and letters home. Crean kept no diary, but the tale of this storm was one he'd long remember. Now a thorough wash and dry of bunk and blankets and saltwater-drenched bluejacket and trousers was in order. And, with the galley stove alight again, coffee and good hot grub was ready to hand.

It had been an eventful week. That the ship had not foundered and gone down was due in equal parts to efforts of the men, the officers, and the green hands of the afterguard. In the shared experience of a desperate struggle, the ordinary distinctions of society diminish to insignificance. A man is taken at face value for what he is and does rather than the circumstances of his birth. When the storm is over the old lines are redrawn, fainter.

The six days following were easy going--five knots or so under sail and steam, with the wind variable and not always fair. The engines ate rapidly through the remains of the coal on deck and the ship settled into a new and better-situated center of gravity suspended between heaven and ocean.

*   *   *   *   *

The temperature of the air and seawater dropped abruptly on December 9 as the ship crossed the Antarctic convergence, the invisible shore of the Southern Ocean. In the messdeck the old Antarctic hands laid bets on who would sight the first ice, and when. It would not be long now.

--*Iceberg off the port bow!*—Sharp-eyed Lt. Evans had spotted the first of the floating ice, two silver pyramids showing far to the west in the intermittent shafts of sunlight. Beyond, the spouts of blue whales hung like clouds of gray smoke. Throughout the morning the icebergs increased in number, dotted all over the open sea in every direction. Closer now, they assumed fantastic shapes—a boar's head, a waterlogged boat, a swan, a woman in mourning with outstretched hands. An ice-sky showed ahead, and then the pack-ice came into view--a vista of broken ice-pans covering the sea ahead. The ship ploughed handsomely into the outlying bands of it, a floating brash that was neither ice nor water.

Every free hand crowded the foc's'le head, leaning over the iron rail for a good look at the cutwater cleaving aside the floating ice as the ship bore into the first really dense stream that lay across her path. The sound of it clattering against her sides made a noise like broken glass shaken in a box, with an occasional heavy *thump* as she shouldered aside a submerged growler. The *Terra Nova* drove straight into a broad field of small ice, acres of twenty-foot floes with upturned edges, dazzling pancakes dusted with powdered sugar floating in a sea of blue-black ink.

These parted as the ship pushed through with the old familiar rattle and crunch, and closed again silently after. A deepening chill crackled in the air, stirring the blood with a feeling of old times.

The sea in all directions became a vast white plain laced with jagged leads of dark water and dotted here and there with still lakes acres or miles in extent, the drifting remains of last winter's frozen sea going north to melt into the Pacific Ocean. Only a well-found wooden ship could survive this transition; a steel vessel would be holed and sunk, an open boat would be crushed to splinters by the drifting, churning masses of floes too small to support a man or a sledge. It would never do to have to abandon a ship caught in the ice; no boat's crew, even one under Crean's command, could hope to survive.

At first this pack seemed a minor obstacle, a brief delay in the explorers' southward progress—the *Discovery* had forced her way through it to the open Ross Sea beyond in a matter of days. The view of the floating pack from the masthead was one of serene beauty. This far south, at this time of the year, "night" was at best a mere idea, a suggestion of the clock with no hint of darkness to confound it. The daylight never wanes. It hangs in the air in a prolonged twilight, a glorious rosy color, reflected burnished-copper and salmon-pink in the still water between the floes, saffron and green in the northern sky as the sun just dips below the southern horizon.

The pack itself grew thicker as the ship drove into it: the pancakes congealed into larger floes, and those into vast unbroken fields until southward progress came to a halt. To save coal the ship was hooked into a very large floe and the fires banked. In the sudden quiet of a Sunday morning, gangs of penguins and the occasional sleeping seal were the only signs of life. The captain read the standard Navy Anglican service to the men religiously from the break of the poop. Crean stood apart from all of them. Catholic—Carmelite, in fact—he couldn't make out the sense of the weekly service read by the Captain. Imagine, a man not ordained even in their bloodless protestant offshoot, reading to the men as though he had Authority. Only the Pope had *that*, and the right to delegate it.

Crean, the only adherent to the original Holy Church, was the only man excused from the *Terra Nova*'s Sunday service. He took his vespers in a private way on Sundays, caressing the brawn scapular that hung from his neck and remembering his prayers. Mother would be proud of him, if she could know. and Hanna's father would accept him into his family. But this was nothing to be boasted of, and neither of them would know.

In the afternoon Gran issued pairs of the long wooden skis to all hands and led them out on the floe to become acquainted with the use of the "planks." The *Discovery* men needed no instruction. The pitch leading up to the Gap from that expedition's hut had been known as the ski slope; any man who had survived a race down that would learn nothing new on the level floe. After class, an Antarctic stillness settled again over the *Terra Nova*, broken at times by the croaks and cries of distant penguins or the crack of a rifle as another seal gave his skin for science and his meat for the larder. To the north, the sun just touched the horizon and bounded upward without having ever set at all. The ship, her decks and engines silent, drifted slowly along in her southward course.

With all sail set and hanging like drapery from the yards, the ship lay waiting, a study for the photographer. It was a view of their ship few other sailors would ever see, how she looked from just under the bow, under full sail. She was beautiful, as Crean had always known she would be. Days were to pass with the ship locked in this temporary prison, with no forward progress. Captain Scott paced the quarterdeck, wordlessly communicating his impatience to the men.

Among the men tensions mounted, along with fears for the expedition's scientific results and concurrent fame. One whole week in the pack and she'd made only fifty miles southing—this would never do. Taff especially had posted his dreams of family life and future happiness on his part in the success of the expedition. Its fortunes depended on the earliest possible landing, in order for a depot to be laid far enough south on the Barrier before the close of the summer season. The long month of December 1910 wore slowly on; each day's delay in the pack meant one day less for the depot journey, and one day more on the march for the men homeward bound from the South Pole.

Waiting for better ice conditions was not the answer. Steam was raised again, and repeated assaults with the iron-shod prow cracked a huge floe and opened a lead. Bowers in particular seemed to take delight in working the ship like a battering ram, to bring her up all standing against a particularly intractable floe. After each crash and impact the masts would whip fore-and-aft and bring up the Owner to see what was the matter. The pack opened, admitted a few miles progress, then closed up again, straining the rudder in its pintles. The ship was forced west, past huge bergs and immense floes miles square and growing ever larger, laden with crabeater seals. Sea-leopards sluiced through the water, making short lazy dives beneath the ship. The men threw lumps of coal at passing killer whales, who seemed to take no notice. When the wind next came up they set sail on the fore and the ship pushed her way north a few hundred yards. She broke free, then wore away east and south, following the leads.   Christmas Eve found her brought up again in a solid sheet of pack in all directions.   The ship lay still, all sail set and hanging.

Bill Lashly and the black gang all messed together just forward of the engine room, and as a rule didn't mingle much with the other men. On the voyage out they had their hands full keeping the steam engine going, their talk all full of reduction gearing and pressure relief.   The four of them hadn't been stoking the fires much; they left that dusty, gritty task fall into the hands of the boyishly enthusiastic afterguard.   Now there wasn't much stoking to do at all.

During the holdup in the pack, the stokers' mess remained apart. While the other men were enjoying a little slack time while the ship lay motionless, the black gang continued on call around the clock for "steam up".   Openings in the ice appeared without warning, and the ship had to be ready to move.

The men's quarters on the *Terra Nova* were not in the foc's'le, but under it, beneath the ponies.   Warmed by the black iron stove fiercely ablaze near its center, the messdeck air on Christmas Night was close, redolent of sweat and the lasting fragrance of pony litter washed down from above during the gale and thick with drifting layers of tobacco smoke.   The whole was warmly lit with lamps and candles.   Here in the heart of a ship, far from the garlanded halls of the civilized world, far from the sea-lanes and the chance of another vessel passing, here the observance of the day comes into its truest expression.   The sailors' thoughts turn inevitably to home and family and girls left behind.   What might Hannah be doing this very day?   Crean took out her few letters, reading over and over the words she'd written to him months before.   She must be thinking of him tonight.   She must be.

And, on every polar exploring ship there must be a feast. The cook pulled out the best of everything his pantry could offer. There was asparagus-and-tomato soup, roast beef and penguin breast to stand in for the traditional Christmas goose, mince pies and plum pudding. The feast was laid out on the groaning board, with beer and whisky to wash it down. There were gifts of tobacco and sweets sent out by the Dunedin Seamen's Mission, and Tom Crean had a basket full of special presents all his own to give out. His pet rabbit had given birth from her nest in the ponies' hay to a litter of seventeen, but for him there were not enough. By night's end he had promised away twenty-two.

A little band was got up, of Anton's mandolin and the sailors' bones and jews'-harps, a backing for the grand choruses of forebitters and Christmas carols. The dangers of the harsh new world lay outside layers of stout oaken timbers. Within, the safe haven of the messdeck, whitewashed and warmed, rang out with wassail songs and stories long into the night. The men's cat snuggled into his hammock for the evening, his head gently resting on the little pillow Crean had made. Ross seals attracted by the noise must have wondered in their seal way, what on earth was happening within this hull that had intruded into their world. Above it all, the sun circled round all the day and night over the unbroken fields of ice.

At midnight the third watch took their turn on deck. By using the old ice-master's trick of alternately throwing the ship aback, then filling sail and pressing the narrow leads, the ship began to make a little headway without the noisy, smoky push of steam. She must be somewhere near the end of a four-hundred-mile wide belt of pack that surged and flexed on unseen currents, opening and closing and seeming to breathe like a living thing. The ice closed around, then opened, closed, opened again. Each day spent languishing here in the ice meant another shortening of the first season's work.

The ice opened out slightly, and the wind came up. The ship was making less water now these days; a quarter-hour at the cranks sufficed. The 29th of December brought a welcome change, a water sky in the south and proof of a swell in the rounded edges of the pancake floes. Steam was raised, augmented by a breeze from the north. The sheets of ice became thinner and more fragmented. A freezing rain fell in the night watch, covering everything on the ship, the decks and davits, the boats and ropes and canvas, with a thin layer of clear ice, as though she had been dipped in glass and set out gleaming in the morning sun. She forged ahead between angular blocks of shortcakes, fields of rounded pancake and isolated belts of brash until at 1:00 a.m. December 30 Lt. Bowers steered the ship into the open water of the Ross Sea. This crossing of the pack ice, at three weeks, was the longest on record.

The *Terra Nova* had proven well the strength of her Dundee lineage. She seemed, as Scott was to remark, a living thing, twisting and turning and bumping through the floe, fighting a great fight. He was equally impressed with the conduct and fortitude of his men, working together, messdeck and afterguard side by side, always cheerful, always willing. Free at last, they set sail for Cape Adare.

Chapter Three

Landing at Cape Evans

The Southern Ocean, 72 degrees 54' South Latitude.

December 31, 1910.

The clouds on the western horizon slowly cleared away, and from the crow's-nest came the joyful shout, *"Land in Sight!" --Where away?—Two points off the starboard bow--* There is no thrill to compare with the leap of a sailor's pulse at the sight of the first peaks of a distant shore above the horizon—no matter what land it may be, or how often he has seen it this way. Crean ran up to the top to see for himself. It was true; the Antarctic continent was in view, the summits of Mounts Sabine and Monteagle gleaming in the distance. So clear and pure was the air that the twin peaks seemed not 120 miles away but almost at hand, bright beacons signaling an end to the slow passage of weeks at sea and the promise of a fresh adventure ashore. Few on board had witnessed this approach before. The newer hands among the afterguard could hardly control their excitement; it sparked from them throughout the older hands in the ship, electric. Crean, always adrift between two worlds--one green, one white--was almost home again. It was the last day of 1910, an occasion for a double celebration. With the sun low in the sky toward the

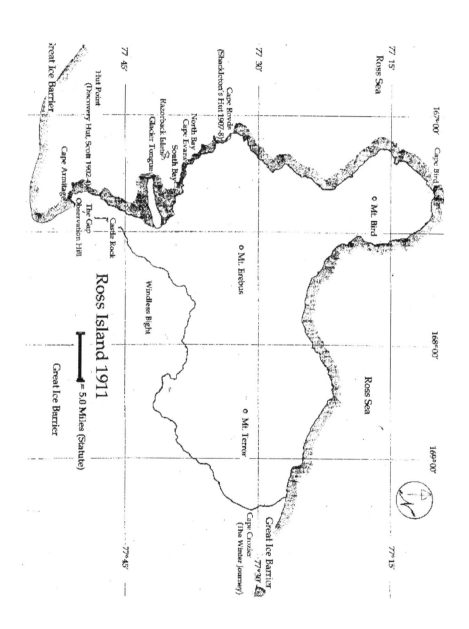

Ross Island 1911

Great Ice Barrier

Ross Sea

Cape Bird

o Mt. Bird

Cape Royds
(Shackleton's Hut 1907-8)

North Bay
Cape Evans
South Bay

Razorback Islands
Glacier Tongue

o Mt. Erebus

Windless Bight

Hut Point
(Discovery Hut, Scott 1902-4)

The Gap
Observation Hill

Castle Rock

Cape Armitage

Great Ice Barrier

o Mt. Terror

Great Ice Barrier

Cape Crozier 77°30'
(The Winter Journey)

Ross Sea

77 15'
Ross Sea

77 30'

77 45'

167°00'

168°00'

169°00'

77° 15'

77° 45'

= 5.0 Miles (Statute)

74

south, the blast from the steam siren and sixteen bells roused all hands at midnight for a general hurrah party to welcome in the New Year.

The first morning of 1911 arrived as glorious as they come in the Antarctic or anywhere else, a bright and hopeful start with clear skies and clear seas with not a particle of ice in sight in any direction. Dr. Wilson took to the crow's nest in his customary early morning ritual, on the lookout for any new species of whale or bird to claim for the expedition. The fine weather continued and some sanitary housekeeping was in order. Lieutenant Bowers loved cold as well as an ordinary man loved warmth. A bucket of seawater and a bar of saltwater soap, taken together on deck, seemed only to make his pink skin red, and keep him happy. Captain Oates made use of the sun and calm and a handful of the seamen to take down the stable-gates and give the ponies a turn on deck.

Mucking out the two feet of manure that had accumulated after thirty-eight days in the stalls was just one of the chores that any good explorer must face. That, and making all sail for Ross Island and the *Discovery*'s old shore station at its southernmost point. There would be no exploration this time of Victoria Land's indented shore; the long passage through the pack had robbed the expedition of anything like leisure time for unnecessary work. Still, the unfolding panorama seen from the crosstrees had lost none of its fascination. Lieutenant Evans kept to the bridge taking rounds and rounds of angles for a running survey of the distant land, refining and perfecting the charts of South Victoria's coast. There was no man better than him for mapping and locating every unknown cape and headland on the vast grid of the globe. If a fellow found himself adrift among uncharted shores, Lt. Evans was the man to have along.

In the evening the smoke from the summit of Mt. Erebus hove into view. The earth's southernmost volcano towered over the only two settlements in this part of the world—*Discovery*'s Hut Point and Shackleton's old camp from his own South Pole attempt. If the winds of past Antarctic winters had not buried them all in drift by now, then one or the other of them offered the best promise of shelter and a new start.

Crean was coming home, after a fashion. So were Taff and Lashly among the men, and Scott and Dr. Wilson. A few years of safe security back in England had only sharpened their hunger for the wide-open country, the shared intensity of adventure that could be answered in only this place. It was calling them with a siren song, and like brave Ulysses with unstopped ears they heard the call and answered. Long before these old scenes came into view, the diminutive cone of Mt. Terror rose up below and to the left of Erebus. The white line vanishing eastward on the horizon was the mighty face of the Great Ice Barrier. Its sheer white cliffs rose straight from the dark sea; nothing more could be seen from the deck of a ship cruising alongside the hundreds of miles of its seaward face. From the crow's nest, the view beyond the windblown cornice revealed an undulating plain boundless and bare, stretching far away into an indefinite horizon. Ice and sky melded into one, with no feature—no rock, no mountain range—to break the monotony. Crean had been one of the first to venture into the stark empty plain. The *Discovery* had found an inlet with low shores and tied up for a few days in 1902; he was one of four sent inland to see what might be discovered there.

Nothing, it turned out, but ice and more ice, white desert with no apparent limit and nothing on it that might sustain or shelter a man. That pioneering foray turned back with nothing to show for their efforts but a new record for farthest south, but that was something. In the field of polar exploring, nations strove mightily for the momentary prize of "farthest north" or "farthest south," since both poles were by now understood to offer their discoverers nothing of value except fame. To the seamen behind the effort even that was denied.

Once the *Discovery* had set up a permanent base at Hut Point at the southwestern extremity of Ross Island, larger field parties had made longer journeys into the back country. Scott, Dr. Wilson and Shackleton had made a long stretch over the Barrier toward the South Pole, returning with little more than a new record after three months' sledging. The distance, the cold, the unending grueling work of it all, had nearly done them in.

Crean himself had been a long way out with a small surveying party seeking to determine the southern limit of South Victoria Land and the extent of the unknown Antarctic continent. Its mysteries had as a result become commonplace, its dangers better understood, if not overcome. Now the great Barrier ice seemed almost like an old friend, but a friend with her own moods and designs, not to be altogether trusted.

The *Terra Nova's* first landing on Ross Island would be at Cape Crozier on the eastern end, where the Barrier crushed up against the land rising in a bluff four hundred feet straight up from the sea. Now from the crosstrees of the *Terra Nova* Crean could see over the Barrier to the well-known landmarks of Black and White Islands where he'd sledged with Lt. Barne and the others in '03. Closer at hand, the old *Discovery* mail post, still showing red, rose up out of the center of the penguin rookery.

A whaler was launched, a landing attempted with the afterguard crowding the regular boat's crew out of their rightful places. With no shelter from the long northerly swell to be found, the unbridled surf broke heavily on the beach; there was no landing to be made. That same swell and a moving belt of pack ice drove the *Terra Nova* headfirst into a little bay, with no room to turn. She was forced to back out into the fast-moving stream, taking tremendous shocks to her already damaged rudder. These were the hazards of shipping down here; a moment's bad luck or an ill turn of the tide, could wreck everything and destroy the work of years and the lives of the men who'd come to explore this grand new world.

With boat and crew safely aboard, the ship headed northwest along the island's barren shore, bound for Cape Bird and McMurdo Sound beyond. Lieutenant Evans was on the bridge again taking a running survey of the coast as she went. The sea was smooth as glass, the world around bathed in sunshine. Clearing Cape Bird, the ship made for Shackleton's old 1907 base to see if it might be put back into use for the expedition, but the shore-ice there had gone out; a landing was impossible. The ship steamed slowly south, looking for better prospects. Farther along, at the very tip of the island, the *Discovery* hut would make a better home. However, beyond the broken, tumbled bluff of the Barne Glacier, the fast ice stretched right across the sound, barring the way south. Just around Inaccessible Island, Scott pressed the ship's iron prow against the ice-foot and sent ashore the ice anchors. The *Terra Nova* had come to rest a mile and a half offshore from a rare bit of exposed rock. It was the morning of January 4, 1911. Scott named the spot Cape Evans after his able lieutenant. After breakfast the two of them, with Dr. Wilson and the carpenter Davies, walked a mile and a half over the fast ice to the shore.

There on the shelving beach they found a level spot and selected a site for the hut.

This place would be home for the winter. Here the great adventure must begin, and who can know how it will all turn out. This much is certain—there can be no better situated a starting place, no better man to lead it than Captain Scott, and none better to drive it to a successful conclusion than these sailing men of the *Terra Nova*. Here at the edge of the world, the provocative allure of the unknown is as palpable as the chill air, but the call of the mundane must be answered first. There will be exploring after the shore station is well established—the stores landed, the hut erected, the ponies housed against the coming winter.

The sailors' work was a varied lot: stevedore today, pony handler tomorrow, draft animal the next day, carpenter and cobbler the next. The ship hooked into a natural ice wharf as close to the shore as she could get. The scantlings of the hut and all its furnishings, three years' supplies for the shore station, all the traveling gear—everything would have to be sledged over the floating ice to the site. There was no time to waste. Within an hour of the setting of the ice-hooks, the dogs were all picketed on the ice, howling and yelping in their rush to snuffle their noses into the snow. Chained to a rope leading from the bow, they raised merry hell when a troop of penguins, heedless of their own safety, came by to see what all the fuss was about.

The solid floe made an acceptable quay about eight feet above the level of the sea. Using the mainyard as a boom, the men began to sweat the cargo ashore, starting with the two huge motor-sledge crates. Mechanics Day and Hooper had already set out their tools and lubricants on the ice. An afternoon in the open-air workshop produced its noisy result; the motors, without silencers, roared to life ready to take on the first of the shore-bound sledges.

Next off were the ponies. They trusted no one. Five weeks tortured confinement at the hands of these men had been enough; the horses were docile and obedient no more. During the passage south while held up in the pack, Crean had taken a fancy to one Blossom caged in his stall, from the look of his head and the bit of character he seemed to have. But here at the moment of release, the pony recognized no master. Now at the horse's moment of freedom, the affection was not returned; no measure of treats and kind words from his handler would change things.

It would take some prodding and poking and more than a little swearing—Crean was no novice at that—to get his horse out of the stall and into the crib of the transport-box to be slung ashore. The horse was too weak from his long confinement to put up much resistance. With a scrape of hoof on decking he inched forward, then with a clatter and a sudden release rushed forward into the box. Lifted off the deck, it swayed in the air momentarily. Blossom squealed in panic until he felt again the solid ice like ground, beneath him. Crean released a toggle and the front of the crib fell away.

The horse stepped out onto the ice. The snow-covered country all around looked like winter in his Manchurian homeland, and with no more ado he flopped down heavily for a good long roll on the ice. Once the long itch was satisfied he got on his feet and allowed himself to be led away with no further ado, to join the other horses already picketed on a hawser stretched over the ice. For the first time it was possible to see all the ponies together in the open air. They certainly weren't much to look at. Crean was from the country, and fancied himself a better judge of livestock than some of the sailors, certainly better than Meares who had been hoodwinked by the Siberian horse-traders into taking these relics for valuable horses. They were bony and spavined, molting swaybacked old relics, white or buff in color the better to show off the shadows of their ribs and the pink skin remaining where the boards of their stalls had worn away the hair. Some of them could barely stand up. Scott had ordered one day's rest for them; they could have used a week.

The long slow weeks spent in breaking through the pack ice with almost nothing to do now began to seem something of a holiday. Now ten straight days of nonstop sledging was just beginning. Even at Blossom's slow pace it would be an endless circuit of out-and-back with every shore-bound article in the hold to be dragged on a sledge across the ice to the shore. Each returning sledge carried a load of shingle for new ballast to balance the lightening ship, fifty tons in all to be manhandled into the tubs and spread out along the bilges. All this must be finished quickly, before the ice broke up under the advance of summer and the makeshift wharf dissolved into the Sound.

The dogs were given easy loads, but the men of the afterguard were allowed no such leisure. Ganged into teams of four, they began pulling the first loads of pony-fodder ashore. It might have been the first time some of these fellows ever raised a sweat; the wardroom certainly smelled like it. They seemed to revel in the drudgery of manhauling in harness that first day, stopping only once at lunch for a monumental tuck-in and once again late in the evening to fall heavily into a waiting bunk on board. Scientists and seamen pitched into the work with equal gusto, each team out to show up the others in the day's tally of round-trips from ship to shore.

The Cape Evans Hut was about to rise from a black sand beach overlooking a small bay ending at the Barne Glacier to the north, well above the highest reaches of tide. Tom Crean and Taff Evans stood on the beach looking south. Familiar landmarks from the old days greeted them from every direction. Tent Island, close at hand just offshore, marked the site of the saw-camp set up on the ice in the spring of 1903 in a vain attempt to free the *Discovery*. Beyond, the white arm of Erebus Glacier Tongue intruded into the icefield from Land's End at the far end of South Bay. Observation Hill towered over the *Discovery* Hut just out of sight beyond the Tongue. Farther south Mt. Discovery loomed, calling Crean back to the old country he had explored in 1903. Just out of sight below it lay the long scarp of Minna Bluff, and just beyond Barne Inlet where he'd tried to land. Across the sound to the west rose the Western Mountains, guarding the secrets of the dry valleys and the polar icecap beyond, known only to Taff himself and his tentmates Captain Scott and Bill Lashly from their great journey into polar history. Not that any of this was about making history; it was discovery, the great driving force of all human endeavor that bought them all here.

What a great lot of work and bother this exploring business was. It went on for years—the planning, the money raising and influence gathering, the buying and shipping, the building of shore stations and laying-out of depots. All of this in pursuit of a handful of dreamlike goals: to be the first to stand here or there, to see what man has never before seen, to add a bit of height to the sum of human knowledge, and sometimes argue about which explorer could claim priority. Here today, the endless round trips along an ice road with a ship at one end and a growing pile of timber at the other hardly seemed like work at all. All the men seemed to be thoroughly enjoying themselves, untroubled by doubts about the value or meaning of their effort.

Lt. Evans' boundless enthusiasm had bubbled over into the general air of the growing camp. Not everyone agreed with his flowery descriptions of the circumstances there on "Hurrah Beach" alongside "Happy Bay,"—the "palatial hut" a-building with the "White Lady" of Mt. Erebus overlooking all, and Captain Scott's looking cool and "quite cheerful" as he set about freeing the ship where she'd run aground. Crean knew his captain well enough to see the exaggeration there, but it was hard to fault the Lieutenant for his chipper kind words and goodwill when they set the tone for the expedition's early days.

By evening of this first day the building site had been leveled and a large green tent erected ashore for the carpenter and his helpers. There were plenty of hammers, and work ashore for all comers. The frame of the hut was already upright and ready for the first layers of boarding and quilted seaweed insulation that would hold at bay the cold.

Piles of food for horses, dogs, and men were growing on the beach. Lieutenant Bowers scurried around with his notebook in hand, ticking off the stores as they came in. The afterguard sweated in harness sledging the pony fodder ashore, an interesting reversal of their customary roles. They seemed to enjoy it, these human beasts of burden, making light of the novelty of the first honest days' work some of them had ever tried. Others, like the two doctors Atkinson and Wilson, already understood the relation of science and drudgery and threw their physical and moral weight behind the work of the expedition. By the end of the third day, nearly all the shore station supplies for the men had landed, with nearly sixty tons of fuel and fodder yet to come.

Even though Scott's figures and calculations seemed to justify it, Crean found the idea of horses as draft animals in the Antarctic hard to fathom. True, the animals came from the Siberian outback where they were hardened to a life in the snow-covered steppes, and Shackleton had enjoyed some success with them in 1907. The sad fact was, there was nothing here for them but death on the ice when their fodder and their usefulness had run out. Dogs at least could be fed from the produce of the sea, seal-meat and penguin, and even each other when all other food gave out. The ponies could scratch in vain at the snow crust in search of a wisp of grass to eat; they would find nothing but ice.

They were making four trips a day and beginning to reveal their characters—some lazy, some fretful, some unmanageable, some with traits that would become legendary. Each of the "shaggy seventeen" had a look and a character that distinguished him from his mates. Few of them stood higher than a man's shoulder. Some were wise enough to figure ways to get out of doing any significant work. Christopher and Hackenschmidt were big and mean. Punch and Nobby were obedient, steady workers. Blossom, with Blucher and Jehu, were the crocks of this uneven lot, better suited for the glue factory than for the hard work they were about to endure. No one but their handlers expected much out of them, but even they were pulling better than the dogs and the tractors. Along the road Crean and Blossom were hourly passed by manhauling parties competing for the humble honors of working the longest or hauling the fastest.

A cluster of tents sprang up to house the camp's growing population, beside the large brown cook-tent and the half-built walls of the new hut. As the days passed, the ice wharf had begun to deteriorate under the spell of the warm weather; holes and slushy weak spots began to reveal themselves. The ice road over which Crean had passed so many times had become a hopeless quagmire. Before the ship went off in search of a new wharf, the last of the three motors was uncrated on the deck and lifted out onto a wooden pad on the ice. As soon as its rollers touched the boards twenty men took up the hawser led from the front end and began to drag it onto firmer ground, but the ice beneath was too rotten to bear the concentrated weight. One of the men on the line put his foot right through and plunged into seawater up to his neck. The next man dropped the rope to haul him out and the forward progress of the motor stopped. With an ominous sigh the ice began to creak and sag, then cracked and slowly gave way with a sickening, advancing gush. First just one corner, then the whole motor began to dip into the hole. Each man kept his grip on the hawser, all of them shouting and cursing and hauling for all they were worth, as though by holding on with human strength they could have changed the inevitable outcome. It was a tug of war the human side must surely lose. First one man, then the next let go the hawser as the motor broke slowly through the ice and sank to the bottom of the bay.

By the end of the eighth day everything going ashore was ashore. The time had come to abandon the ice road. The shell of the hut was nearing completion. Patent fuel and bales of fodder stacked like bricks enclosed a roomy stable for eleven ponies along its south side. Overhead the skua gulls wheeled, their screeching calls an occasional accent to the racket of hammer-blows and men singing at their work. These were happy times. The work, the shared endeavor toward a lofty goal, was its own reward.

Scott was pleased. The fits of temper and moodiness that had brooded in him during the long passage through the ice had been replaced with smiles and recognition all around. So rapid was the progress on the shore station that Sunday January 15 was declared a day of rest and the men were left to lie-in until eight o'clock, a just reward for a job well-done. The balance of the day was given over to make-and-mend and a leisurely stroll up the nearby slopes to take in the lay of the land. In the *Discovery* days this place had been known as "the Skuary" after the thousands of gulls that called it home. Now it was home to twenty-eight explorers; the hard-frozen wilderness of Ross Island had been settled. The grace notes of Anglican hymns drifted up from the men gathered on the foreshore for Sunday service. There could hardly be a more beautiful place in all the world.

After that one day's rest it was back to the grind, not that a single soul ashore was complaining. The very idea of standing watch on board the ship now seemed like so much leisure. There, a man knew when his trick would be over, and where and when a snug bunk awaited him. Nothing to it at all--pointless in a way, with so much yet to be done.

Two days later, the hut was finished. It was much more than a "hut". It was a virtual palace inside and out—certainly more comfortable than the *Discovery* hut would ever have been--and the men moved in officially. A steady stream of them trooped bearing the raw materials of bunks and shelving, spring mattress and sleeping bags, books and the impedimenta of science and survey.

* * * * *

It took a moment for the eyes to become accustomed to the darkness of the men's quarters just inside the entry door. The corner to the right was given to the galley, shaped and dominated by a huge black iron cooking range. The kitchen pantry was easily the most colorful spot in the entire hut, with long shelves stacked high with cans and boxes and packages—blue Demerara sugar, red dutch cheeses, the bright yellow of Fry's concentrated cocoa. Right beside stood the big cook's table from which would rise the bread of a thousand meals. The men's table stood four-square right in the center of the room—a trestle, a workbench, a smoking-stand, a gaming table—and at its end the hut's only sewing machine. To the left opposite the galley were a row of four bunks, wire mattresses supported on metal frames. The one nearest the bulkhead was chosen by Taff Evans, and hard by this his *cobbo* Tom Crean chose to make his home.

The wardroom was deeper inside the hut, past the bulkhead of packing cases stacked like bricks to make a flimsy wall between the men's quarters and those of their officers. Their messdeck side was as private as a foc's'le, where jibes and criticisms of their seniors could be freely shared, easily heard, and resolutely ignored by every true officer in the wardroom. Just as on board a ship, the men's quarters were their own, and whatever was said or done there was no concern of any officer.

Already music from the gramophone—Caruso, Tetrazzini, a Norwegian tune for Gran--began to fill the air. With the hut now fully occupied, the focus of the work shifted immediately to preparations for the present season's depot journey. There were still two months of sledging weather yet before operations must close down for the winter. The plan was to leave as soon as possible and travel a far as possible—82 degrees South was the goal—there to leave an advance depot of stores for the next season's work. Camping gear was served out to all who would be going south—felt boots and slippers, sweaters of Jaeger wool, summer windproofs and fur mitts, two pairs of finnesko for each traveler. Crean and Evans took charge of fitting out the sledges for travel. No one else on hand could know better the demands of life on the trail.

The next stage was already beginning.

Chapter Four

Trial on the Sea-Ice

Erebus Glacier Tongue.   January 24, 1911.

Crean had one night only to spend in warm and noisy luxury of his new spring bed before leaving for Hut Point. The fresh smell of that bed—clean horsehair and wool, the lingering scent of bleach in the sheet—would not last. By evening the hut was filled with drifting layers of tobacco smoke, the rank aroma of unwashed sweat from twenty-eight men newly confined to a life indoors. After lights-out, a single candle cast dancing shadows of the night watchman's nodding head on the folds of the galley curtain. Crean would not have thought the ticking of a handful of clockwork instruments in the wardroom could make such a racket, until the mild sound of them was completely overwhelmed by the snoring of Bowers and half the afterguard. Already he was longing for the clean air, the cool and quiet of life on the trail.

In the morning after breakfast he'd harness the docile Blossom to an empty sledge and head out over the fast-ice still clinging to the shore. They would keep company with seven other teams stretched out in a slow-moving line along the narrow trail toward the Glacier Tongue. The *Terra Nova* was already waiting there to meet them. She was as far south as she could get toward the *Discovery* hut, the first way station along the south polar trail. A landing had already begun in earnest at the Tongue, the southbound stores loaded out of the hold and directly onto empty sledges. The dogs were to pull them at once to sounder ice below the bare black turret of Castle Rock looming on the hillside high above like a medieval fortress.

Growing piles of southbound stores littered the ice there at Camp One, awaiting the arrival of the ponies to carry them onward a hundred-fifty miles past Hut Point and well out into the middling reaches of the Barrier. A good stout depot at eighty degrees South was Scott's ultimate goal for the waning season, or farther along if the horses held up. Out there man and pony food, oil for the primus stoves, and replacement gear would lie in wait over the winter, under cover of the polar night and a good thick pile of Barrier snow, to be picked up in spring. By the time the depot party returned to Cape Evans for the winter, the ship would have long since departed to winter in the tropic waters of the South Pacific. Perhaps the *Terra Nova*'s crew had the right idea after all.

Of the seventeen surviving horses, only eight would be going on the depot journey over the Barrier. They would scratch in vain for a wisp of grass beneath the snow, but there would be no food at all for them that they hadn't hauled along themselves. Their sharp little hoofs broke right through the surface crust; their wooly pelts were not enough to keep them warm in a blizzard.

There were differing opinions about their best use. Captain Oates, the only real horseman among the men, wanted to take the weakest and slaughter them out on the Barrier, leaving their corpses to line the trail like mileposts. The meat from their butchering would be cached to feed the dog teams when the real push south was underway in the spring. Scott

90

was too much a sentimentalist to think of the ponies in such a cold and calculating way. Some of the crocks would be going south—Jehu, Weary Willie, Crean's own Blossom--along with some of the better horses. Not all of them were expected to make it home. The goal was to place the depot at the farthest possible distance along the trail; strength and endurance would be needed. A shortfall now would mean more work and greater distances between depots for the men returning from the Pole next year.

Crean's last letters home were in his pocket, written and sealed and ready to hand over to the captain of the *Terra Nova* to post when the ship reached New Zealand. In them he tried to answer questions asked months before, but his own handwriting with its carefully scrawled lettering and short terse sentences he knew had not the eloquent turn of his voice. Hannah must be waiting, waiting to hear from him. The folks at home would want to know his whereabouts even if they had not the maps on which to pinpoint his whereabouts, and Mother would want to believe he was keeping warm. Of course, he told them all, everything would be all right. Everyone's letters home did the same.

It was well the ponies departed when they did; one day later the last of Cape Evans' fast-ice connection to the south broke away and drifted out to sea. One could never count on much of anything in the way of sea-ice in summer. The rendezvous with the ship at the Tongue had gone without incident. By the end of the third day everything was off-loaded onto the ice and the ship sailed away.

It is always the same with the men of the King's Navy embarking on some mission, no matter where they might be bound. Cheer and cheer returned, a waving of hats between ship and shore until distance mutes the voices into the sigh of the southern breeze, and each from the other disappears from view.   Crean and Taff Evans would be parted for a while, the one to go south with his horse to lay out the depot on the Barrier.   Taff remained aboard with the geologists, bound for the Western Mountains across the sound.   The newcomers would have to be broken in, and they could have no finer teacher of the rigors and ways of life on the trail.

After landing the geological party there the *Terra Nova* would sail east along the Barrier face as far as Edward VII Land.   There Lieutenant Victor Campbell and his Eastern Party would be set ashore to finally explore the mysteries of that barely-seen, never-visited unknown realm. Now *those* fellows would have their hands full—an entirely new landing complete with hut, stores, stoves, sledges and ponies, the entire equipage for another wintering party, albeit five men and two ponies only.

The Southern depot party setting out turned their attention quickly to the task at hand.   In all, the job was expected to take seventy days' sledging out and back until the first of April, quite late enough in the autumn to be abroad on the Barrier.   Twelve men, seven ponies, thirty-eight dogs, and three tons of supplies had been landed from the ship at Camp I on the Glacier Tongue.   After breakfast the men made their first move, past the sloping head of Hut Point and the knoll above where Vince's cross had for nine lonely years withstood the blasts of the Antarctic gales.   There would be no stopping at the *Discovery* hut.   It would be *keep on, keep on* while the sea-ice held.   Camp II went up briefly to rest the ponies off Cape Armitage, before crossing the thin ice of the still-frozen thaw pool off the cape and onto the Barrier itself for Camp III.   This last, far enough in on the Barrier that the ice on which it stood would not likely break off, came to be known as Safety Camp.

The wind off the Barrier beat into the men's faces and scoured everything else down to one flat, level plain. In the distance two mounds rose above that plain like boulders from a sand beach, like nothing that nature would have left there. These proved to be two of Shackleton's tents from 1907, nearly filled now with snow. Excavated, they gave up an abandoned store of unfamiliar rations still fit to eat—Rountree's cocoa, Bovril, Brand's Extract of Beef, sheeps' tongues, cheese and biscuits. Nothing here that would not have been common as dirt back home, but each new flavor and texture promised an unexpected luxury in the months of hooshes yet to come.

Dr. Atkinson was trying manfully not to show it, but he had been limping all the way around Cape Armitage. In the frenzied effort to get everything safely landed in the shortest possible time with a minimum of fuss or complaint, he had chafed his heel. He wouldn't be known for a slacker; he kept on working, ignoring the pain of it. Now it had suppurated so badly he could hardly walk. Behavior like that might have been expected of a seaman, putting up a good show rather than be seen as too weak to push on. It might mean the difference in a man making the Pole, or not-- but he was an officer—and a doctor! He certainly wouldn't be walking out onto the Barrier another hundred-twenty-odd miles and then back home again.

It was the sick-list for the doctor, and a sure blow to the seaman who would have to stay behind at the *Discovery* hut to keep him company while the others went on to lay out the depot. Crean was the unlucky sailor, but he had too much respect for his Captain, too much affection to make him say the words *this is an order*. He had earned a place in the advance party. Of all the men on hand Crean, alone with Scott and

93

Wilson, had *ever* crossed the icebound wasteland ahead. Only these three had the experience, the firsthand knowledge of the hazards underfoot and ahead, that lay in wait. Crean had been Scott's Captain's Coxswain in the interval between the expeditions; he'd earned a place of more distinction.

He knew every man there could read the disappointment in his face. Another man less experienced on the ice—Cherry, or the seamen Forde or Keohane—could do the job just as well. It wanted little but attention and company. *Anyone* could have stayed behind to play nursemaid to the man, a surgeon no less. Dr. Atkinson should have better known how to care for his own infirmities, but perhaps, like anyone else, he'd never admit to an infirmity that would keep him out of the game.

No matter. An order's an order whether it's spoken as such or not. The advance party would be gone a month and a half; they'd get on fine without him. There was plenty to be done right here at Hut Point. In the years since Shackleton had used the place, snow coming through a broken window had filled the hut quite to the rafters and compacted into a solid block of ice within the walls. A shame it was in this condition, barely usable for any purpose other than as a landmark. The bare wood of its siding showed through the once-bright terra-cotta paint blasted away by years of wind-driven granular snow. On the crusted snow outside, ancient footsteps still showed in relief. The white wooden cross, stark against the black basalt of Arrival Heights, still stood erect. *"Sacred to the Memory of George T. Vince",* lost from *Discovery*, far from home. The cross still cast its gnomon shadow around the clock and the old reliable Hut Point wind still poured through the Gap between Crater Heights and Observation Hill.

After the last of the pony sledges disappeared from view, Crean

94

looked into Atkinson's eyes, and the doctor into his. A long, silent moment passed between them. It would be the first of many. They were opposites in more ways than it was possible to count—social standing, education, formality, polar experience, common sense. More critical than any of these—one of them liked to talk, loved the sound of his own tongue, the ebb and flow of gossip and blarney he'd mastered as a child. The other spent his words like a miser, kept all thoughts and ideas to himself unless they were drawn out of him against his will. How the two of them would fare in the enforced intimacy of six weeks alone together at the Hut could only be guessed. Crean might likely go mad with loneliness from having no one but himself for conversation, and the doctor be driven to the same end from the incessant chattering with no particular point. The prospect of it, though not quite torture, was not far removed. How either would retain his sanity was anybody's guess.

From the outset Crean had plenty to keep him occupied and clear of the doctor's taciturn company. A great mound of pony fodder had been abandoned temporarily at Safety Camp, to be sledged at leisure over to the hut and covered over with snow for future use. The hut, filled to the rafters with four years worth of frozen snow, was uninhabitable and would remain so until someone—Tom Crean—cleared it out. The invalid was unfit for either task. The chink-chink-chink of the pickaxe on the rock-hard ice and the scrape of a coal-shovel against the wooden floor might well be the only sound for weeks.

In the end, their enforced isolation was a good thing. Six weeks is a long time for any two men to spend alone together. A talker like Taff would have worn Crean's ear down to a nub with his incessant swaggering tales half-fact, half-fiction. There was no danger of that with Dr.

Atkinson; still, he was not altogether silent, and the two found there was much to be learned from each other.

The excavation of the hut was like an archaeological dig. Each new yard of floor exposed seemed to contain some hidden artifact of a bygone civilization—Shackleton's hastily abandoned final meal here, old books and older newspapers there, the remnants of the stage lights from the *Discovery*'s Royal Terror Theatre. Most important of all—tinned and dried foodstuffs would add some variety to the ordinary sledging rations lately hauled in from the *Terra Nova*. The inevitable needs of science must also be met by the digging of holes through the sea ice for Atkinson's trawls and dip nets.

Once the floor was cleared, the two men gathered up abandoned packing cases and partitioned off the larger of the rooms, and setting up their tent within its shelter, moved in. Except for Shackleton's brief stop here in 1907 this was the first time anyone had *ever* called the place home. With tin matchboxes pressed into service as blubber lamps, the first layers of seal and penguin soot were soon added to the soon-to-be-blackened walls of the chilly interior. Outside, the sea ice filling the bay as far as the Glacier Tongue north began to break up and drift away until open water lay just a few hundred yards offshore. There an ice-dock awaited the *Terra Nova* when she returned from her eastward excursion to King Edward VII Land with some astounding news.

The ship had been unable to get close enough inshore to land Campbell and his Eastern Party at King Edward VII Land. Discouraged in that ambition and steaming back toward Ross Island along the ghostly cliffs of the Barrier face, she had put into the Bay of Whales for a quick look at the Barrier ice up close. There was another ship tied up there! It was the *Fram*. Amundsen had absconded with her from his announced voyage to seek the North Pole and had instead come south under a veil of secrecy. Now his terse telegram to Scott in Melbourne was beginning to make sense.

His plans were now no longer a secret; the Norwegian was headed for the South Pole. It was a brazen attempt to forestall Scott's long-planned and very public assault on that very same goal. Here was a challenge no one on the *Terra Nova* had foreseen. Campbell reacted with anger, as did they all. Who was this foreigner to come trespassing here in the Antarctic, to challenge the British on their own ground? Scott had opened the route to the Pole, and now by rights it was his to finish.

After the bare formalities of a state visit—the Norskies were European, after all, and some neighborly pleasantries here in this remote desert were in order—the *Terra Nova* was off again. Campbell and his men had become, in a rapid reorganization, the Northern Party. They would be landed at Cape Adare during the ship's homeward passage to her winter quarters in New Zealand, there to make the best of their circumstances and add to the store of knowledge about that almost-as-remote part of the world.

Along their way, they called again at Hut Point, and handed off the news to Crean and Atkinson to relay on to the others. The ship did not tarry long. Crean's farewells and his final letters home would be the last for at least a year until the ship returned again in the spring of 1912. A year is a long time for any suitor to be away. Whatever chance he had to confirm his betrothal to Hannah lay in this one letter to a trusted friend. *--Please speak to her father on my behalf.--* Beyond these inadequate written words, there was nothing more to be done but wait out that year for the reply.

The ship sailed away, this time for good. Crean stood on the ice-foot with the wind ruffling his already-graying hair, watching the ship steam slowly away, waving his last goodbye as she grew smaller against the horizon. Then she was at last lost from view. *Godspeed*, and none could say when these men would meet again.

By the third week of February the Depot Party might be expected to turn up at any time. After his five-weeks' confinement the doctor's foot was well-healed; he was able as any man to get around. Anticipating the depot party's imminent arrival, he and Crean set off around Cape Armitage to greet them. They met up with Scott, Wilson, and some of the others bringing in a single pony, Jimmy Pigg.

They had just arrived at Safety Camp. The news from the hinterland was not encouraging. The depot party had fallen thirty-five miles short of their goal of 80 degrees south latitude. The shortfall would mean three and a half days' extra marching for weary travelers homeward bound from the Pole. Blossom and another horse had died on the trail. Their meat was now depoted under mounds of snow, cached away to fed the dogs in the coming spring. The five surviving horses still out on the Barrier were not doing well, but they ought to arrive in due course with Bowers, Oates, and the Norwegian Gran. With Scott there was never any time to be wasted idly when there was work to be done. He had determined that the time waiting for their arrival would be better spent hauling more supplies from Safety Camp farther out onto the Barrier. This meant manhauling, and Crean was enlisted.

At last he was being put to some good use out on the trail, where he belonged. The next way-station "Corner Camp" lay thirty-odd miles east out on the Barrier. From there on, the crevasse-fields near White Island were assumed to be safely behind, and the trail bent around to its true southward bearing. Crean joined Scott and Cherry in one tent; Atkinson moved in with seaman Forde and Lt. Evans in the other. They would be manhauling in harness, dragging the loaded sledges behind them over the level plain that was the Great Ice Barrier. Jimmy Pigg, the one horse at hand, was given a reprieve from his late exertions and allowed to walk unburdened behind the sledge. Somewhere out ahead they would be meeting up with the others.

Something about this life on the trail erased most of the distinctions that in other circumstances would have come between the sailor and his tentmates   Scott was his captain, not his friend. That fact would never change, but it could be softened, rounded over by the spare simplicity of life on the trail. Cherry was of the landed gentry, unranked and young enough to be open to true friendship. Settling into the warm depths of his reindeer fur sleeping bag that night after a last pipe and the small quiet talk of men together before they drop off to sleep, Crean knew he had been away from this life too long. The floorcloth crackled beneath him when he turned; the wind sighed and sucked at the green canvas of the tent. Outside Jimmy Pigg snuffled and stamped, lonely for the companionship of another horse.

The old camp routines of the trail and tent came easily to Crean. Beginning with his very first *Discovery* marches onto the Barrier, he'd logged 131 days in the field, more than almost anyone else and certainly more than any of the other seamen. He was an old hand at this, pitching the tent under the windiest and most miserable of circumstances, tending to the gear or lighting up the primus and filling the cooker--whichever duty called. The whole scheme was a decided improvement over the way things had been done on *Discovery*. The tents and all the gear now were set up for four-man units. The new reindeer fur one-man sleeping bags were a decided improvement over the cumbersome three-man bags used in the old days. It was a great comfort now to have a bed of one's own. In the warmer summer weather still remaining, the unwanted body heat of two companions in so intimate a confine would have been a perfect affliction.

Within the tent on the polar trail all the men, whatever their rank, are just *men*. Between them flowed a heated discussion about the news of Amundsen's setting up camp at the Bay of Whales for his own assault on the Pole. This was an unsportsmanlike affront, to sneak in unannounced and try to beat Scott to the fulfillment of his long-sought ambition. The Norwegian had not bothered to bring much elaborate scientific equipage; he was here for the glory of it and nothing else. He had thrown down the gauntlet with his cryptic telegram at Melbourne: "Am going south." Scott had gamely responded for the benefit of his men, that the threat of a rival expedition would not alter his plans. In truth they were set in motion long before and too complex to modify or accelerate. Now that the Norwegian had called it a race, let the best man win.

His countryman was now suspect. Gran's every lapse of judgment or failure to follow orders with alacrity became another shortcoming from which Scott could not conceal his annoyance. In the beginning nothing the boy could do would earn him praise, or even a momentary respite from his commander's scrutiny. The sailors felt for him, understood his plight, but were too much of the mess deck to ever really make him a friend. Gran slowly redeemed himself in countless small ways, but he would never be chosen to be one of the southern party to bring home the goal to England.   At the end of all the talk, there was nothing to be done about the matter except to continue with the original plan of the expedition, and may the best men—from the *Terra Nova* of course—may the best men win.

The men in Scott's tent were by now the more experienced and the faster travelers. Outward bound they made Corner Camp on the 26th, passing Bowers and the others still coming in at a distance along the way, and depoted another six-weeks' provisions and some pony food.   Leaving the others to lead Jimmy Pigg along at a slower pace, Scott's sledge turned for home going at a great rate.   They covered twenty-six miles that day, camping only ten miles in from Safety Camp.   All the stragglers from One Ton Depot on the Barrier, the dogs and the last of the ponies, caught them up that night.

The depot journey had been just what Crean needed to feel the part of the explorer again.   Any man can live in a house, but only the few can call the ice their home and mean it, every word.   The crunch of the snow beneath the floorcloth, the hiss of the primus and bubble of the hoosh-pot, the snapping of the tent-canvas under the blow of the southern gale—it is all enough to soothe a man to sleep each night and wake him peacefully in the morning.   Sure, there might by then be a quarter-inch of rime covering the bags and everything inside the tent, but it brushes off.   Cold, yes, but really not much colder than the inside of the hut and a whole lot cleaner and brighter.   Then it's the slish-slish of the ski on the soft snow, the clatter of the runners over the sharp sastrugi, the welcome call of lunch-oh!   in the middle of the day.

The survival of any of the ponies in this weather remained in doubt, and it was imperative to get them back to Hut Point without delay. Of the eight ponies taken out on the Barrier, Blossom and Blucher were dead and buried. Another was now so near death by exhaustion he might not make it the few remaining miles to the shelter of the *Discovery* Hut. The path through the Gap was too steep and rubbly for the weakened ponies just come in from the depot journey. They would have to be led down to the sea ice, rotten as it was, out around the thaw pool of open water that always bedeviled Cape Armitage, and then on to the hut along a sea level route.

Bowers left Safety Camp first and led Uncle Bill—named at the landing for Dr. Wilson-- safely down on to the fast ice to wait there in the lee of the Barrier for the other three horses to catch up. Crean and Cherry came along shortly after, leading Punch, Guts, and Nobby. Each horse was towing a heavy sledge to stock the *Discovery* Hut with food and oil in anticipation of an extended layup there waiting for the sea route to Cape Evans to freeze over for the winter.

They all joined up at the ice foot and struck out over the sea ice, following in the dog track left by Wilson and Meares, who had gone on ahead, leaving the horse party would follow in their wake at a leisurely pace. Frost smoke hovered over the sea-ice, a hint at the open water to be expected off Cape Armitage ahead. Crean had been out around the Cape himself only a few days earlier and seen the thaw pool out there wider than expected. A good long circuit farther west ought to keep everyone safe.

The dog teams could still be seen, black specks in the distance breaking a trail for the ponies. They made an unexpected tack to the right, then disappeared into the dense dark fog covering everything in that direction. The fog crept slowly toward the Barrier until it enshrouded the horse party and obscured the barely visible dog track. In the flat light, the footprints disappeared altogether. The sky was clear overhead and the summit of Observation Hill remained in view above the mist, a landmark by which to keep the course. As long as they kept out a weather eye for the edges of the thaw pool, the horse party could navigate around the Cape to safety. Moving onward, they crossed the tide crack separating the newer sea ice from the old fast ice clinging to the Barrier edge. The new ice was at least seven feet thick and to all appearances quite solid.

They pressed on. The ponies, worn out from their six weeks on the Barrier, were not going well. Small cracks began to appear beneath their feet, only a half inch wide and solid on both sides, but there was water in them—not a good sign. In another mile the cracks became unpleasantly common. The horse party stopped at a working crack. The gap was no more than an inch wide; the floes on either side of it scraped up and down against each other, a barely perceptible motion. There was no doubt about it; the ice was no longer fast. Pinned in on three sides by the Barrier and the islands, it might hold together until they had all reached solid ground again around Cape Armitage. Or, once under the influence of the open water to the northwest, it might break out without warning and carry them all out to sea.

Bowers made the wise decision to retreat to the relative safety of the fast ice. A few hours' march back along the trail the cracks between the floating ice pans were no longer in motion. When the four ponies could walk no farther, the men stopped to pitch their tent and settle in for an uneasy night. After another half-day's march in the morning they'd be home free.

Crean and Cherry threw up snow walls to shelter the poor animals from the wind for the night while Bowers, the peggy for tent, busied himself making supper over a broken primus stove. In the half-light one bag looked much like another, and the batch of cocoa he thought he was boiling was made instead with curry. Crean drank his right down, barely seemed to notice. Camped on the ice after a long day on the trail, one hot drink was much as good as another. So what if one was a little hotter that expected; it would keep a man that much warmer for the night.

At 4:30 a.m. Bowers, awakened by an unexpected rustling outside, left the tent to make sure his pony had not gotten into the oats. The scrape of his jacket on the canvas of the door broke into Crean's uneasy sleep. He felt the gentle rocking of the floe, the low rumbling grind of ice-edge on ice, the plaintive neigh of the horses in the distance. *Distance!?*

Bowers was outside the tent, shouting. Crean, suddenly awake, knew in an instant what the trouble was. He jumped out of his bag and into his boots in a moment. The almost-firm pack on which they'd pitched camp just hours before was breaking up around them. The cracks that had once been nearly invisible had spread and the solid ice sheet was now a field of small floes separated by jagged leads of black seawater. The floes, spinning lazily in the still-confined waters, were heading out to sea with the camp aboard. The tent was on one, the horses and sledges on another. Bowers jumped across the gap in his stocking feet and quickly dragged the sledges close before they drifted off. The home floe split again but the tent, the sledges and gear were safely all together on one piece, fifty yards across and already crumbling away at the edges. Two horses were on another. One pony had vanished. Guts was gone, and his pony wall, with only a streak of black water to show where they had been. The other three--Nobby and Punch and old Uncle Bill--stood by calmly, awaiting orders from their masters.

The low mist shrouded everything more than a few yards off, while the summit of Observation Hill still showed clear above. Somewhere miles back on the trail the fast-ice still held, but they would have to get to it. The three men did not need to think up a plan to get started; first get the ponies onto the same floe as the gear and afterward hold council for what to do next. It was still early in the break-up. The two floes bearing the camp and the animals were slowly rotating, touching at one edge, at least for the moment. The horses, with no idea of the danger and their impending doom, followed at the gentle urgings of their masters from one floe to the next.

Strike camp *now* and load the sledges for an escape. Never mind that at the moment it appeared the only hope of survival must surely involve abandoning everything—horses, sledges, tent and all--to its fate and lighting out for shore. Lt. Bowers and Cherry were in something of a panic; Crean went calmly about this business, like any bluejacket acting as though he'd done this sort of thing often before.

The course of action was quickly decided: all or none. Under Bowers' command, the plan was to never separate, but keep the gear, the men, and the ponies, all together. They would move in a unit, dragging the sledges and jumping the ponies from floe to floe as they made their way toward the Barrier edge across the moving ice. All the expedition's plans depended on having enough ponies, tents, bags and men, for the polar advance in the spring. Bowers would never willingly give up any of it. As long as it lay in their power to preserve what was in hand, these three men would give their all to save it.

The moving broken-up sea ice was still somewhat confined, the floes drifting, slowly spinning. For six hours the horse party worked their way along, coming at last to one large floe, a piece of the Barrier newly broken off and floating like an iceberg with a sloping top. Only forty feet of open water lay between them and the safety of the Barrier. The men marooned on it might almost as well have been on the moon. A herd of killer whales had gotten a whiff of fresh meat ready for the taking. The lead was full of them. The water was fairly boiling with their furious careening and charging, blowing and roaring, flashing white teeth and beady black eyes and blood from half-eaten seals everywhere. The ponies, ever-patient, ever-trusting, took no notice. Without warning the ice beneath them split in two.

After a hasty retreat to a safer floe, the men fed the ponies and held a council of war. Someone must go for help, across the moving ice to the Barrier and Safety Camp, where some of the returning depot party might still be camped. Lieutenant Bowers as senior officer would not leave his charges behind even though it could mean going, like any master, down with his ship. Crean and Cherry both volunteered at once to make the dangerous trip to shore. Cherry with his poor vision would be unable, if he lost his spectacles along the route, to find his way.

Crean it would be. With no further ado he said good-bye and left. He knew from *Discovery* days that the ice, once broken up and started, could vanish forever out to sea within hours, never to be seen again. The only hope would be a happy coincidence of floe touching floe as they hurried along on their ocean migration and by chance laying out a fairly direct route for him to the fast ice miles behind to the east. With each passing moment, the likelihood of such luck grew less. Bad timing or a faint heart could doom them all, and perhaps the expedition's chances of success as well.

By this time the day had come into full bloom. Looking back, Crean saw his companions drifting away into the distance beyond spreading pools and lakes of open water. The sound of the pack in motion—the creaking and grinding of floe on floe, the splash and gurgle of running water, the hiss and blow of killer whale—grew louder. Another man might have found the outlook hopeless, but Crean was no ordinary man. He was pretty lively, blazing a convoluted track over the spinning, spreading patchwork of ice that still at random places touched. At times he paused, waiting for the moving ice to connect and make a path for him, stamping his feet and swearing like any sailor to keep warm.

One last black lead lay between him and the low vertical bluff of the Barrier edge. The floe on which he stood moved slowly westward, rolling against the fast-ice like a wheel, touching and then bounding away. If he was to gain the shore, then he must make a leap across the gap to a small sloping shelf at the water's edge, the only place that had a prayer of holding him. If his faith did not desert him, he might hang on for dear life, cut himself a step with his rigging knife, and then another and another. One slip here would cost him dearly--a disabling plunge into the freezing water, a quick death by drowning. His friends would drift away with the departing ice, lost forever. No one in the expedition would know more than that they had gone onto the sea ice and floated to their deaths.

He leapt and landed, and did not fall. With one hand he steadied himself, with the other scooped out a first footstep, then another, up the steep face of the fast-ice. Chunks of hardened snow, loosened by his hand, tumbled down the steep face and splashed into the black water. He did not slide back down. Each step lifted him above the last until he gained the lip of the bank, braced himself, and with one mighty heave threw himself over its edge and onto the flat, secure face of the Barrier.

The effort had almost done him in. It was good he'd kept up the pace over the floe; the long hours picking out a way over the moving ice had cost him his vision and slowed him now. His unprotected eyes had nearly gone snowblind from picking out a path across the constantly shifting ice. Squinting, he worked his way along to the northeast until he found his own outward track, and made for Safety Camp. Just before it went entirely, he made out up ahead a black figure on skis coming out to meet him. He knew by the voice it was the Norwegian.

Scott was surprised to see Crean coming back to the camp with Gran from the southwest, having supposed the pony party were already safely housed at the hut. He lost no time in putting together a rescue-sledge and setting out for the Barrier edge with Oates, and blind Crean in tow. Out on the sea-ice, Cherry and Bowers had been following Crean's example, taking advantage when they could of floes touching in the right direction, working the gear and the horses toward the Barrier edge. They had made it to a secure floe jammed up against the Barrier edge and waited there for help to come. They could have left the camp and ponies and saved themselves at any time by using a sledge as a ladder to climb the low bluff, but Bowers would never abandon his charges, not until the very end.

The ice remained in its position until the rescue party found them. Crean saw nothing but heard the passion of anger and relief in his Captain's voice shouting down to Bowers from the bluff Barrier edge. *"I don't care a damn about the ponies and the sledges. It's you I want, and*

I am going to see you safe up here before I do anything else."

The men at least were safe. The floe, slowly turning, inched closer inshore as the gear and sledges were handed up. Oates cut a bridle-path into the ice down to meet a landing-place where few feet of open water still remained. Just as success seemed assured, the wind changed, the ice shifted and a lane of black water began to open--2 feet, 6 feet, 10 feet, 20 feet. The men on shore, unable to do anything more, made supper. The ponies on their floe sailed slowly out towards the sea on a course parallel to the barrier, still huddled together calmly awaiting their masters to bring them their nosebag breakfasts in the morning.

Their floe came to rest again, pinned in a mass of loose ice a few miles to the west. There was still some hope. The rescue camp moved again. Crean, helpless, followed along in its wake. Out on the broken ice a mighty drama played itself out. The sledging gear was already successfully landed; the time had come to lead the ponies to safety. They might be dull, but they were no fools. They had no intention of jumping this black lane of water while the ice on which they stood was firm and secure. Still, with the right cajoling and a hearty smack on the flank, they might be successfully persuaded to make the leap. They'd all of them jumped wider leads than this before--but suddenly weary, or newly aware of the horrifying circumstance to which he'd arrived--Punch balked.

For reasons known only to himself, he hung fire at the very edge, lost his footing, and slid into the freezing water. He had not the strength or a decent foothold to work himself up over the floe edge. Panicked, he thrashed helplessly in the water. The commotion would bring a killer whale to seal his fate in one bloody moment. Oates stepped up and with one quick blow of a pickaxe to Punch's brain ended his agony. His awful squealing softened the deadly sounds of impact, of shattered bone and pierced soft tissue. The hissing and blowing of killer whales on the hunt filled the sudden silence. There was no time to mourn his loss; two ponies remained. After near-miss of a jump Nobby landed safely on the Barrier. One ashore, one yet to go. Birdie's pony, Uncle Bill did not have the legs for it. He leaped, fell short, slipped into the black water. He met his end as Punch did, with a pickaxe to the brain.

Crean heard all this, but saw nothing. Snowblind, helpless, he held tightly to Nobby's halter on the Barrier edge, listening to the grisly scene played out below. Four sledges, one pony, the gear, and three men were safe for another season's work. They'd done all that was humanly possible.

Now all that remained was to bring the tattered remnants of the depot party to safety at Hut Point. This meant a difficult scramble up and over the heights, through the Gap and down to the hut. With the two surviving ponies sapped of whatever strength they'd ever possessed, it was left to the men to portage the sledges up and over the seven hundred foot pass to the hut. Worn and weakened, dejected, defeated, they arrived there March 5, and for the first time since the establishment of Safety Camp five weeks before, all the men of the Depot party were together again.

Chapter Five

Roughing It: Life at Hut Point

Hut Point.   March 1911.

Crean's fondest memories of his Antarctic days did not include a comfortable sojourn in the *Discovery* Hut.   Some of the coldest hours he'd ever spent were right here in this place as one of the captive audience for the performances of "The Royal Terror Theater" staged for the entertainment of the men of the *Discovery*.   The flames of the stagelights and the warmth of the sailors' bodies all gathered in the drafty room had done nothing to relieve the intense cold that seemed to dwell within it. The patent stove intended for it had never been installed, so that the temperature on the inside—and it was known to go into the minus-forties--was the same as on the outside at all times.   This shadowy uninhabitable den had been made darker when board skirts had been lately added to enclose the veranda for the ponies.   It was just not a place a wise man would want to call home, unless he was stranded on this lee shore with no way to reach the relative luxury of the house at Cape Evans. Spare as the temporary accommodations were, they would have to do until the open water barring the way home froze over solid enough to travel over

At its construction in 1902 the *Discovery* hut was already a relic of outdated thinking, a misplaced cabin designed for a settler's use in the Australian outback, landed and built on these Antarctic shores. What it lacked for insulation against the cold it made up for in extreme draftiness, but even the unrestricted flow of the Barrier breeze through it was not enough to clear the air of the greasy soot of burning penguin blubber.

Even though Crean had spent his weeks with Dr. Atkinson clearing the place of its accumulated ice and the rubbish left by its former occupants, it still remained a long way from comfortable. The furnishings were simple, most of them improvised from castoff goods restored to usefulness with a new purpose. An abandoned door was propped up for the cook's table. Shackleton's old blubber stove—little more than an open fire burning in an old kerosene tin set on bricks in the middle of the floor--wanted some improvement before it burned the place down. The *Terra Nova*s knew what to do. Fitted with a flue of sheet-iron from the scrap heap, the fireplace now sent most--not all--of the greasy blubber smoke outside. A bulkhead of packing cases divided up the interior into three rooms, each with its own atmosphere of heat and blubber soot and occupied by the men according to their tastes for warmth and cleanliness. Cleaned, heated, and fitted out as well as it would ever likely be, the hut was now ready for the extended stay of a dozen men, a pack of dogs, and the two surviving horses. Homely, and home it would have to be, until the sea froze firmly enough to admit an overland passage to Cape Evans.

The connecting road along the ice foot north to the winter station hut was closed. Open water still lay between the two outposts. There would be no direct communication, no returning to its relative comfort and security until the open sea froze over for good. It might be some time: during the *Discovery*'s stay the sea had not permanently, irretrievably, frozen in the ship until April. Crean remembered well how the ice had formed and gone out, formed and gone out again. Until it was finally frozen solid enough to make a dependable ice road, there would be no rejoining their comrades at Cape Evans. No man had ever tried the overland route across the crevassed glacier ice sliding off the flank of the volcano. The danger was just too great. As for the horses, they would just have to wait. Sea ice was wanted, firm and level, and nothing else would do. Now in early March it was open water all the way, and for who could say how long? There would be no traveling anytime soon, and no communication or supplies of any kind to be expected from the North.

Crean's work during Dr. Atkinson's convalescence had restored the place to a state almost as clean as the day it was built. All that changed with the onslaught of ten more unwashed ruffians coming in from the field at the end of the Depot journey. As the incoming stragglers took up residence, they set up neighborhoods around a packing-case partition. Some of the officers laid their beds under the ice-encrusted window illuminating the floor just north of the blubber and meat locker. The name "West End" implied a more elegant address than the place could actually claim. Past the kitchen, through a curtain to the coldest nook of the hut, three of the noblest souls—Wilson, Bowers, and Cherry, along with the dog-driver Meares, made up their beds in "Virtue Villa." This place shared a wall and the associated noise with the stable for the two surviving ponies. The sailors were the smart ones, claiming the warmest place hard by the blubber stove to sleep right through whatever activity swirled around them there.

By chance rather than choice, the lot of them kept close company. Until the sea-ice might freeze and grant them safe passage home to Cape Evans, there would be no going far from Hut Point. A walk of a mile or two for exercise, or else through the Gap to bring in one of the frozen seal carcasses stored on the other side. Oily smoke from the blubber stove and the matchbox blubber lamps soon coated every surface, including windproofs and whiskers. There was no escape from the greasy soot and no cleaning up until one black-faced man looked much the same as any other. Each was known by the sound of his voice, the choice of his words, or the roll of his gait coming in after a hike up Observation Hill looking for a signal from Cape Evans. They had already been all two months without a wash, a shave, a change of clothing, or even so much as a hair-brush. No one really minded the absence of grooming. Dirt is a relative thing, and the blubber soot set the standard by which all other sorts of filth did not even register.

The men would have to make do with whatever supplies they had themselves carried ashore in February, or had been left at the hut by the two previous expeditions—mostly a large supply of *Discovery* and *Nimrod* biscuit, some of it ten years old now. To this they'd add the meat of whatever penguins and seals could be killed and stored before these had made their own departure for the north. There was plenty of cocoa for the taking, to be boiled up in buckets. All of it would be cooked over the blubber fire adding its own distinctive greasy, fishy flavors. For variety there was a modest stock of luxuries in the form of raisins, oatmeal, sardines, and jam--nothing further in the matter of diet until communication with Cape Evans might be made.

The optimists believed the sea might well freeze over within a few weeks. Crean knew the score; there'd be no departure any time soon. Vince's cross, in memory of the seaman lost in a gale here in 1902, stood as a reminder that here one did not tempt fate, or the weather. With the sledging season closed for good, there were more men than there was work to keep them busy. There was no longer any urgency to the work of making the hut more comfortable. As long as seals remained plentiful and easy to secure, no one would go hungry.

On into the autumn the seals still hauled out at the tide crack at Pram Point. The hunting was no sport; it was a brutally simple game that hadn't changed since *Discovery* days. The brutes were easy to kill. One mighty swing of a heavy maul in a crushing blow to the creature's head, and the doomed seal sank heavily to the ice. Crean's fourteen-inch dagger just reached its heart. The hunters stepped back, dodging the gush of blood that squirted from the hole to spread and congeal on the ice. Then quick—skin the beast for its blubber, gut and clean it before the carcass froze solid, and load the meat onto sledges for manhauling up through the Gap and down the ski-slope to the hut. The liver and the steaks went for the men, the offal and the cheaper cuts were stacked like logwood to feed the dogs. The blubber, cut into strips, would feed the fire and fuel the improvised lamps. Coming back to the hut Crean, reeking of the slaughterhouse, brushed from his jacket the frozen blood in a shower of crystal red cascades to stain the virgin snow.

* * * * *

Crean could be friends with anyone in the most trying of circumstances, even those whose rank made them his superiors, but he never relaxed the formality of *"Sir"* in direct address. No officer ever achieved the level of familiarity the seamen reserved for their peers. In the close quarters and shared privation he was getting to know some of the fellows, better than he might have on board a ship. Now that he was spending a part of every day in company with Dr. Wilson, he saw how the man made no secret of his trust in Providence that no matter how difficult the circumstances, all would turn out right in the end.

The young bucks of the afterguard went to "Uncle Bill" for solace and advice. Something about his quiet, austere manner made him seem kindly and wise. Perhaps he was, but to the seamen his erudition and reserve made him harder to approach. They found in the two Lieutenants--Bowers and Evans—the salt-blasted common sense that earned their confidence more readily. Both had found their station in the world through the hawsepipe—the seaman's way. Common courtesy dictated that they always be addressed as *Mr.*—to their faces, in the shared community of the hut and later of the trail, even in the enforced intimacy of the tent.

Dr. Wilson wore many hats in the expedition: zoologist, official artist, explorer, inventor, cook, confidante and peacemaker. From his talented hands flowed a stream of watercolors, true renderings of the Antarctic's many fleeting images--the mysterious transient beauty of cloud, ice, drift, aurora—that mere words could never describe. He went up on Observation Hill daily to sketch up weather and sea effects, to be colored at leisure indoors and Cape Evans. Some of the men went with him and tried to learn the art, but none could match the sure tracery of his hand or the quiet self-control that colored his every word and directed his every move.

Lieutenant Evans spent his days in the refined work of a different indispensable kind, that of chief surveyor and mapmaker, always busy improving on the spotty and indifferent charts turned out by earlier expeditions. He still played the role of overgrown adolescent with his feats of strength and practical jokes, keeping up a roistering banter with every comer. He was a good sort, but it would be hard to see him in full command of any part of the expedition. Captain Oates, Dr. Atkinson—now that they had each other to not be talking to, they both seemed happier. Good old Bill Lashly was another quiet one, steady as an English oak upright through any gale. Cherry—Mr. Garrard--in particular had become a special friend since the ordeal on the sea-ice. He was such a youthful bounder, full of curiosity over every detail of Antarctic life, of boyish admiration for Crean's experience in these matters. As for the others, they were all good enough men; Captain Scott had chosen well.

There were still desultory attempts at improving the hut with scraps and debris salvaged from the trash heaps, but they yielded small results. The explosion of Gran's experiment with the remains of the *Discovery*'s discarded acetylene lighting system nearly beheaded Meares with a piece of flying tin. Oates tried his idea next. *"If this blows up, the hut goes with it."* Ever tactful, Uncle Bill joined him at his endeavors and in a day or two the whole scheme simply vanished, to the great relief of the others. With a stock of candles left over from *Discovery* and the dim and smoky light of blubber lamps, the old acetylene plant returned to its proper place atop the rubbish pile outside.

The spirited debates and arguments—none of them ending in hard feelings—the stories and speculations, for a while kept at bay the inevitable boredom that comes with waiting, waiting. Sleep became everyone's primary entertainment, and a good twelve hours out of the twenty-four became the standard. Each night just before lights-out Crean, Keohane, and Gran cleared a place beside the blubber stove and spread their bags on the wooden floorboards. Comfort was a relative thing. Most nights the temperature of the air inside stayed well below zero despite the constant crackling flame of the stove. A bed on the snow outside would have been warmer underneath, and cleaner. Quieter too, when the two ponies under the verandah started kicking up a fuss. The twelve men were just getting settled in to this routine and accustomed to the domestic hardships that had become their lot, when four more men were spotted coming in over the ice from the west.

After an absence of months, Taff was coming home, at least to the *Discovery* hut, as close as he could get until the sea-ice froze over. He was bringing with him the three geologists he'd led into the Western Mountains; now they'd get used to the constraints of shore life in a crowded, evil-smelling house. He'd taken them all over South Victoria Land, up glaciers and down, into the desert-bare dry valleys he had himself discovered with Scott and Lashly in 1903. For the scientists it the land was practically virgin territory like nothing else on earth, known only to the very lucky few.

It was well the stragglers all arrived when they did. Two days later the weather broke, stirred up the open sea to high waves that blew the frozen spume right over the point to rattle noisily over the Hut's wood roof. By morning an inch-thick coating of salt ice covered the beach, the hut, the dump heaps and the ruins of the weather-shed.

Hunger—or the boredom that satisfying it tended to relieve--was the driving force at Hut point. Never mind that there was plenty to eat;

with more seal meat coming in almost every day no one would starve, though a few might be longing for variety in their meals. With sixteen large appetites now to feed, and not much in variety available, they took turns cooking over the smoky blubber fire. As a rule breakfast was seal hoosh, cocoa and biscuit; lunch was chupatties and flapjacks made from flour and biscuit dust with butter or cocoa; supper was seal fried in butter, biscuit and cocoa. Cherry broke into the only tin of sardines to make a Hut Point variation of "whales on toast", but forgot to mind his blubber stove until the Cabin biscuit burnt to a cinder. Supper that evening was a concoction by Evans and Wright intended for stew, but generally regarded as "glue." Wilson's attempt at Welsh rarebit never melted away the long ropes of cheese that left it barely edible, though tasty to those who gave it a try. His feed of seal steaks fried in penguin oil, redolent of rancid sardine, was easily voted the worst attempted. Some of the men, with effort, managed to eat their share. On April Fool's Day Birdie Bowers handed out mugs of chaff with a thin layer of hoosh on top. No one ever seemed to tire of cocoa at every meal.

There was not a change of clothes or bedding to be had, no chance of a wash. Even Bowers had to do without. A manlier existence could scarcely be imagined, except perhaps a few more nights out in the field, away from the foul stale air and too-close comfort of the hut and its blackened sleeping inmates. One more sledge journey remained to complete the season's work. One more load of supplies had to be sledged to Corner Camp thirty miles out on the Barrier. What a relief to be returning to the rugged, simple life abroad on the veldt he'd come to love despite its hardships. It promised air crisp and pure, aurora firing the sky overhead, the coarse and close and wordless companionship of a handful of men whose shared trials forged a bond unmatched by any other.

Eight of them set out under command of Lt. Evans. They would be manhauling on skis the whole way, with a load of four cases of biscuit and a bag of oats for the ponies. Crean shared his with seamen Forde and Taff Evans, and the prickly geologist Wright. In a fit of patriotic fervor on St. Patrick's Day the big Irishman upset the hoosh-pot over the floorcloth. Scraped back into the pot newly flavored with grimy residue and a few stray reindeer hairs, the stew was only a little less palatable than it had been before. If the more delicate of his tentmates declined their portion, so much the more for Crean.

Except for the recurrent frostbites and snowblindness that crippled each man in turn, the eight days out and back were uneventful. There was nothing new to be seen, just the undulating white plain of the Barrier ice with a long line of coastal mountain ranges disappearing into the distance to the right, and the smoking peak of Mt. Erebus and its little brother Terror rising beyond Windless Bight to the left. Thick weather prevailing and minus-forties temperatures gave the newest hands their first taste of real cold-weather late-autumn sledging.

The extremes of temperature, as cold as any yet recorded on the Barrier, kept any pleasure in the outing to a minimum. It was impossible to light the primus with gloves on, so bare-skin fingers turned the adjusting screws and burnt like hell against the dreadfully cold metal. A good hot supper hoosh and a mug-up filled each man, not only his stomach but his chilled blood, carrying with it the warmth of the stove and the company. A man could feel that heat coursing through him, right to the ends of his frozen toes, if only for a little while. Enough to prepare him for the worst ordeal of autumn sledging, worming his way into the frozen sleeping bag, thawing it with his own body heat as he went. It took three hours each night, and once a man was snugged down, he was not inclined to leave that comfort until morning. That first step outside was another tribulation; his clothing, clammy and damp after a night in the relative sauna of the tent, froze solid with an electric shock the instant he stepped outside. Six days of this were enough to cure Crean of any nostalgia for the manly rigors of the field.

The Depot Party arrived back at the hut on March 23, glad to partake of even its paltry luxuries. Frostbites had been a daily occurrence, and their kit upon returning was pretty nearly frozen solid. The cold at the hut had been even worse—everything including the hut itself was encased in a sheath of solid ice. Fierce winds had stirred up the sea into a froth and carried the spray clear across the point, where it froze on every surface, every object. But not the sea. Here, where *Discovery* had been trapped in solid ice for two years, open water still stretched to the horizon.

With everyone reunited back at the hut, the sixteen men crowded together to begin their Spartan life in earnest. It was introduced with an unseasonable warm spell, which combined with the warmth of the blubber stove to melt the ice out of the attic overhead. The resulting water flow turned the floor, newly greasy with seal blubber, into something of a snipe marsh. The tropical rain-showers within, attended by the sound of water dripping into pails and pannikins scattered about the hut, posed a noisy paradox: here in the Antarctic, rain never falls unless it falls *inside* the house.

Cold weather returned to dry up the worst of these miseries. The days, ever shorter, began to follow one another unheralded, their passing barely noted. For those who kept diaries, there was less and less to say. With all its homely amenities, the hut was still a cold place. The wind off the Barrier flowed constantly through the Gap, and then through the gaps in the hut's uncaulked siding, but the sea refused to freeze.

The doubtful pleasures of this extended stay in such primitive conditions began to wear thin. All were growing anxious for a change. The sea began to freeze. An oily-looking skin of ice grew to a few inches thick--not quite enough to carry a man--before a change of wind swept it all away. It began to freeze over again, and by early April was thick enough to bear a man walking gingerly, sagging like a stretched blanket under his weight. The new ice seemed strong enough to inspire a hopeful crew to start hacking a trail for the ponies down through the ice foot--a bitterly cold job but a welcome one, for it signified an end to the camp life at Hut Point. Crean was to be among the foot party, the first to be leaving, but bad weather delayed a start.

Damn! By morning the ice had gone out and black water lapped at the ice foot. Had anyone been abroad on the sea-ice that night, they would now be in the bellies of the killer whales, or else lying on the bottom. So much for hopes of an early return to the relative luxury of Cape Evans. To make matters worse, a new spell of unaccountably high temperatures again began to melt the ice still trapped in the hut's roof. Soon a score of tin basins rang with the impact of droplets falling everywhere, until the temperature might drop and freeze everything solid again.

Everyone was anxious to get back to the base at Cape Evans, Captain Scott most of all. As soon as the new ice looked strong enough to bear, he called for another try. Nine of the sixteen men would be going, leaving the others to stay behind with the dogs and ponies to wait for firmer ice. Crean was among the men that set out April 11 with two sledges. It was a long haul overland first, up past Castle Rock without a breather and then down onto the sea-ice beyond Hutton Cliffs in a final push for Cape Evans. In fair weather the fifteen miles could be made in a day, but this little jaunt was to become an adventure in itself. The seven men staying behind helped them out with a pull up the old ski slope. It was snowing, and by the time they reached the third crater a mist hung in the air. The "relics" turned back; the departing men camped for lunch to wait for the air to clear. There was no trail here. A way down would have to be carefully scouted, the sledge held back to prevent a runaway. No one wanted to repeat poor Vince's fate and go hurtling off the cliff-edge to a certain doom. After some searching they found a way down to the ice foot, a respectable drop of thirty-odd feet. Crean rigged a fall with the Alpine rope looped over an ash stave driven into the iceslid down over the cliff edge to the ice foot below.

Once down on the sea-ice, salt crystals on the surface made for a tough pull out to the Glacier Tongue. There was just light enough to pick out a way. Luckily the new ice held them well; they reached and crossed the tongue without incident, to camp in a hollow for a meal and await a clearing of the weather that never arrived. After dinner Scott decided despite Lt. Bowers' vigorous protests, to push on over the new sea-ice through the rising blizzard. He tended to rely overmuch on luck in some of his decisions and try to make up the difference with sheer human endurance. Going out onto the sea ice at this point might not have been the wisest decision, but it was the Captain's.

The ice on the Cape Evans side had apparently formed in the

last day or so.   Just inches thick, the greasy ice sagged beneath the weight of a man's foot and rippled before the advance of the sledgerunners. Nothing about it was solid or inviting, but the men were too far along in their journey to let a little danger slow them down, too anxious for a hot supper and a warm night in.

It was only a few more miles to the hut.   The ice past Tent Island ought to be stronger, if only it could be reached before the blizzard closed in for good.   But the wind swept in with a growing fury, driving the snow in great sheets across the path.   With the stars and the shoulder of Erebus lost to view, the men kept blindly on, steering by dead reckoning with the wind astern.   Under a gale like this, the young ice might go out at any moment and they would all nine of them be swept away and drowned. It would be a quick and painless death, unless Captain Scott's luck stood its turn to serve in his favor.   For one brief instant the black summit of Little Razor Back Island raised its head off to the left, and the straggling party made for it.   They had to settle for camping on the sea ice for the night just as the first toes were going to frostbite.

Pitching a tent in a gale is never easy.   Still, with practice—and Crean had plenty of that exploring the Barrier in 1903—it was only another job of work to get done before a man could take his pipe and relax. The canvas billows and thunders like a topsail torn loose from the yard, and were it not for the sure grip of bared hands would be carried away.   It was the ice underfoot that was a concern.   Six inches of it was plenty in a calm, but in this gale it could easily go to pieces without warning, and without any chance of survival for the men on it.   There were no floes on which to take refuge and scarcely any snow to weight down the valences of the tent.   The shrieking of the wind through the rocky outcrops overhead gave the only clue that the island was still close aboard. It was a small relief to know that, even with all the other miseries, the camp would not be drifting out to sea. One experience like that was quite enough for Tom Crean.

No one slept much. The sea ice held. In the early morning light, while the blizzard still blew all around and obscured all but an intermittent glimpse of the black rocks close at hand, the tents were moved to a tiny ledge on the island barely wide enough to accommodate the two tents. Above, steep cliffs rose to the island's summit. Below, this *terra firma*, if only the merest toehold on the island, proved to be a snug enough harbor, out of the wind. There was nothing to do but sleep and wait out the storm. On the third day the weather cleared enough to admit travel. It was an easy five miles now.

As the return party came closer to Cape Evans, Crean could see the black figures of men moving about. Looking up from the business at hand, one man rose and stood rigid. He spoke to the other man, then dashed into the hut. In an instant the entire crowd housed within came streaming out to welcome the castaways home.

The hut now sported a house number, a framed wooden "1". It was the first and only house on its street and in fact one of only three in the neighborhood of Ross Island. It promised luxuries in untold abundance, splendors of comfort and appointment to the travelers just returned from eighty days of rough-and-tumble camping. The shelves of the larder fairly groaned with sweets and spices, novelties of soft bread and well-cooked meat, cheese and butter. Cutlery and crockery added a long-forgotten touch of the civilized world, but for all its seeming elegance, the atmospheree inside the hut seemed stale and stuffy, altogether too civilized. The acetylene lighting showed up every bit of dirt, and it was not a pleasant sight. Here one had to be on the lookout for muck on his boots that might be tracked inside, or grease on the seat of his pants when he sat down anywhere.

Almost immediately Scott organized a relief party to bring fresh provisions back to the pony-keepers back at the *Discovery* hut. They were in no danger, but it seemed almost criminal to deny them a taste of civilization and a change of reading-matter now that the state of the sea-ice admitted travel between the two outposts. Crean and Bowers hankered already for a sleeping bag out on the snow, or the even blubbery atmosphere of Hut Point, and volunteered to go.

It was a good opportunity to be training a few more of the novices in the arts of Antarctic subsistence. The mechanics and biologists were, like everyone else, expected to learn the skills of the trail; Nelson and Hooper could have asked for no better teachers. The cheery old south wind welcomed them heartily at the Glacier Tongue, blasting their faces raw all the way to Hutton Cliffs. It calmed down to a glorious night, but there would be no making the hut until sunrise, so they pitched the tent on the nearest piece of ground. The slope there would not offer the best in comfort.

Lieutenant Bowers and Crean took the lowest spots in the tent better to make their mates more comfortable for a proper rest for their first night on the trail. During the night, the sleepers in their bags all slid imperceptibly down the slope, until Crean was half outside under the valence—still sound asleep and entirely unworried by the steady stream of bitterly cold air flowing over him. Bowers was continually in awe of Crean's capacities: *"It takes a lot to worry Captain Scott's coxswain."*

They reached the *Discovery* hut the next day, and the novelties in foodstuffs they brought in got a great reception, especially the sugar.   The presence of the two new fellows among the castaways was met with less enthusiasm.   There was to be a rotation of men; some of the newcomers were to stay behind and tend the ponies until the sea froze solid enough to walk them home, some of the old hands were to be relieved to the comforts of Cape Evans.   The route was much the same as before: up the ski slope with help, past Castle Rock and the craters, and dropping onto the sea ice below Hutton Cliffs.

Once Crean and Scott had lowered themselves and pulled the rope down after themselves, there was no turning back.   The ice between them and Cape Evans had better be firm enough to walk on.   By the end of the descent, everyone was quite cold—pitch tents and brew hot tea as quick as possible.   Freezing fingers clutched at the hot pannikins until the warm glow spread, and even the toes felt warm before the cup was empty. Thus warmed, they set out again, determined to make the trip in one day this time.   Scott was showing his fondness for making sledge-pulling into a competition to see who were the best men, and so they made a race of it from the Glacier Tongue to Cape Evans.   Crean was in the Owner's team, and they held the lead the whole time—this was always the Scott's way, to push on and on, to prove who could come in first--arriving in a sweat. The frozen sweat on their windproofs fell away in showers of ice when they entered the hut at last.

The sledging season was at an end.

Chapter Six

Winter Quarters at Cape Evans

Cape Evans. April 23, 1911.

Sunset takes a long time in the far south. The half-disc of the sun works its way along the northern horizon, slides slowly westward lowering imperceptibly as though it would stay longer if it could. Once gone, it is gone for good, until at springtime three and one half months hence it peeps again above the horizon, abashed at its long absence. For Crean and Taff Evans, this long eventide marked the start of a third polar winter.

In years past the unspeakable cold and darkness of the long polar night had driven some men to madness, but *they* were not of the Royal Navy. Captain Scott's men knew well there was nothing to fear. If anything, the end of autumn heralds the onset of a new season of calm routine, of less work and more sleep, a time for leisure and introspection and recovery. The polar night begins with a long twilight, an extended sunset brushing the edges of the high clouds with lines of pure gold, enriching the clear heaven beyond with amazing rivers of orange and lavender. As autumn wanes the fading light deepens into a pitchy black dusted with a million southern stars, but even the darkest days are still brightened by a long faint red glow in the northern sky at noon.

Unnoticed, a routine takes hold, the daily round of chores and obligations.

On May 13 five men and two ponies hove into view, barely visible in the distance as they descended from the Glacier Tongue. The mere appearance of them stirred the greatest excitement the hut had known for weeks. Here was proof the bay ice was firm, the absentees at Hut Point and their two ponies all accounted for and fit enough to travel. Even more important, here was a change of company, a cause for celebration. The idle hands dressed for weather and went out to greet and then usher in the stragglers.

Lashly, Hooper, Day and Keohane took up their old bunks again, doubling the population in the men's quarters. It would become a little more crowded in the busy room, but no one minded very much. Compared to the messdecks of the *Discovery* and the *Terra Nova*, there was plenty of space here and more than enough comfort for all. Each man had his own spring-mattress with a head- and foot-board and time to make use of it. *What more could a man ask?* The inconveniences of less elbow-room and more chatter and smoke were more than offset by the warmth and novelty of fresh conversation provided by the newcomers.

Bill Lashly was a tough one to get to know. Of all the stokers on board the *Terra Nova*, he was the only one landed for winter quarters. He had the machinist's instinct for mechanical things—whatever couldn't be repaired, he could make from scratch. It wasn't until he was on shore and the ship departed for the winter, that he became truly one of the men.

Even then, it took a while. He was a quiet sort, not given to bragging or idle talk, which put him at a disadvantage in the crowded, noisy confines of the Hut's messdeck. He took better care of himself than most of the others—never smoked, never drank—but put to the test he could swear with the best of them. He'd been married for years—since the *Discovery*--but never said two words about his home life. Taff had only recently been spliced to his Lois, and to hear him go on about it one would think he invented the institution.

Lashly was one of the men, but even in the crowded busy space of the messdeck he found a way to be sequestered away from the seamen in a makeshift stokers' mess, the narrow cubicle behind the galley stove he shared with young Hooper the motor mechanic and Clissold the cook. It was not that he was unfriendly. More that he was older, a stoker, perhaps wiser from his upbringing. Who could say? This much was sure about the man: when Scott went out on the plateau in 1903 and needed two men on whom he could absolutely depend to pull through—Lashly was one of the two.

Taff Evans was the other. Scott did not select from among his officers for his companions for that daring, arduous journey; he chose from the roster of his men. In so choosing, and then in living daily for weeks on end on the hopelessly barren desert of the plateau, he learned what no other commander in the RN was likely to ever know. It is the *men* on whom their seniors depend; the best of them might come without pedigree, but they still are the best of *men*.

Funny how it is, two old salts come together after years apart, after different passages in different ships, and take up where they left off without a moment's thought. Crean and Evans stuck together, when they could. In the field they might be placed in different tents, spent long hours engaged in homely domestic tasks, with never or in widely separated branches of the expedition's scientific forays, but when at the end of their travels they always came together again. Back at Cape Evans they placed their bunks athwart each other. Like an old married couple, they spent long hours together with never a word passing between them.

* * * * *

Captain Scott, inclined to build upon things that had worked for him before, continued some of the routines first established in *Discovery*'s winter sojourn. They gone well then, and they would do for the men now at Cape Evans. He established a series of lectures, to be given twice a week on the wardroom side of the bulkhead. Attendance was purely voluntary, but any man anywhere in the hut could hardly miss the presentation in progress. The seamen sat in on the first two lectures but gave the remainder a pass, put off no doubt by the title and presumed aridity of the third—"Physiography by Griffith Taylor". Weights and measures of the men were to be taken and recorded at regular intervals, as much for the entertainment value as the scientific. The *South Polar Times* was re-established as an occasional magazine of art and entertainment—certainly not just for news, since every one of the men knew almost every thing as it happened. Cherry, the newly appointed managing editor, posted a tin box for submissions beneath the hut's only looking-glass.

Before the gathering darkness assumed full control, football on the ice alternated with the lecture series. The teams fielded for the May 1 season opener—Messdeck vs. the Afterguard--were a mixed bag of talent. The official rules for scrimmages didn't carry much weight this far from home. Everyone seemed to be offside, and the more so the better. By the end of it—even though the halves were only twenty minutes each—everyone was pretty well knocked up, and felt their bruises for days after. New teams stood for remaining games in the season—the young vs. the old, the married vs. the single, the Britons vs. the Colonials, until the failing light made even these games impossible to play.

They hadn't come all this way to play. They'd come to work. A man who hasn't a useful thing to do with his time becomes a listless, irritable shell of himself. Each day began when the night watchman awakened the hardest-working man of all. The cook is the most important man on board any ship; a bad one can stir a mutiny among the men, a good one is better respected than the captain. There is a special talent in keeping a hungry crew satisfied by turning the limited possibilities of a ship's or a shore-station's larder into an endlessly varied series of filling menus. Tom Clissold managed the task with ease and an endless supply of good humor.

Upon rising each morning he put on his boots and stepped outside for a bucket of coal to throw on the embers and stirred the fire to life, then out again to fill pots of ice to melt for coffee, tea, and porridge when it showed on the menu. Before long the yeasty, seductive aroma of fresh-baking bread wafted through the room, along with the fishy smell of penguins' grease and the sizzle of their frying eggs. Every morning at breakfast Griff Taylor would lean through the door of the messdeck and announce his predictions for the day's weather. *--Who cares? What of it?--* It might blizz or not, and certainly blow, and possibly clear to a calm, all on any given day.

With breakfast snugly tucked away, pony exercise was the order of the day—weather permitting—or grooming and maintenance if not. These animals were the mainstay of the spring season's advance. Only twelve of them remained of the original nineteen that had boarded the

Terra Nova in New Zealand.   These all lived in a stable built against the south side of the hut, with outer walls of brick-laid fodder bales and cubes of patent fuel, roofed over with tarpaulins.   Its innermost recesses glowed warm and yellow from the penguin fat fires burning within Oates' patent blubber stove.   Walking down the narrow passage, Crean passed a line of sleepy equine heads, seemingly resigned and patient, but as likely as not to take a nip as he passed.   One of them took special note of his coming. Whenever Crean felt the need of a quiet moment—hard to find with Taff in the next bunk—he got his new horse out of the stable for a stroll.

Now that Blossom was a heap of pony-meat buried on the Barrier, Crean spent his days exercising his Bones.   It was exercise for man as well as beast—long walks alone on the ice beneath the stars or the waning moon, with words and whinnies meant only for each other.   This chore--if Crean could even call it such--easily filled the hours before lunch.   The two shared many a private conversation abroad on the ice, though it was more of Crean's discourse with the pony's tacit approval, quiet familiarities in a private language no others could quite understand. These were the basic ingredients of a fast friendship with never a thought for a future fate that would inevitably one day part them.

Bones was of middling height, just a few inches shorter than his master at the shoulder, well proportioned like a small horse and not at all stump-legged and sway-backed like so many of the others.   Freed from his wooden stall and led outside, Bones was keen to relieve his itches with a vigorous roll in the snow and then make a break for it.   A long brisk walk would follow, accompanied by the Irishman's soothing rich brogue, or a sad song under those same stars shining over Ireland and home.   The horse almost seemed to understand the haunting words. . ." *he's wishful like me, to be back where the dark Mourne sweeps down to the sea.*"

If all the sailors and their charges seemed to be on the best of terms, it might have been because the men, so much removed from the comforts of shore-side romance and domestic life, gave the best of their love to the animals instead. Through the still darkness of the calmer days, the shuffling sounds of hoof on snow and low muted voices could be heard in the distance telling of other ponies at exercise, sometimes miles away. Their idle jaunts done, the men and animals returned to the hut, each to his respective mid-day meal. By noon the messdeck table was spread and the men reconvened for lunch, a simple affair that never wanted for conversation. For old Bones chaff and oats or oil-cake with snow, and for Crean huge amounts of bread and butter, cheese and jam, with plenty of tea and cocoa.

Once the business of eating was completed, pipes were lit without further formality. There was a thankfully unlimited supply of Navy cut tobacco. The pleasant bluish fug of its smoke drifted in layers back and forth through the passage to the wardroom, freshened on occasion by a fresh blast of cold Antarctic air as someone made his way out through the porch. By two o'clock the men were all dispersed again to their various duties. At times Crean and Dr. Atkinson walked in happy silence out to the fish-trap on the floe. During their weeks of shared solitude out at Hut Point had overcome their differences to forge a stronger bond of friendship. Now on a lucky day they would bring home upwards of forty fish to be served out for breakfast the following morning.

Crean was spared the sacrilege of partaking in the weekly Anglican service that was not his own, but inside the hut there was no escaping its hymns. The songs themselves were not so bad, but the singing of them—led by the captain with his uncertain tenor voice and variable in pitch between the choruses—could be painful to hear, and not for the words of the verses. His search for perfection in the singing of "Onward Christian Soldiers" kept them at it for two painful Sundays in a row. That row gave way to the racket of Cherry's typewriter working up the pages of the next issue of the *South Polar Times*. Then there was the *scrape scrape* of the geologists at their rock-polishing, the unending *tick-ticketing* of the weatherman's clockwork recorders, the endless cags and lectures and relay of orders, all of it silenced when a stout pony-kick threatened to cave in the walls shared with the stables.

The gales of mid-May blew eighty and then a hundred miles an hour, rattling wind-blown gravel from the ramp against the roof while the whole hut shuddered and creaked. These were no days to be abroad, but Crean never failed to step outside the porch and feel his way to the stables alongside the hut to bring his Bones a special treat. That done, it was back into the hut with its chatter and smells and smoke, to wait out the storm's assault on the thin boards that kept this home secure.

The extended campaign of the autumn depot journeys had worn down much of the sledging gear, which would be needed in top condition for the spring. There was much to be done: sledges to be rebuilt, sleeping bags and canvas tanks to be stitched together from the hides and bolts brought down from the north, boots and finnesko and tents all in need of repair. Every man had his job to do. Taff Evans had the reputation of a cobbler; Crean of a master tailor at the treadle sewing machine. Both trades were required to stitch reindeer hides into sleeping bags, and the photographer wanted a record of them working in the hut. Ponting's job was to create the photographic record of everything that every man in the expedition was charged to accomplish. Some he caught on film engaged in their everyday work, others were requisitioned to pose and perform for the "camera artist." All the men obliged the photographer by "ponting" for him on demand.

A flash momentarily blinded everyone in the room. The camera captured a quiet moment over the mess table--two rugged men of equal size, clad in matching jersey, half-hidden behind piles of luxurious fur, their eyes intent upon their work. Between them a pipe lay unlit for the moment on a tobacco box. Behind, white crockery neatly stacked on shelves hints at coffees yet to be shared. Many were the hours the two have spent working side by side like this, spinning yarns of past campaigns and pulling stitches as fine as any shore-side seamstress. The seamen were always willing to lend a hand to the academics in these matters of the domestic arts. A little blarney is all it took to get something made or mended, and all the scientists learned something or other of the sailors' arts.

As suppertime drew near, someone would sit down to coax a little music out of the Broadwood pianola in the wardroom to make the men happy as well as hungry. With 250 rolls in the cabinet—Wagner, Gilbert and Sullivan, Strauss, the Washington Post March, ragtime tunes—there is a little something for every taste. Seal and penguin were the staples of almost every meal, alternating with frozen New Zealand mutton twice a week while it lasted. The basic courses followed: soup (all too often tomato-based), fresh-baked bread, pudding for dessert. With supper over and the tables cleared, pipe smoke filled the air and the men sat down to books and games or that oldest of standbys, yarning. Gran organized a ping-pong tournament and for weeks the wardroom and the messdeck beside resounded with the clatter. Chess came into vogue next, then backgammon, and late in the winter bagatelle. One game yields up to the next with no apparent reason, but cards never fall out of favor in the messdeck—whist, poker, patience.

Just before lights-out comes at eleven, Dr. Wilson could be heard through the doorway, cranking the gramophone. The needle scritched into its groove and the rich voice of Clara Butts floated through the quieting rooms:

> *"Abide with me; fast falls the eventide*
> *Darkness deepens, Lord with me abide. . ."*

The cards, shuffled one last time, slid into their cases; all around the two rooms books slapped shut, bedsprings creaked as the men turn over and in for the night. The bubbling of the acetylene plant went silent, the hiss of the flame jets fell to nothing. In the darkened corners of the hut barely heard puffs of air put out the scattered candle flames, releasing slim trails of smoke into the still air.

The night-watchmen were always assigned from the ranks of the afterguard to keep an eye on the ponies, record the hourly changes in weather and aurora and stir the fire in the galley stove to life before calling the cook in the very early hours of the morning. It was this stove, kept going night and day for two years, that kept the men's quarters always cozier than the quarterdeck. Late in the night, when the coals burned down and his tea went cold, the night watchman nodded half-asleep. Should his pipe fall from his fingers and clatter to the floor, or his dreaming shout wake the sleeping hands, it was safe to "score one" off the brass from behind the blanket draped for a curtain. After all, no officer should expect better treatment from the men when he intruded into their space before the mast, even if that "mast" was only a wall of packing crates in the common space of the hut.

So the days of late autumn passed, each steeped in cold and darkness outside the hut's four walls, yet somehow brighter within and full of warmth and hope. In many respects the men had all become one big family—Crean and Evans were close as brothers--sharing more than just a common household. No holiday or birthday was allowed to pass without a celebration of some sort. Captain Scott's forty-third was honored in June with a magnificent cake, but the big festival approaching was Midwinter's Day. It had been the polar year's greatest holiday in *Discovery* and Shackleton's Cape Royds hut, and this first winter over at Cape Evans would prove no exception. For days preceding June 22, certain souls managed to prepare a few surprises, and on the morning of the big day paper chains and Japanese lanterns were lovingly hung from the rooftrees over the messdeck.

Could Crean keep a secret? Of course he could. Any man who wanted to get on in the King's Navy learned eventually when best to keep his mouth shut. Some, like Taff, loosened up too much when there was strong drink about, but then fell into line in the dry valleys of an Antarctic hut with a gang of officers just abaft the bulkhead.

The real Christmas in the pack--25 December 1910--had been a placid, truncated occasion. Here at Cape Evans, Midsummer's Eve would stand in for the holiday. It marks the darkest, longest, coldest night of the year, and a true cause for revelry. Lieutenant Bowers' idea was to make a Christmas tree in absolute secrecy and haul it unheralded into the wardroom at the penultimate moment of that night. Secrecy was of the utmost importance. Given the close quarters and constant traffic through the messdeck, it would be almost impossible to keep. When Bowers enlisted a handful of men in the top-secret production of a Christmas tree for the Midwinter celebration, he knew he could count on their conspiracy.

Penguin feathers glued to strips of split bamboo, and those strips stuck into holes drilled in a ski-stick stood on end into a plankwood base and then graced with tiny tapers, made a tree. There was no green in it. A close investigation would not please the nose with hints of tannenbaum, but the mind's eye surprised by its sudden appearance could make out wisps of childhood memories long forgotten. It's the surprise of that makes the greatest gift.

The day felt like Christmas, but it was instead late June. Back home in Ireland the hills were blooming white with the rhododendron and purple heather, and Hannah—God bless her—must be thinking more of the garden than her long gone sailor cast away on a cold and barren shore. Crean's time here's half done, and if it's well-done he'll come home with a promotion and a raise.

The day was declared a general holiday, though of course the essential routines would never be neglected. The ponies knew something was up when they were brought a special hot mash, and for Bones a handful of Captain's Biscuit. Volume III of the *South Polar Times* was published after lunch, to everyone's delight. It ran to fifty pages, the text of the stories and poems neatly typed out by Cherry. Like those of the first two volumes put out by the *Discovery*, it existed for the time being as one bound volume, though this one was elegantly cased in elaborately carved and finished venesta-board covers made by the motor mechanic.

Dr. Wilson had noticed the bond between Crean and Taff Evans, and called attention to it in one of his sketches for the *South Polar Times*. It was a clever rendering of the history of Cape Evans, of the travels and trials of the men during that first autumn, done up as an ancient Egyptian hieroglyphic. Orders from above had dictated that the two men must go their separate ways for a time—Taff Evans to the west, Crean to the south. *"Kreen-an-Ephans,"* the translation read, *"the Cobbos parted."*

Clissold was all day putting together a feast worthy of the occasion. Buzzard cakes were broached at tea, and hut hung round with Union Jacks in anticipation of the fandango to come. The meal began at 7:00 with an appetizer of seal soup, followed by roast beef with Yorkshire pudding, fried potatoes and Brussels sprouts only a little the worse for their stay in the deep-freeze of the outdoor pantry. For desert, a plum pudding--flaming of course--mince pies, caviar of cods' roe, burnt almonds, crystallized fruit, chocolates. Champagne flowed in the wardroom, beer in the messdeck.

After the feast, the big table in the wardroom was upended and its legs removed to make room for rows of chairs. The photographer set up his magic lantern, transforming the room into a makeshift theatre for "Ponting's Antarctic Picture Show". The men trooped in and shuffled into their seats. A hush fell over the room when the acetylene flames were doused. Wild applause greeted the first of the gorgeous still pictures flashed onto the folding screen, calmed with the following shots of penguins, icebergs, ice effects, the men themselves at work and play, the ship in the gale, the ship at the ice-wharf—all most pleasing to these men of the sea.

When the picture-show was over, the men retired through the

curtained door to the messdeck. The table was restored for snapdragon and milk punch, and the speeches over it began. Lieutenant Bowers sidled to the last place in the speaking order, and in his turn rose to say that, as he could not make a funny speech, he would *show* afterguard something funny. At his cue, four seamen marched in from the messdeck bearing something no officer expected—the Christmas tree!--hung about like the real thing with candles and candied fruit and little presents for everyone, officers and men included. The secret had been perfectly kept—the surprise was complete.

The gramophone played itself silly all night until the effects of unaccustomed liquid refreshment began to reveal themselves. Some retired to bed early despite the revelry that filled the room. The normally dour and taciturn Soldier Oates fairly bubbled with good humor, and insisted on a set of Lancers with Anton, the Russian groom. "Pat" Keohane became more Irish than ever, and true to form agitated for a political argument.

--I'll drink to that!-- Of course Taff would, he'd drink to anything with a bottle of Bass in each hand to prove his point, sharing deep confidences in a heavy whisper with anyone who would listen. On the opposite side of the store-case bulkhead, it's plain the afterguard were more in their cups than they'd ever allow the messdeck to become. Then came the inevitable songs--old favorites and some composed on the spot, some sad, some good for a laugh. Here in the warm security of the hut, the memory of life on the trail took on an easy, rosy glow that inspired the occasional poetical effusion, recited this day from the newly published *SPT*. Sledging was work, good hard clean work that made a fellow feel like a man, like he had done something noble and worthwhile that will

never be found in the bosom of *"home-life's silken chains."* *"I long to be mid snow-swept plains,"* said the poet, *:In harness, outward bound."*

The seamen went for a walk to get clear of the noisy, crowded, smoky hut. Outside, the aurora gave its most glorious display yet. Mysterious flashing lights danced overhead--fold upon rippling fold of dazzling curtains, great leaping arches of vibrant color leap across the still night sky. No breath of wind disturbed the quiet over the land, no moon or cloud obscure the unearthly show above.

In the still silence of this deepest of nights every footstep rang on the hard ground, the tide-crack moaned and then cracked sharply in its slow motion rise and fall. From the distant hut the muffled noise revelry within the spread over the crystalline night. A door slammed in the distance; another soul has come out to take in the wonders of God's heaven and earth.

*   *   *   *   *

In the messdeck the next morning, some heads were found to be too heavy raise, eyes too red to open, *"the morning after the night before"*, as they said at home. No matter. As the speeches had all noted, the halfway point was passed and the real job just beginning, with much yet to be done.

Dr. Wilson, Cherry, and Birdie Bowers had been preparing to mount a winter journey overland to the penguin rookery at Cape Crozier for months. Nothing of the kind had ever been contemplated, let alone attempted, in the brief annals of Antarctic exploration. The very idea was daunting in the extreme—to set out on an expedition using only the camping-resources at hand, to be gone for six weeks in the near-total darkness and untested and unknown extremes during the middle of winter in the coldest place on the planet. Only a small handful of men could be so foolhardy, or so dedicated to their science, to even dream of attempting it. The rare three such men did indeed exist; they had come to this place, and had elected to be the brave ones to make the attempt.

Wilson's passion in life, as far as science went, lay in the study of birds, and his dedication to his science knew no limits. He had a theory, hatched during the *Discovery* expedition, that these Emperor penguins represented the missing link in the evolution of birds, an idea that could possibly be proven by the study of their embryos in the egg. The principle problem lay in the fact that these bred and laid their eggs in the remotest of locations, in the very deepest and darkest heart of the Antarctic winter. If one was to study their embryos, then one must travel to their rookeries when they were laying, and there was nothing else to be done but go. June 27, a week after the lush excesses of the Midwinter feast, was set for departure.

Bowers and Cherry, inspired by Wilson's zeal, would be his willing accomplices. Scott, with some misgivings, approved their journey, but only after Dr. Wilson promised to bring them all home alive. They left in complete darkness overland dragging three sledges laden with five-weeks' supply of oil and provisions and the necessary gear for camping and securing the eggs. A part of the plan involved the building of a rock-and-snow hut at the Cape, and feeding and warming themselves in it with a locally-gotten supply of penguin oil for an improvised stove in the hut. It was hard to belay the thought that only fools would even attempt such a journey as this, dangerous in the extreme. Who could survive such extremes as they must surely encounter, and for such a meager goal—birds' eggs! Their return would not be expected for five or six weeks at least, before anyone would even think of looking for them.

It was hazardous enough even close to home. One evening in July Atkinson failed to show up for dinner--only then was it realized that he had been missing for hours, somewhere out in the blizzard that had suddenly blown up. Crean, Evans, and Keohane headed north with a lantern, creeping along the tide-crack, looking for a sign of him. They tumbled back into the hut half-frozen two hours later, caked with the driven snow. They had seen nothing. With the added help of Dmitri and the dogs, they set out with a rescue sledge into the storm again. Search parties went off in all directions, until the hut was nearly empty. At 11:45, the surgeon, badly frostbitten, stumbled in, alone. He had been blown off-course after a visit to the weather-screen out on the sea-ice, spun round and round by the blizzard and left to wander distraught and disoriented over the ice. These things happen to the most hardened explorer. A lucky break in the storm placed him near the familiar landmark of Tent Island, and a moon in the clearing sky finally led him home.

Winter had settled in for good. The blizzards and gales blew through like ships of the line, blasting away mercilessly one after the other in an endless succession. The blow of July 10, the worst yet—Force 11 wind, a near hurricane fit to send a man flying off his feet, his gear scattered to the other end of the earth. It brought with it a new extreme of deadly low temperatures—minus 39 degrees. The new wind speed record, 77 mph, was broken in a few days by 82 mph. A man could only touch at his scapular and pray for the fates of the poor men who had chosen these days to be abroad on the ice.

In time the gales, like any at sea, will blew themselves out, and

145

the sailors returned to their customary watches. Bones and his handler Crean were both were craving a little exercise, a little quiet time to themselves. The horse tossed his head in agreement, gladly took the bridle, and the two headed out into the darkness, up the ghostly pale snow sloping past drifted over mounds of long-buried stores. Suddenly Bones began to convulse violently, racked by quickening spasms of pain, a piercing squeal, a breathless panting, a look of utter panic in the eye. He lurched unsteadily forward, fell to his knees, tried to lie down but the unseen pain would not let him.

By the time they reached the stables the animal was in a horribly wretched state. No sound escaped him. This was awful; Crean hadn't kept and nursed his horse through the winter, befriended him in the tenderest of ways, to see him suddenly suffering for no reason, perhaps to death. Oates gave him opium pills to ease his pain; beyond this there was nothing else to be done. Crean warmed blankets over the blubber stove to lay over his friend. It was all they could do. They never left their patient. Gradually the spasms seemed to diminish; at 2:30 in the morning Bones raised his head, then stood up, as though some nightmare had come and gone. He began to nose at some hay and then at his neighbor in the next stall. In the morning he coughed up a ball of fermented hay containing a length of tapeworm and a strip of his intestinal lining, and after a few days he was quite recovered.

Beyond these excitements, the days passed uneventfully, punctuated by alternating blizzards with attendant worries for friends abroad on the ice, and calm. The Crozier party returned August 2 after an absence of five weeks. Three more weather-beaten men could not be imagined. Their story unfolded as they sat at table for the first time, alternately filling their bellies with prodigious amounts of food and falling asleep over their platters. This tale of survival would admit no rivals. They had endured the lowest temperatures yet recorded by man, where the ice had rolled like sand beneath their sledge-runners, and matches were too cold to light. Their sleeping bags had frozen into solid lumps of ice, their clothing hard as iron sheathing around their tortured limbs. The light of a single naked candle had lit their way across Windless Bight. They had done what they set out to do, secured three penguin eggs and brought them home, to the advancement of evolutionary science.

In early August the two motor sledges were hauled out from their garages, fired up, and noisily started in their trials. Out in the stable Bones had taken to voicing his displeasure with his circumstances by kicking furiously at the boards in the back of his stall. Crean tacked up sacking over the wooden walls, curing the noise if not the habit. The muted light of the long dawn grew stronger with every passing day. The sun was due shortly to reappear. By mid-month its rays from below the horizon it glittered on the shoulders of Erebus with a rosy splendor. Even the ponies noticed, growing more restive with each day's lengthening noonday glow. Two more weeks would pass before the sun rose above the headland to the north and shine directly on the hut.

The first ray of sunlight to strike into a man's eyes at the true end of a long deep night and a slow enticing dawn chills him to the core. He stands transfixed; all thought, all fear and sadness are swept away, and a tide of hope floods in to take their place. It is only a passing moment; the work of the day is still at hand, and wants his attention. The new light seems to reveal just how much work is yet to be done; in its electrifying presence, the pace begins to pick up.

The lecture series had continued all winter. Oates' talk, on horse management, was required listening. A cavalryman, he knew more about the ponies than anyone on the continent. *"They have no reasoning power at all,"* he said, *"but they have excellent memories. There is no use shouting at them; they associate the noise with some form of trouble, and will set out to make more trouble."* Taff had come up with and idea for pony snowshoes for his Snatcher. Put to the test, they seemed to help in the deep snow, but not the hard ice to be expected on the Barrier. The ponies wanted hard work to become again accustomed to harness and heavy loading. September was still far to cold to consider venturing the animals out onto the South Polar Trail, but manhauling parties were sent out to test their own mettle early. A few went out under Lt. Evans just to see how the depot at Corner Camp had fared through the winter. Scott himself, anxious to spend a few days out of the close confines of the hut, took a jaunt across the Sound to the Western Mountains.

Though it was still early spring, Crean, Oates, Wilson, and Cherry set out with their ponies October 6 to add sleeping bags and sacks of oats to the stores at Hut Point. It was a pleasant outing, taking only five hours to cover the fifteen miles. The hut was comfortably warm on their arrival, with Meares and Dmitri already encamped there, preparing a pemmican of seal meat for the dogs. They had established telephone communications with the base at Cape Evans, laying a bare wire out over the sea-ice behind them as they went.

The sun was scheduled to rise and shed its cool rays over Cape Evans August 24. The geologists, romantically envisioning a glorious sunrise, trotted up the Ramp for a look but came home hours later disappointed. It shone on the flanks of Erebus perhaps, but not on those standing on the beach facing the empty sea to the north. The sailors stayed in, turning tricks at six handed euchre. The sun would come in full soon enough, and then never leave the sky.

Scott was pleased with the *Discovery* seamen who'd returned with him for another go at the Pole. *"Crean,"* wrote the Owner to his wife, *"is perfectly happy, ready to do anything and go anywhere, the harder the work the better. Evans and Crean are great friends. Lashly is his old self in every respect, hard-working to the limit, quiet, abstemious, and determined. You see altogether I have a good set of people with me, and it will go hard if we don't achieve something."* They brought with them a wealth of experience learned not only in the earlier days, but also from the hard school of the navy that taught a man how to face any situation that could possibly occur. Though Taff Evans was the clear favorite, Crean and Lashly were not far behind.

No one knew better than Crean the many moods of Captain Scott. Their conversations, since 1901 had been limited to the bare necessities of the moment for a long line of moments. The natural separation of commander and seaman ensured that the spoken words betray no intimacies. Scott was a man at once tender and sentimental to a fault, and but he could lash out with brutal reproaches when displeased in a critical manner. He held high standards for himself and everyone chosen to take part in his plans, yet was at times strangely tolerant of ill-attended details, even in the deadly environment of the frozen south. If pride was one fault, humility was another. When in the wrong he was sometimes willing to admit it, even make amends, but he put a great deal of effort into finding out the best means to accomplish his ends.

Now they were sharing living space in a way they never have

before, albeit across a flimsy bulkhead of packing cases in a cramped and crowded hunt at the end of the earth. Only one who had spent years in his presence, under his command, could have seen Scott's strengths and weaknesses and come to know and respect him not for what he should have been, but for what he was. Crean was one such man; Wilson was another.

Captain Scott was nothing short of a marvel in his capacity to think through and fully understand the intricate needs of all the expedition's disparate aims. Before his departure for the South Pole, he must leave clear orders for five separate units—the ship, the western geological party, the northern party, the shore party remaining at Cape Evans, and the various phalanxes of his own southern push. He had to compose detailed instructions for each of these, considering all the possibilities each might encounter over the four months of his absence. That he could do so with such clarity, such grace, was little short of a miracle. Crean knew nothing of these details, only of the magnitude of the combined undertaking, and the unique wisdom of the captain who brought order to it all.

The success of it all depended on trust, on the understanding that every man among them would perform his duty to the utmost of his ability. Scott's written orders left much to the judgment of his lieutenants, fully relying on their maturity and experience to ensure that their intent would be fulfilled. He was like that with his seamen. He understood that they would not require management, only a statement of his intent, to go about their end of the expedition's business. Each of his men was like his own right hand, in the best rendition of naval discipline. The captain indicates what he wishes to have done, and it is done. This wide-spread net of trust and reliance had much to do with the harmony of that first year in the ice, and its legacy, the second.

The motors roared to life and rattled down onto the sea ice October 23, 1911. These crawling tractors were a novelty in the Antarctic, and certainly an improvement over Shackleton's Arroll-Johnson motor car. As a pioneering experiment in transport they proved to be ill-adapted to the task at hand. At best they moved steadily at the rate of a brisk walk; each required two men, a driver and a steerer on foot. After a mile or so at this pace, the motors overheated, and wanted a half-hour's cooling off before setting out again. They left Cape Evans two days ahead of the others in order to make some headway before being caught up by the ponies on the Barrier. After some adjustments they were on their noisy way to the Glacier Tongue to pick up some loads previously manhauled out, and carry them forward. Three days later Simpson rang up from Hut Point. The motors were marooned on the sea ice under Hutton Cliffs, unable to get forward without assistance.

Crean was in the party sent out to help them, and the experience did not endear him to this new mode of travel. The motors, forced by overheating to shut down after only seven minutes of ineffective crawling over the slippery ice, required a team of men to get them started again after each stop. The men camped in the *Discovery* hut for the night, woke in the morning to a fine breakfast hoosh cooked over the improved blubber stove, and headed back out over the frozen sea to rescue the motors.

Once started, the motor sledges rattled along at their deliberate halting pace around Cape Armitage and finally up a beautiful snow ramp onto the Barrier itself, to continue slowly on toward Corner Camp and points beyond. The assistance party cheered them on, knowing full well the din of the engines fairly overwhelmed the sound of human voices in the distance. Led by Crean and Evans they marched at a quick-step back to the *Discovery* hut for lunch, and made Cape Evans for supper.

There was no end to the work to be done there, gathering stores and loading the remaining sledges for the expedition's final departure for the South Pole. In a lighthearted break from the routine, four men "ponted" one last time for the photographer. He wanted live-action motion pictures to show the folks at home how the explorers lived and traveled on the South Polar Trail. Scott and Wilson, Crean and Evans, showed him how it was all done--pulling in harness, pitching the tent, cooking with the primus, then breaking camp, packing up, and hauling it all away. All this was done on a lovely day, all with fictitious loads to bear. Would that it might always be so easy! The images of this routine would become all too familiar after four months on the trail.

By late October all was ready for the start of the final big push for the Pole. Ten men and ten ponies stepped over the tide crack and onto the sea ice off Cape Evans. Toward the end of the line Bones and Crean ambled off gently, followed by Captain Scott with Snippets. Ten minutes later Taff Evans with Snatcher passed them at speed, and the race for the Pole was on.

Chapter Seven

The South Polar Trail

Cape Evans.   November 1, 1911

This was the big day, the culmination of a year's—no, a decade's—striving toward an heroic goal worthy of a nation's dreams. Everything that had gone before—the *Discovery*'s first noble attempt, Shackleton's near miss—only foreshadowed this, the final necessary strike at the heart of the Antarctic.   Crean had been a part of it since the beginning and was honored to be among those now starting out on this mission.   The longed-for moment, this day of departure, had at last arrived. Each man in his own inner mind carried the hope that he of all the others would be chosen for the final assault on the South Pole, for this advancement of human knowledge, for glory.

It was also another ordinary day of work.   The shining honor of the moment was somewhat dulled by the realities of horses to be taken in hand, of last-minute inventories of gear to be packed or left behind, of deadlines and tonnages to be met now against a future success at the South Pole itself.   Every detail had been thought out, every need accounted for, every step of the way ahead plotted.   The world ahead unfolded like a new map.

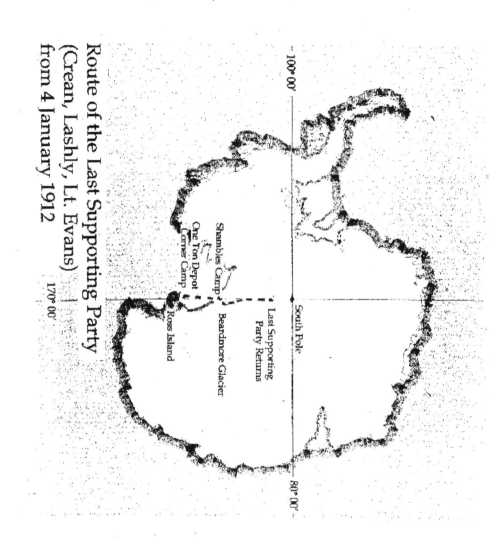

Route of the Last Supporting Party
(Crean, Lashly, Lt. Evans)
from 4 January 1912

100° 00'

South Pole

Last Supporting
Party Returns

Shambles Camp
One Ton Depot
Corner Camp

Beardmore Glacier

170° 00'

80° 00'

Ross Island

154

The tractors had gone out to join them in late October, chortling over the sea ice and up onto the Barrier at their customary leisurely pace. On the last day of the October Keohane and Dr. Atkinson took charge of the weakest of the ponies and set out on their slow walk south. Nothing much was expected of Jimmy Pigg—the sole survivor of the disaster on the sea-ice--and Jehu. It was generally acknowledged that they would be among the first to give out and be shot beside the trail to become meat for the dogs and the men.

November 1 was the big day of departure for all the rest. That first night out found the horse parties all together at the *Discovery* hut. The veranda there would be the last shelter any of the horses would ever know and even that was not enough protection for the weakest of them. The crocks spent the night under its sheltering overhang, stamping and neighing and raising an awful racket, keeping everyone awake.

Seen from the ski slope, the pastoral landscape surrounding the *Discovery* Hut resembled a seaside farm on the shore of Dingle Bay, with sparkling fields of white snow instead of Kerry's fabled green. Dark figures moved about the yard of the peak-roofed homestead; here and there were horses as if in a pasture, a few dogs roaming about the grounds chasing the wild birds, bales of fodder stacked beside the road leading south. Stony mountains rose from the far shores of the frozen bay, their sharp ridges softened by drifted snow. If only a whiff of new-mown hay might come breezing through the Gap, the illusion through half-closed eyes might be complete. All seemed calm and unhurried in the day and a half's leisure spent in waiting for the evening of November 3 and the first of many night marches in the final push for the South Pole.

* * * * *

When all was ready the horse-drawn sledges, coming quietly along over the ice from the shore, started to form a line to pick up their next loads. One of the motors, trundling along a little way off, backfired with the sound of a gunshot. Cherry's pony Michael, spooked, squealed and jumped sideways in a panic and leapt up wheeling and thrashing the air like a boxer. The sharp little hooves cutting through the air would brain any man coming close.

Crean stepped in, caught the whips of the reins, hauled the horse down with one violent thrust and nearly threw him to the ice. The horse made a lunge to the right, then gave up, suddenly calm under the sailor's steady hand. --*Here you go, son*--, he said, handing over the reins to the younger man. --*You just hang on for all you're worth. Make 'em know who's in charge.*-- It was all over in a moment.--*I mean, Sir* --and no damage done.

Cherry was still a little breathless. The horse could have cut him up or worse, run off with the sledge and started a stampede. --*Thank you, Crean.*--

Some order must be imposed. Scott's plan was to send off the ponies in three detachments. The crocks set off first, to be caught up and passed during the day's march by the middling teams of Snippets, Michael, and Nobby led by Scott, Cherry, and Bill Wilson. The final four were known as the "Fliers," the best and strongest horses and for those reasons the last to leave the safety and security of the hut forever. One of them was the very devil on four hooves. Christopher was the largest of all the horses, and he would not be harnessed, not without a fight. It took four men to control him, hobble and throw him, and strap on his harness

156

while he was down, then stand away with a firm hand on the lead while he leapt to his feet and kicked out at anything nearby. Once nominally under control he became a trifle more tractable, and set off at his own brisk rate, dragging Oates and the heaviest sledge off at a smart pace in the wake of the others. Bowers' Victor was almost the same trouble, though not *quite* so vicious, and once under way led his short-legged master along at a furious pace.

The other two fliers, Crean with Bones and Taff Evans with Snatcher now set off sailing right along in their wake. This detachment pulled straight through never stopping for lunch, overtaking the crocks before the end of the day's march. First one, then another was in the lead. This was no Galway race; there would be no roses for the winner, only an early stop at the evening's camp for a leisurely supper.

Goodbye to the old hut, goodbye for good. It would be many a long day before any of the men would find comfort in its shelter again. From here on out it was pitch tent, strike tent, for every single day's rest and sleep. The lucky ones would be sent home early, when their strength had given out and they were no longer useful to the expedition's loftiest goal. The strong would go on, each as far as he was able, but only the few would be chosen to make the Pole.

The traveled way out to Corner Camp was becoming as familiar to Crean as the road from Annascaul to Tralee. At his left hand the smoking hulk of Mt Erebus rose in its snow-covered grandeur, throwing its long shadow over the Barrier. To the right the stony headlands of the three nearby islands rose out of the ice plain covering McMurdo Sound. Beyond, the mountains of the Britannia Range stood out in bold relief, lining the way south until they disappeared in the distance.

In the world of near white that was the backdrop to every view, each man became a silhouette, a black-on-white cutout shape as familiar to his mates as the face seen close up. Each had his own peculiar height and stoop, a distinctive slouch when standing, a gangling armswing in a walk. Wilson's head was known by the swelling headband of the rolled watchcap Oriana knitted for him, his legs spread at a consistent angle, his arms always akimbo. The soldier walked with the rolling gate, a telling reminder of his old wound from the Boer War. Bowers stood short and stout, Atkinson long and lean, Cherry of a middling height with his shoulders always sloping down. Taff lumbered along like an uncaged animal, long-armed and loose-limbed, with a muscular grace always in view despite the thick overcovering of his jumper and windproofs.

Crean couldn't see himself, but the others knew from his sturdy shape and purposeful stride who was coming from a long distance off. Being among the last of the contingent to depart, he had a view of the whole parade, a string of dark hulks stretched out in a long column over miles of white snow. It gave the impression of a somewhat disorganized line of ships with very unequal speed, an unnerving resemblance Russia's Baltic Fleet making its long slow way to defeat at Tsushima Straits.

Among the motley crowd of horses, Bones at least presented a shipshape outward appearance suggesting a workmanlike suitability for the daunting task at hand. Like his master he was of a medium and sturdy build, a good if not exactly beautiful specimen of his type, of a mild demeanor given to sudden and indelicate outbursts of temper or affection. He was comfortable with the idea of following in his owner's lead, but was known to take an unexpected turn of his own at times with no warning or explanation. The horse's dun coat grew thick and shaggy to keep him warm in the searching winds out of the south, the fringes of his mane hung down over his face to sweep the snowflakes from his eyes. And, like his master, he was sociable and gregarious in company.

Night marching became the order of the day; with the sun circling in the sky over the mountains to the south, the surface would be harder, making for easier going. Even so the horses' small sharp hooves sank deeply into it; the sledges towed along behind dug into it, plowing up low immobile wakes. The sun's warmth at noon gave extra measure to the ponies' rest during the day. At times that warmth was overwhelming—sweltering, the air breathless, the glare intense, the tents too hot for comfort, the bags damp from sweat.

The motor sledges had already demonstrated their mechanical fragility, their basic inability to maintain an equable running temperature. After the investment of a good deal of patience and ingenuity to get them started in the frigid air, they very quickly overheated and wanted a break from their labors. In light of this weakness they had been given a few days' head start and were still out of sight somewhere ahead on the road to Corner Camp. Judging from Lt. Evans' upbeat note-- *"Hope to meet you at 80 degrees 30'"*—left for those following in their wake, they were apparently having some success, rattling onward at a steady pace and hauling their loads like good docile draught animals.

It was hard to fault the Lieutenant for his chipper kind words and goodwill when they set the tone for the expedition's progress. His cheery optimism lent its inflection to everyone's recollections of these early days. The one place it failed him, and everyone else, was in regard to the success of the motor-sledges in getting the necessary stores far enough south to really be of use. The appointed rendezvous was far out on the Barrier, well beyond One Ton Depot.

Within two miles of the cairn posting that note a pile of petrol tins appeared by the wayside--a sure sign of trouble. Four and a half miles on, the cold metal hulk of a motor-sledge lay forlorn and abandoned in the trail. The cause of the breakdown was an old familiar trouble spot, the big end of No. 2 cylinder. It had finally broken for good; the only spare one had already been pressed into use. With their motor dead, Day and Lt. Evans went immediately to manhauling, carrying forward petrol for the second machine and six bags of forage for the ponies. There was evidently still hope for the other motor-sledge.

One more march brought the pony party in all of its strung-along glory into the depot at Corner Camp, where the animals took on their full loads for the first time. This place now seemed almost a suburb of the *Discovery* hut. The neighborhood was known and comfortable, and close enough by--one good long day's walk--to seem an extension of the home front. Another note from Lt. Evans mentioned problems with the remaining tractor, now dimly visible with its handlers in the distance.

The white waste vanishing beyond them was known but to a few. A handful of the men present had been out-and-back before on the autumn journey to establish One Ton Depot. Crean himself had spent two months out there exploring with Lieutenant Barne during the *Discovery* expedition. They had learned then that the Barrier was in constant motion, flowing inexorably toward the limitless basin of the Ross Sea. The surface of the Barrier may have moved along, but the mountains were unchanging. Up ahead, just past the long sweep of Minna Bluff, lay the great ice-filled bay receiving the stupendous turbulent outfalls of Barne and Mulock Inlets. It had been impossible then to work through the chaotic ice to the land, but he had learned a few things that might come in useful on the Beardmore Glacier farther up the road. Each new day along the trail would open up to him well-remembered vistas of the frozen continent, peaks and headlands he had been among the first to investigate. Among the present-day explorers, many were altogether charmed by the very notion of being even here, where so few had come before.

In two more miles, the horse drawn sledges came upon the other broken-down motor. Lashly and Hooper had now joined Evans and Day in manhauling. This early failure of the motors was no great surprise, but it would cut into the amount of supplies brought forward for the use of the men homeward bound. The cold deserted tractor's carcass made a depressing sight; it had barely made it beyond Corner Camp. No longer would the stillness of the Barrier be shattered by its incessant complaint.

Luckily Scott's plan was not entirely dependent on their success. The heavy loads they had been intended to pull would now be dragged along by men. Sooner or later everyone would be manhauling, but the motor party were obliged to begin their efforts here, still well north on the Barrier. These four would be going along ahead of the ponies and the dogs, breaking the trail and marking it with snow-cairns for those coming along in their wake.

The wind was rising as the last of the ponies struggled into camp. The moment Scott called a halt to the day's march, the fliers' tent made camp in a quickstep routine. It took all four men to throw the flapping canvas over its pyramid frame and hold it down while a neighbor cut snow blocks to weight down the valance. One man was peggy for the week, another filled the cooker with clean snow and passed it into the tent along with the makings of the hoosh. The other two became masons cutting and laying blocks of hard snow into pony walls shoulder high and ten or twelve feet long to shelter each horse from the shifting Barrier wind. After supper each night Crean was back outside with the currycomb brushing away the frozen sweat of the day's labor from Bones' shaggy pelt. There were feedbags to be filled with oats and chaff, a thick woolen blanket to be thrown over the horse and snugged down, a song and a kind word for an old friend. After a supper of steaming hoosh and cocoa and a good long pipe musing over the events of the day, Crean was outside one more time to check on his Bones, and then to bed.

The snow walls hastily thrown up by their keepers at the end of every day's march gave the horses but little shelter from the southern breeze. After supper a gale came on, rising to Force 8 in the watch below. Crean stirred from the comfort of his bag and left the tent more than once to clear away the snow drifting ever higher behind the pony walls until it threatened to cover the poor beasts. Despite the modest shelter, the animals were pretty well bunged up. All the next day the travelers were forced to lie up while the white drift whirled about the camp, singing the old familiar windsong through the green canvas walls. One week out, and the expedition was already losing a day to the weather.

By the following evening the storm had begun to abate and Castle Rock came again into view well astern, above the drift. Such fine clear weather was not expected to last. The "Funeral Cortege" got under way at midnight. Followed in due course by the others, they were off and into a beautiful night's sledging. The slower ponies had cleared the trail left by the manhauling motor party days before, and left nothing for Crean and Bones to do but follow along at leisure. The mountains of White Island to starboard were long familiar from the slow paces of this march and his earlier one with *Discovery*'s mission in 1903. To port, it was only the blank empty plain of the Barrier.

Just coming into view beyond the distant figures of the crocks, Crean saw something new. It was a flag, a piece of black bunting fluttering in the breeze over his long-dead first horse. Blossom was buried in this place beneath the snow, a casualty of the autumn depot journey from which the sailor had been denied his place.

The dogs, traveling easily, caught up with the slow-moving entourage somewhere past Corner Camp. Speed was their best asset, but one that could only be managed well by only a few men. Their excellent showing made light of the plodding slow work of the ponies, and the early utter failure of the motor sledges. The next few days of bad light, a wretched pulling surface covered with soft down flakes of new snow, and a stiff headwind made traveling a miserable business and the camps cheerless and silent.

At least the men of the fliers' contingent got to sleep in of a morning and take their breakfast in the tent while the others bustled about in the cold feeding their animals and preparing for a long and miserable march. They would pay for such leisure later in the day with a cold lunch drawn from a pocket and eaten on the march. These four men made an interesting mix—two ratings, two officers; a soldier among seamen; three talkers and a quiet one whose few well-chosen words had much to say.

Bowers was a happy companion to have on board. The smallest man had chosen the largest, ugliest, and most excitable horse to lead, and seemed to revel in the challenge. Victor took four men to harness him, Oates' Christopher would not be put in his yoke without a real fight. Taff's horse Snatcher was more like Bones, strong and compliant except for the occasional unexpected outburst of unruly behavior. The four sledges moved quickly along in a bunch, not stopping until they came up to the others at the end of their ten miles a day--plus a few extra yards to make up for the days already and yet to be lost to the blizzard.

The keepers of the Baltic Fleet messed together; it was their shared misery to rise and hit the trail well before any of the others, and come straggling into camp much later with all their camp-work yet to do. Their crocks were managing their ten miles a day as well as the others, albeit with less vigor. Twelve days out, all the horses were showing definite signs of wear even though, having fallen at last into their routine, they began to go a little better. Some even earned new nicknames: Jehu, he of the Funeral Cortege, was now known as "the Barrier Wonder"; Chinaman, "the Thunderbolt". Their endurance was exceeding everyone's expectations, even Oates', despite the increased drag of the sandy surface underfoot. The dog teams were not much bothered by the adverse conditions. They pulled their assigned loads easily, leaving well after even the fliers at the beginning of the day, and arriving ahead of them all to camp each night.

A snow cairn marking the buried remains of Blucher from the autumn depot journey still raised its rounded, diminished head over the Barrier between the bold new trail markers thrown up by the manhaulers ahead. Cheerful notes left for the Captain by Lieutenant Evans boasted of the splendid mileages posted each day by the manhauling party out on the Barrier ahead.

On Wednesday, November 15, all the pony party arrived at last at One Ton Depot, 130 miles from the *Discovery* hut. The big cairn marking the spot was much the same as it had been left last autumn, trailing a winter's accumulation of drift in a long line 150 yards to the northeast.

Scott had determined to give the ponies a day's rest here, before proceeding south with increased loads and a new daily requirement of thirteen miles. The day off was a welcome relief after two full weeks' uninterrupted traveling. Much time was given over to make-and-mend, to reading and dozing in the mild air. Very distant land could be seen all around to the west; Mt. Discovery had come into view again, and the Royal Society Range. The expedition was well away from the land where a gap in the far-off mountains showed the mouth of the Barne Inlet. From this distance it looked as though the Barrier ran smooth and level into it, but Crean knew better.

In Scott's carefully laid plan, everyone had been traveling lightly since leaving Cape Evans one hundred fifty miles and two weeks ago. They had been saving their strength for this moment when they would take on the full loads buried under the Barrier snow for the winter here at One Ton Depot. Taking advantage of the full day's rest and layover, Lt. Bowers directed the excavation and distribution of the foodstuffs for ponies, dogs, and men, of the carefully rationed oil for the primus stoves. These were all loaded onto the waiting sledges, leaving just enough behind to serve the returning support parties on their way home from the polar advance. A note from Lt. Evans and the manhauling party breaking the trail showed them to be five days ahead, going at a faster rate on foot than the ponies could manage. Maybe Scott was right—the way south would best be won by "good old British manhauling."

They set off again from One Ton in the usual order with the ponies now bought up to full loads from the depot, and all going better than expected. The crocks appeared done-in and ready to give out at any time,

165

yet they kept on plugging.   Perhaps they understood that each day's good work meant a stay of execution.

The weather became much more pleasant; for days on end the temperature dipped only once into the -20s.   At first the sun shone constantly, gloriously wheeling round the sky, burning everyone's face to a deep and weathered brown.   Sledging, whether manhauling or horse leading, solitary or in teams, becomes a silent business.   The animals when not overtaking one another march along in file; words between men can only be exchanged in passing.   The monotony of the Barrier trail gives way to realms of inner life, to plans and memories, philosophies and dreams.   The clear weather was short-lived; when the sun and the horizon disappeared altogether on overcast days, even the tents were silent after the march.

Some time after departing from Camp 15 Crean finally passed the invisible line of 80 degrees 5', his own record for farthest south, the one he shared with Scott and Wilson alone of the men of the *Terra Nova*. Everything from here on out would be, for him, all new land.   All new, but in appearance much the same as all the other land down here—stone, ice, and sky.   A long line of mountains disappearing into the distance off the starboard bow slowly closed with the trail ahead.   The details of it changed almost imperceptibly with every passing day.   Farther peaks showed above the white horizon ahead, the known landmarks drop away behind.   Off in the distance, well out from the land, a dark spot on the Barrier horizon resolved itself into the details of a camp, a tent and the dark figures of men moving about.

Lieutenant Evans' manhauling party had been waiting at 80 degrees 32' South latitude, as arranged.   Six days they had been camping

166

at the spot, waiting for the others to catch up. To pass the time they had erected the tallest cairn the Barrier had ever borne. Fifteen feet high, it had been dubbed Mt. Hooper after the erstwhile mechanic, a monument for a year or two if not for the ages. A beacon to welcome the returning parties into home territory, it was visible from nearly twenty miles away. The manhaulers were thin as rakes, had grown fearfully hungry even on the full Barrier Ration that easily satisfied the pony handlers. It was the first indication of just how physically demanding extended manhauling would be. Still, under Evans' leadership the four men were cheerful as ever, and anxious to be off on the trail again with some company other than their own.

From this point forward three depots containing provisions for the returning support parties, each some days' journey from the next, were to be laid out in a north-south line over the Barrier. Mt. Hooper was designated the Upper Barrier Depot, the first to be laid south of One Ton. It was stocked with Summit Rations, Emergency Biscuits, two cases of oil--three one-week food units for the use of the three advance parties on their return from points distant toward the Pole. There was nothing left in the depots for the ponies---none of them would be going home. After giving these supplies a proper stowage, the whole entourage moved forward another three miles: sixteen men, five tents, ten ponies, twenty-three dogs, and thirteen sledges.

The ponies were growing thinner—poor Bones now fully deserved his name—and moving ever more slowly even under their reduced loads, showing very conspicuous signs of running down. The weakest of them would not last much longer. Neither would the dogs' supply of biscuit. Even the dogs were growing ever leaner, ever more hungry, and unduly

167

interested in the weakening ponies. Meares, captain of the dogs, was not regarded kindly by the drivers of the Baltic Fleet.

Jehu the Barrier Wonder was the first to go. At the beginning of the journey he had not been expected to last two days, yet here 192 miles along he had outstripped the first to go of Shackleton's ponies. His usefulness as transport had ended, and as food for the dogs had begun; his time had come.

He met his end at lunch-oh. There was no way to ignore what was about to happen. It would be in full view, well within earshot. Oates led the pony a little way back on the trail. Inside the tent, Crean turned up the jet on the primus; the hiss of it did not hide the crack of the pistol shot, or the sudden great silence that overwhelmed the camp. It was a sad occasion, as all these coming executions must inevitably be. Still, it was all a part of the plan. That night the former motormen Day and Hooper made up the first detachment to be sent home, guided by the snow cairns marking the way across the frozen wastes when the trail ran away from the sight of land.

Thick weather, and the slow fading of the ponies, began to shadow the southern advance; the men's spirits fell. *"A tired animal makes a tired man."* Still, there was steady progress. The thirteen-mile mark was turned by the end of each day, despite the continuing oppression of the overcast and bad light and a vacant plain of ice. There was no sense at all of forward motion, of anything accomplished beyond a daily accumulation of tick-marks on the sledge-meter. Careful navigation showed they were nearing the land once again, though none of it could be seen. Mount Hope and the mouth of the Beardmore Glacier were no great distance ahead, the mountains of the Queen Alexandra Range were somewhere out of sight to starboard.

If a man feels he cannot live without a constant flux of change and variety in the world around him, he should not come to this place. It is a world where color shows only as shades of white, where faces and voices become deadened from constant close association, and the most blessed hope for tomorrow is that it is somehow different from today. Tom Crean knew all that and came here anyway, back to this place by choice, the inevitable result of decisions made too long ago to be regretted now. He knew also that there would be an end to this, that in time a world of magnificent vistas, of vast mountain ranges and endlessly wide plateaus would open to him again. He had only to keep on.

Adrift in this haze of fog and murky obscurity, the men were taken by surprise at the sight which greeted them when the sky cleared at last on November 29. The triple peaks of Mt. Markham were hard abeam, showing up in the daylight night through the first rifts in the cloudy haze. After three hundred miles of featureless barrier swathed in a gray haze of impenetrable gloom, this vision of solid earth was truly a wonderful sight. The following day was the first in a week of sparkling clarity where every detail of the land surrounding was bathed in glorious sunlight. Here was the view everyone had struggled and come so far to see, the new land so few had witnessed, crisp and bright and magnificent in every aspect. Enormous mountains bore giant glaciers cascading down like frozen rapids in a stream, surely the hand of God at work in every detail.

Camped at 82 degrees 21'S, they were four miles beyond Scott's farthest in 1902. This was new land for all of them now. Terra nova, indeed. Only Shackleton's pole party had been this way before. Here Wright's pony met his end, and his flayed and butchered remains fed first to the dogs, the remainder laid to rest under an upright sledge now no longer needed. *"Chinaman died today of senile decay"'* his master wrote, " *complicated by the presence of a bullet in the brain. Poor old devil. . ."*

Scott was trying various combinations of men to gauge what teams might work best together, and who might be fittest for the Pole. Already it was becoming clear who would be favored. Titus Oates would soon be leaving Crean's tent to go over and join the Captain; Cherry was coming in, bringing his youthful innocence and enthusiasm, his love of words--a welcome change from dry sarcasm of the dour soldier. Of the eight ponies still able to go on, Bones and Nobby were acknowledged the fittest. Christopher, the former pacesetter, had in these latter days lost all the fire of his youth; he would be the next to go.

Just at the moment of the shot, he jerked his head. The bullet only wounded him. Startled, he jerked free, ran squealing back into camp trampling tents and upsetting hoosh pots in his panic. Spurting blood everywhere until captured and subdued, he was forced back to meet his executioner once again. This time the bullet did its work and the horse found his final rest in the bloody snow. Unlike Jehu, he made good eating, very tender like good beef to the taste and sight.

One day later it was Bowers' beloved Victor; two days after that, Cherry's little Michael. By this time all the ponies were in marked decline. Their ends, and the end of the Barrier stage of the journey, were clearly in view. Each man had become attached to his animal during the cold dark months of winter walks, the weeks of constant company and daily care and grooming along the south polar trail. Each sad end came with the crack of the bullet, and left the company diminished by one. It was hard to see them go this way, to end up as feed for the dogs, but still it was all part of the plan.   With the excess of horsemeat at hand everyone went to bed at night as full as he wanted to be.

According to the sledgemeters they were only two days' march from Shackleton's Gateway marking the mouth of the Beardmore Glacier. December 3 the men roused at 2:30 a.m. to find a change for the worse in the weather, thick and snowy outside the tents. The weather cleared in the afternoon, revealing a landscape of incredible beauty, a range of snow-laced mountains close at hand riven by enormous icefalls and high passes leading into the mysterious interior of the unknown continent.

The grandeur disappeared as the blizzard came over them again. The men pushed on through it, making ten miles for the day before settling into their reindeer bags with a good hot meal.   The snowfall continued unabated four straight days, big wet wind-driven flakes of it piling up relentlessly, sticking tenaciously to everything it touched.   The tents weighed down with heavy snow began to sag inward to settle on the men in their bags.   They broke free at intervals to feed the ponies and shovel away the huge drifts growing long in the lees of the pony walls.   Oates remained outside tending to his charges for hours at a stretch, long after Crean had returned to the soggy shelter of the tent.   Each man entering brought fresh loads of damp snow inside, where it promptly melted into little pools of chilly water on the floorcloth to soak the fur bags.

The small heat of the primus was not enough to dry anything.   The clothes were wet, the food was wet--the matches, the sledges, the dogs, the ponies shivering under their green blankets—everything was waterlogged. The tobacco pouches could not keep out the infernal meltwater; inside, their precious contents became a sodden, pulpy, and--worst of all—unlightable mess.   Still, there was plenty of food to eat and time to sleep.   This was no time to go on short rations, with the long climb up the glacier just ahead.

The slushy drifts, left unchecked, would have entombed Bones to his shoulder and sapped the life right out of him.   Three or four times each day Crean left the sopping comfort of his reindeer bag to bring his horse a feed and a kind word, to shovel away the snow and wring the worst of the meltwater out of his green horse-blanket.   Four endless days went on like this--no change, no letup in the constant blizzard, while precious time blew away in the storm. The sailors debated among themselves: who is the Jonah?   Someone or something has got to be to blame for this miserable setback.   It must be—no names are mentioned, every man and beast has done his utmost.   It must be—the cameras!

On the fifth day, the weather cleared.   The snow—four feet of it--had covered everything.   The sledges had been buried for days, completely out of sight.   The camp lay in the middle of a vast waste of soft snow untold miles in extent.   There was no way out but that which they could forge themselves by brute force and sheer willpower.

Bowers and Cherry, followed by Lt. Evans and the manhaulers, led the way out, wading into the chest-high snow to clear a path.   The lead pony pushing into the drift right behind them had it worst; the heavy sledge at his heels plowed up its own wake through the lower drift.   The horses alternated leading and following, up to their bellies in the broken snow.   There was so little the worn out animals could do.   None could last longer that a few minutes in the lead.

When Bones was no longer moved by kind words and encouragement, it took a smack on the flank, and then another, harder.

Then beating—anything to get the beast to move. Forget the bond between man and animal, the genial companionship of the trail. These were desperate measures from desperate men. When the beating no longer worked, when one horse was too done to take another step, the next was brought up into the lead, until he too collapsed. They plugged on, hour after hour, not daring to pause for lunch, but there was only so much to be gotten by leading, urging, cajoling, swearing, whipping. The horses, overcome by the effort, were sinking down in the snow after five or six yards hard-pulling, collapsing in their tracks. For all of these animals, this awful march would be his last. There would be no food at the end of the march, only a bullet to the brain for each. This was the end for the horses; the pony food had given out during the blizzard.

Here, just short of Mount Hope, it was clear the ponies had given their all. They could do no more. The Barrier stage was over.

Chapter Eight

The Glacier

Shambles Camp.   December 9, 1911

The Great Ice Barrier had known no sound but the crackings and crumblings of its own inner turmoil, and the sweep of the searching wind over its desolate plain.   Then came small groups of men adding their own low voices to the wind's song, and the barks and sighs of their draft animals.   All these sounds arose from, and died away to, the splendid isolation of this remote and frozen desert.   Then came a new sound, harsh and alien to even this grim landscape, one with no place here.

--Here, Bones, let's go.--   Taking the leather bridle in his mittened hand, Crean led his horse a few steps back along the trail they'd just plowed with so much grinding labor through the soft, deep snow.   He took a biscuit from his pocket and raised it to the pony's lips.   *--There, now, old boy.--*   A pistol shot rang out.   The sharp dagger of its sound pierced the ear, and the heart.   Three more shots cracked through the desolate silence of the great Barrier plain that day, one by painful, sorrowful one until the last horse was dead.

There was little talk, certainly no laughter in the camp.   The few words to break the awful silence between the shots were those of patient coaxing mingled with the uncommon love that sometimes joins man and beast who have shared a great deal. Each shot signaled the end of one labor and the beginning of another in a long and seemingly endless trail. Each pony sank to his knees, and then to his side, and then rolled lifeless onto the bloody snow. Each must now be butchered for his meat, tough and stringy though it would be, before his carcass froze solid.

The blood ran into the soft snow and congealed there in bright red blocks. On another, later, day these would melt to make the broth of a good soup. A little way back along the homeward trail, small groups of men huddled over the stiffening corpses. Others busied themselves about the camp, pitching tents and lighting primus stoves for the evening's simmering hooshes to be amplified by pounds and pounds of fresh pony meat. Even full bellies would do little to allay the despondent air settling over the camp, so worn, so mournful, so far from home.

The steady breeze off the Glacier could not dispel the sickly smell of spilled and clotted blood that drifted over the camp and invaded the tents. The feelings of the entire party, as they surveyed their miserable position and their prospects, could be expressed in two words—*Shambles Camp*. Their position was a desperate one. Could they have seen themselves from the vantage of one of the skuas flying from time to time overhead, they might have given it another name—Hopeless Camp. It lay in the center of a vast shallow basin filled to its brim with sticky, slushy snow. The hard-won trail so bitterly forged these last miles with the ponies would seem but a scratch on the surface, the camp itself a hole, the butcher shop a red stain on an otherwise unblemished blanket of pure white. In every direction, the outlook is the same—north, south, forward, back, there is only a mire of snow as deep as a man's chest. There are two choices, stay and wither, or plow onward into the morass and with great and painful striving lengthen the pitiful scratch.

There could be no waiting, and no turning back. The expedition had come this far, and but for the long blizzard would have been four days up the glacier and well ahead of schedule. Now on December 10, 1911—forty days out from Cape Evans--here was nothing for it but to press on.

The first order of the new day was to rearrange the loads and cache whatever was unnecessary to carry forward. With the horse transport now become food, there was a stable's worth of pony-gear to be left by the wayside, along with a good many oddments of clothing and incidental supplies. All the rest of the gear was loaded onto four sledges. The dog teams would advance one more march before they were sent homeward with orders to come out on the Barrier in February to help the last supporting party in. Everyone except the dog-drivers was now manhauling. Before the march began Scott reassigned the men, taking Oates from Crean's tent into his own. He was testing the men, assembling a team for his final march to the Pole. Already it was becoming clear who would be favored.

Shackleton's Gateway opening so grandly onto the lower reaches of the Beardmore Glacier still lay two miles ahead, two exhausting miles of uphill wading through the waist-deep snow. Bill Lashly and Lt. Evans had been manhauling since the breakdown of the motors outside of Corner Camp, but everyone was at it now. The sledges ploughed along behind, runner-deep in the soft snow beneath until it became firm enough to bear, cleaving the snow in a slow-motion bow wave that left in its path a glittering mockery of a wake. *On, two, three—heave!* It was the old pulley-hauley again--a concerted heaving at the traces to get the sledges moving, a headlong struggle to keep up the hard-won momentum that inevitably ground to a halt.

The long climb—2,000 feet above the Barrier--gradually rounds over and levels off into the pass. With each step forward a further vista of the new land comes more clearly into view. A wide valley below--twenty miles across at least between soaring walls of stone—fills with the vast sweep of the Beardmore Glacier, the highway leading upward, always upward, to the plateau and beyond. Even the mighty Barne Glacier paled in comparison. No man here had ever seen anything like it.

Lofty mountain ranges at either hand direct its course. Wide tributaries pour into it like rapid mountain streams, tumbling down from hidden valleys above in dazzling cascades of broken ice flattening into its calm-appearing surface. From this distance the broad back of the glacier seems smooth and promising, its corrugations and crevasses barely visible. Far beyond, the distant peaks to the south shape its course between them. Dropping down from the high polar plateau, its surface ripples and eddies and shatters into a torrent of gigantic blocks of ice in the rapid of the Shackleton Icefalls nearer its source.

The men paused at the Gateway summit, stood silent. This then was their reward. The storms at sea, the darkness of winter's night, the long blank days on the Barrier trail were all but forgotten here--for a moment. After 425 miles of the unrelieved white plain desert of the Barrier, they were at last able to look upon great red granite cliffs towering in silence above them. Taking up the traces again after lunch, they started into the gentle descent toward the mighty glacier. What troubles lay ahead now must be imagined, and might beggar all imagination. It would be best to face the difficulties at hand, and let those that come later sort themselves out then.

Six miles made the day's mileage to a camping spot with a magnificent view right up to the inland ice. Some of the loads would be left here in the morning to make up the Lower Glacier Depot, now stocked with three weekly Summit units of provision, two cases of emergency biscuit, and two tins of oil. These were to be picked up by each of the returning support parties to carry them homeward as far as the Southern Barrier Depot at Mt. Hooper. Twelve men were here advancing forward, each in his heart determined to be among those four chosen to man the final assault. No one knew yet who would be returning to this spot first, somehow found out to be not quite fit enough for the Pole.

An improvement of the surface brought about by the night wind made the next day's pulling less demanding. The dog teams came forward a few more miles to the lunch camp before turning north for home. Their loads were distributed among the manhauled sledges. These were full loads now—800 pounds per sledge, two hundred a man. A few last notes were hastily scribbled and handed over to Meares, and with a whirl and a rush they were off. The dogs, no fools, were eager to be homeward bound and were soon lost to view. There were no draft animals at all now, only the twelve men to take up the first full loads most of them had yet drawn.

Two skuas hovered over the lunch camp, having followed the south polar trail from Cape Evans, attracted by the garbage and pony offal strung out along it. Pitching the tent in the evening, Crean broke through a crevasse hard by the door. Better now than while up in the night. He threw an empty oilcan down, listening. The sound of it rattled against the sides of the hollow pit and echoed for a terribly long time, fading into a hard, blue, fathomless silence.

The morning march gave a good long view of the wearying days to come. Getting the sledges in motion was the worst of it. Starting was worse than pulling. It required a dozen or more desperate heaves at the traces to jolt the sledges from their frozen beds. Once in motion, the momentum might carry the sledge a few hundred yards before the men, breathless from their exertion, began to slow down. It was a regular "sweat and swear" day. Crean's sledge first stuck ten yards from camp; nine brutal hours later they were little more than half a mile on. The work was as hard as any he'd ever done, and the reward of a thick hoosh at the end of the day fell well short of assuaging the hunger that was coming to dominate all thoughts during the day's march.

Scott's four-man team seemed to be the strongest—always in the lead, and always pulling ahead. There were daily mileages to be made, no matter what, if the goal of the South Pole were to be reached. But there was also the need to outdo the competition. Shackleton and his men—Frank Wild among them—were the only ones to have been in this place before. Their distances and dates would have to be met, and overmatched; it was a matter of pride, as well as necessity. There was also the matter of the Norwegian interloper, Amundsen. He must have intended to reach the plateau by this glacier—it was the only known route--but there was no sign of him. Perhaps his dogs had failed him; perhaps he'd given up the race.

Crean's sledge pulled into lunch camp in second place--Atkinson's was always last--despite their bravest efforts. In an experiment, the two lead teams exchanged sledges for the afternoon march. Sometimes a flaw in a runner made more drag, or perhaps the loads were unequal. Each team thought their new sledge the heaviest, but Scott's men still continued to walk away with the lead. Perhaps it was true—perhaps the men of the supporting teams had not quite the strength to keep up, to carry on. But this much was also true—Scott was a driver, of himself and of his men. He had an artful way of making it known that his expectations for himself and for all of his followers were high, and they must at all accounts be met.

Four men would be sent back from the next depot, and Crean knew already who two of them would be. Keohane and Cherry had been steadily weakening under the endless daily effort. There was no doubt about it--they moved slowly in camp, their eyes lacked the fire, their voices the lilt they'd once had. Their weight loss was readily apparent even under the baggy folds of their windproofs, but the same was true of everyone. There was plenty of food, but it wasn't enough. In the other tents Lt. Evans and Lashly had been manhauling four hundred fifty miles already and were showing obvious signs of wear. Setting up camp at night was a blessed relief after a long day trying to keep up the quickstep pace set by the Owner. A constant high wind swept up the glacier that night, gradually blowing away a layer of dry, powdery snow to leave a better surface for easier travel in the morning. Even so, the work was getting harder, and a good stout breakfast in the morning no longer kept the ravaging hunger at bay.

Each day's sun swung slowly round, casting ever-changing shadows across the black mountain faces towering over the Beardmore. Spectacular new landscapes rose ahead, to be slowly brought athwartships and then recede behind: Mt. Kyffin and Mt Hope, the portals of the great iceflow; Socks Glacier coming down on the right, marking the spot where Shackleton's last pony had disappeared down a crevasse. He'd gotten more work and better distance out of his ponies—at least that one. Alice Glacier sweeping into the Beardmore at grade; Wedgeface on the port bow. So new was the world around them that no scree had gathered at the feet of the huge cliffs leaping skyward from the glacier's sides.

Narrow crevasses lay in waiting underfoot, but none swallowed more than a leg. Making good mileages every day now, the men were catching up Shackleton's distances; at this rate, they ought to overtake him and make the pole handily. As the party gained elevation, the depth of the snow diminished--first twelve inches, then nine, then patches of hard blue ice began to show through. The climb was, if not pleasant, at least manageable. Blazing sunlight cracked the lips and hardened the face to a scaly brown leather. A man had to be careful of his eyes in this light. He wouldn't know until the burning started, and then it was too late to stop the damage. Crean knew the feeling well—like ground pepper laid in under the eyelids, and no relief to it but the passage of days and sleepless nights. Every man had snow goggles in his kit, if only he would remember to use them.

On Sunday December 17 the men traversed a series of huge pressure waves abreast the Cloudmaker. Up, up they went until the sledge balanced on the crest of a wave, poised for a descent. Bowers aimed it carefully, gave a nudge, and with a mad scramble all four men jumped aboard. It started off slowly, picking up speed. In a moment it was out of control, a runaway express with no brakes bumping and clattering ever faster over the hard blue ice. Every bump threatened a capsize, a tumbling roll that would have broken the sledge to bits and a few bones as well, but there was no stopping it now. What could they do but laugh like schoolboys on holiday until the sledge came safely to a halt in the trough of one wave, and they had to take up the traces for the long trudge up the next. The spell of gloom from Shambles Camp was finally broken, and the men began to talk of Christmas coming soon, daydreaming of a full belly for at least that one day.

Here in the shadow of the mighty Cloudmaker they'd place the Mid-Glacier Depot, laid out in the morning under a cairn and a red flag on a bamboo pole. The twelve men had come a long way together. They had risen altogether 3,000 feet from Shambles Camp. Blessed with a span of fair marching weather, their distances increased daily, even with the steepening climb. The way, however, was neither clear nor easy. Shackleton had found trouble to the east, so the Owner when he could laid the trail toward the west side of the glacier. He was a tough one for setting the pace and marking off the miles, and it was a hard slog for the others to try to keep up.

The expedition was coming along according to plan as the lengthening days' marches brought it up to speed. That plan included in it the necessity of weeding out the weaker men as they went along. Scott's own tent was assumed by most to be the team that would go on to the Pole. He had Dr. Wilson, Captain Oates, and seaman Taff Evans in his tent, all fit and pulling like horses themselves. The everlasting hunger hadn't slowed *them* down much. Certainly they were the quickest on the march, always ahead and increasing their lead as the day wore on. Among the others trailing along behind, the greatest honor accrued to those who could come nearest the Pole. There was keen competition between the tents to prove out who, collectively and individually, were the better men. Both the supporting teams were satisfied as to their own superiority. They were all pulling very hard.

December 19 saw seventeen miles for the day, even with a long lunch for a round of survey angles by Lt. Evans. The following day they covered nineteen and a half miles, climbing eight hundred feet along the way despite the fact that in Crean's tent Bowers and Keohane were both snowblind, making hauling for them a double agony. The weights were so heavy, the surface so gritty, that if any of them eased up for even a second the sledge stopped dead and it was all they could do to get it going again. A hundred yards without grinding to a halt was a good show, but if they were going to keep up with Shackleton's distances, there could be no slacking up now. They were all beginning to feel the effects of too little food to sustain their struggle. The dreadful cold, increasing as they rose, cut right through the close weave of their windproofs, chilled the beads of sweat gathered on their backs.

Regardless of the shows of bravado and bursts of energy for Scott's benefit, some of the men--Cherry, Keohane, Teddy Evans, Wright--were close to the limit of their endurance. Crean himself was not so sturdy as he once had been; the thinner air, the constant cold, the unending uphill slog, the empty belly that never knew satisfaction—they weakened a man in spite of himself.

The issue of who should go forward and who should go home involved more than the physical condition of the men. At such a distance from home, and following a route that led away from visible land and out over the trackless wastes of the Barrier, each returning party would need a navigator. Atkinson would have to return at some point; his services as a physician would be needed at Cape Evans to tend to the needs of the shore station and the various field parties as they came in. Some of the men were noticeably weaker, and would no be able to go on. Cherry's dependence on his spectacles was a liability to consider. Crean, P.O. Evans, and Lashly had all the seamen's knack for make and mend, at improvising necessities from whatever was at hand, skills that were lacking in the officers and would be wanted on the trail ahead. Besides, they were three *Discovery* veterans, with the unconscious self-assurance of men who had faced a thousand dangers and could face hardship with a laugh and disaster with equanimity. Crean himself had impressed young Gran as *"a man who wouldn't have cared if he'd got to the Pole and God Almighty was standing there, or the devil."*

At an elevation of 6500 feet the glacier widened out to a broad river of ice miles in width, and the mountains rising above the valley no longer seemed so imposing. Here where the great ice flow squeezed between Buckley Island and the Dominion Range, the men found a maze of crevasses in their path. When the cracks in the ice were too wide to jump, the men would tread gingerly on the snow bridges that in places crossed them. Sometimes these gave way without warning, but the harnesses were something a man could trust his life to. Before starting, Scott looked up the glacier. *"Well,"* he said *"There are crevasses. Someone has to fall into one first."* He was the one, but by day's end everyone had taken a fall, two of them to the length of their harnesses. It is no pleasure to be suspended there between two walls of ice, spinning helplessly while one's mates peered over the edge above shouting down catcalls and words of mock encouragement. Each found the whole thing rather funny until his own turn came around.

At the end of the day's march they made camp, pitched their three small tents in the midst of the wide white glacier. At either hand towering snow-clad peaks looked down upon them. Their tracks behind disappeared into the ever-falling distance; untrodden icefields rose in gentle slopes ahead. The end of the long climb was almost in sight, the start of the barren level plain of the high plateau just beyond.

Bowers worked late in the evening of December 21, rearranging the stores and bagging units for the Upper Glacier Depot. A mournful air settled over the three tents that night. The twelve men had come so far together, had suffered and struggled to advance a common ideal and shared between them a bond transcending that of mere friendship. The four told off to head for home—Dr. Atkinson, Silas Wright, Cherry, and Keohane—could not hide their disappointment, but the final success of the expedition's highest goal demanded this parting, at this place.

*   *   *   *   *

In such close company, private moments are hard to find.

--*Crean, here. Take these.*-- Cherry had an unexpected gift, drawn from the interior of his own ditty bag.

--*What?*-- It was a pair of Jaeger wool socks, the knit of them fresh and tight, as though they had never once been worn.

--*Take them.*-- Crean's eyes were drawn from the socks, held out by Cherry's ungloved hand, up the windproof sleeve, across the stooped shoulder, to the eyes—the puffed watery eyes, for a brief moment unguarded by the thick lenses of the customary spectacles. For one long moment, Crean considered. The boy'd been cursed with a weak constitution; he'd have his own need of good stout wool on his feet; it's six hundred miles of a long walk back to the hut, starting tomorrow. Without

186

good socks to warm his feet, he'd surely suffer frostbite to his toes, then go lame and never make it home.

That's what makes the gift. The sacrifice, if sacrifice indeed it must become. Not which man might need the socks more, but who has the greater need to see his friend succeed. This far out on the Polar journey, success and survival are spelled the same. Homeward now, or forward and back home again. It is all one goal.

--*And this.*-- With a knife Cherry made a small nick in the hem of his scarf, then ripped it longways down the middle and handed half over. No further words need be exchanged. Spoken words would only diminish the gift. A long deep look, eye to eye--soul to soul, though neither sailor thought of it as such--is enough. Crean took the socks and the half-a-scarf, removed his glove for one unguarded moment to feel the smooth weft of them before folding and then slipping them into the deep recesses of his own ditty bag. He must give something in return, but there is nothing, nothing that can be spared. No one has brought along any surplus. The long journey has meant that no man brought more than the barest minimum of to maintain his own survival. --*Thank you.*--

The canvas of the tent shuddered at the touch of a fresh breeze. Voices sounded just outside, just before a gloved hand opened the flap of the door and Bowers' bare head pokes through. -- *'Tis cold out here. make room for another.*-- Keohane followed right after, dusting the snow from his shoulders as he crawled in. With the practiced ballet of four men in a low tent, they each of them wriggled into the chill cocoon of their sleeping bags, praying for sleep but hoping at least for rest. Crean's bed was, for this night, just a little bit warmer.

* * * * *

In the morning, Cherry and Keohane were gone. Before leaving they threw up a snow-cairn over the depot and marked it with two ten-foot sledge runners and a black flag. Beneath were two half-weekly food units, and all the crampons and glacier gear--ice axes, crowbar, alpine rope—that were no longer needed. The gentler slopes of the glacier and the flattening summit of the polar plateau lay just ahead. Scott was optimistic. *"We ought to get through."*

The returning party were soon lost to sight in the shifting tumbled ice of the upper glacier. In some ways they were the lucky ones. The way for them was now downhill, the return so much sooner to the real solid walls of a hut and the plentiful food that awaited within, but there was more. With the sudden diminishment of the company, an undeniable sense of isolation and danger took hold of the plateau party. They were five hundred miles from the hut, and the tenuous thread connecting them to the place had just grown thinner. The new world ahead was as dangerous as it was beautiful; the siren call took on a new, more sinister, tone.

Now there were only eight to hear it. Crean was still in the running for the final dash. The vacancies left in the tent were filled by Bill Lashly and Lieutenant Evans, called "Teddy" by his peers in the wardroom "Sir," by the seamen, even in the close quarters of the tent. Even though Lashly with Lt. Evans had been manhauling much longer than anyone else, he was hard as nails and still going strong. Lashly was a quiet one—a married man, a teetotaler, but he knew his way around the ice. He knew how to swear, too—taught Crean a few new tricks, though of course the two seamen had to be circumspect in their language around

188

the other two. The lieutenants were the finest of men, both of them always ready with a joke and a laugh, but still they were officers.

After the last farewells, the two advance teams made ten more miles uphill until they were at last well clear of the land, and raising new nunataks on the level ice plain ahead. The following morning was an uninterrupted slog to top the first of a series of enormous pressure waves. Here there were crevasses into which the *Terra Nova* herself, masts and yards and all, could easily have disappeared. At 7500 feet, the thin cold air here was beginning to wear down even the Captain--and everyone was stiff and weary at the end of a long day's march. Still, they had been making good mileages every day, had caught up their schedule and finally overmatched Shackleton. There was no sign of Amundsen at all. The Pole was almost in hand. Though still rising, they had cleared the head of the glacier and were properly on the South Polar Plateau. The route lay clear and level ahead. Behind, the summits of one or two mountains lately passed could still be seen. It was an eerie sight.

There is no desert in the world so bare, so empty and devoid of any scrap of life or stone to delight the eye or interest the mind. It goes on like this for hundreds and hundreds of miles, to the far side of the continent, with nothing so much as the nunatak peak of a buried mountain to mark a way across. The coldest of wind sweeps the drifts of snow across its expressionless face in every direction. There is no way out but the return of the way in, where the meager depots are planted at the slimmest of margins, to guide and sustain the traveler home.

Christmas Eve 1911 came as a fine sunny day, and gave them a rise of 400 feet after a march of fourteen miles on a proper course for the Pole, and a keen glow of anticipation for the feast they had promised themselves on the morrow. There was to be no holiday, for the schedule admitted no delays. It was, as Bowers said, *"a strange and strenuous Christmas, with plenty of snow to look at and little else."* The day began as had so many others--rise and shine, breakfast with a little pony meat added to the hoosh for the occasion, pack, harness, go. They were still mounting the pressure ridges, climbing another 240 feet before lunch camp.

Christmas Day was Lashly's 44th birthday. He marked it by dropping straight to the length of his harness. The men of Tent #2 were marching steadily along, diagonally across the depressed lid of a crevasse when without warning he dropped out of sight. The jerk when he reached the end of his harness pulled Crean and Bowers both backwards off their feet and nearly dragged them and the sledge into the depths with him. In that one moment it would have been all over for them, and for the expedition. Crean's harness, caught under the sledge, pinned him to the ground. The two lieutenants released him, and the three of them dropped a bowline over the edge to their shipmate. Spinning in space between the blue-black walls of ice over a bottomless pit, he had ample time to study the walls of the chasm, growing colder by the minute. Once Lashly was topside, Crean wished him *"many happy returns of the day"*. The stoker wound up and unleashed a torrent of unrestrained profanity that only a man well-versed in the art, and driven beyond the farthest extent of his endurance, could deliver on this holy day. Even Crean was astonished.

By lunch camp they had done over eight miles. Bowers, peggy for the tent, came up with a stick of chocolate for each from his secret store, and two spoonsful of raisins each for their tea. Refreshed and happy, the two teams set out with renewed vigor on the afternoon march.

Scott, fairly well wound up, led the way, on and on. Checking the sledgemeter, he found it at fourteen and three-quarter miles. *"How about fifteen for Christmas Day?"* That was the Owner, always asking a little bit more from his men, and so they went, and gladly, but happier still to call it a day and pitch the tents.

Bowers had another surprise for his companions. He had managed to keep concealed, all the way from Cape Evans, sundry treats and delicacies to brighten just this day. The first course was a good fat hoosh with pounds of pony meat and extra ground biscuit. Next, a chocolate hoosh—cocoa, sugar, biscuit, raisins—followed by plum duff (how could one celebrate Christmas without a duff!), a two-and-a-half inch square of it for everyone, with a good mug of cocoa to wash it all down. For dessert, four caramels and four squares of crystallized ginger apiece. This was a feast like no other, leaving all the men so stuffed they could scarcely move. There were toasts over the cocoa, handshakes and cheerfully shouted greetings and good wishes of the day. Visits were exchanged between the two green tents, these lonely sentinels at the frontier of the unknown world. Bowers spoke for all of them, turning in that night. *"Good night Teddy. If all is well next Christmas, we'll get hold of all the poor children we can, and just stuff them full of nice things, won't we!"*

Though no one really understood it, the altitude had joined forces with the cold to break them all down. The men slept well that night, and thoroughly warm. Then up, breakfast, back to work. But the spring in their step was soon lost, and the sledges dragged more heavily. The months of unbroken grinding effort were taking their toll, though none would ever confess it.

From the crests of the pressure ridges they could see far behind to the southeast the last nunataks of the Dominion Range, between which the icecap flowed in glaciers to the Barrier. For five days they found it heavy going, making distances of only a dozen miles or so over the frozen plain. The second sledge was clearly running down, lagging far behind Scott's by day's end. The Owner had the four men depot their skis, stuck upright in the snow so they wouldn't be missed on the way back home. It was clear now who was going on, and who would be returning.

With their steadily diminishing loads, the sledges were becoming, in effect, too large. Scott had determined to use the morning of New Year's Eve to dismantle and shorten the sledges. It had always been the plan to cut down the twelve-foot sledges to ten, once the reduced loads became light enough. Shorter sledges would be easier to handle, and less weight to drag onward.

This kind of work was the natural domain of the sailors. Crean, P.O. Evans, and Lashly emptied their tent of all but a floorcloth and the sledge. With the improvised canvas workshop heated by a primus, they set to work in the coldest, highest, Godforsaken mechanic's shop in the world. Bowers went over to the other tent for the duration. From time to time his high-pitched voice could be heard across the way, making some point or other to the other officers who had no skills to bring to bear in this task.

It was fearfully cold work. The sledge, far too long for the available space, stuck out through the tent's open door. The small heat of the primus escaped into the plateau breeze. Each sailor carried in his dittybag a sledging toolkit, a neat array of chisels and rules and diminutive hammerheads with a common wooden handle, all carried in a folding leather wallet. These, with blunted sailors' knives and marlinspikes better suited to rigging than woodwork, would have to do. It was another "cold-hand" job, a matter of cutting through the lashings, hacking across the hard ash runner grain made harder by the cold, and lashing up the shortened runners and deck-laths again.

No one could handle these tools through the mitts; it was gloves or nothing, and the gloves gave scant protection from the cold. A man's fingers were soon white throughout, completely numb, and another man's fingers took their place. It was clumsy work, and no surprise when Taff's right hand and the tool it tried to control took a quick slide across the icy wood and plunged the blade deep into the flesh of his left.

The wound bled profusely, the droplets freezing as they struck the floorcloth. With enough pressure and a filthy bandage, the red tide was stemmed for the moment. There would be no need to alarm the officers; someone might think it cause enough to send him home with the supporting party, and he'd come too far along to let that happen. The lower deck would be represented at the Pole, and he would be the man to do it. He'd always been Scott's right-hand man in the traces, and Crean would never be one to deny him the right, even when he could plainly see his friend was weakening—weren't they all?

With the work completed and the sledge shoved out the door, the sailors huddled mutely, shivering violently within the thin shelter of the tent while the hissing primus brought a pot of water to a merry boil. Half a day's inactivity, even with an ending in the doubtful comfort of a balding fur bag, was enough to nearly freeze a man--not superficially, like an easily remedied frostbite, but deeply, wholly, into his very core, body and soul. Each sip of the steaming tea brought Tom Crean blessed relief--first to his lips and mouth, then the stomach aching deep within, then the heart itself and the blood it pushed through arms and thighs to fingers and toes, reviving each to life and some small measure of hope.

Now there was time for another round of celebration for the keeping of the New Year, a fond exchange of wishes for a happy and prosperous year and success in bagging the Pole. It lay out on the plateau ahead, only 180 miles away. After a stick of chocolate in honor of the day, it was into the harness and --*Ho! for the Pole*-- and another day's slog across the unchanging plateau, pushing always toward that elusive goal.

One never knew quite where he stood with the Owner. Four would be going on and four told off for home, and the day for the division was close at hand. The best and strongest should be going forward. It only made sense; the Pole party would have another three hundred miles to their tally than those sent homeward now. Each man looked at all his fellows, calculating their chances, judging their strength. Crean knew he was, by that measure, among those who should go on. Scott was a bulldog, always had been; there would be no stopping him now, not at this small distance from the goal of his life. Wilson was clearly up to the job. Bowers, the same; there was no diminishing of his boundless energy, even with the thousands of extra steps mandated by his short legs. Look at the two Evanses—the Lieutenant was without doubt weakening, and the Petty Officer had lost much of his former body weight, and now had quite an injury too. As for himself with Lashly, they were about equal--both well worn, both still up to the job. It was only another one and a half hundred miles, then lightly laden and with the Pole in hand, sprint for home.

On the morning of January 3, 1912, the Owner went across to the second tent and stood beside it in silence. Inside, the tent was full of tobacco smoke as the men took a moment's ease after breakfast. A man needed the stimulation of his 'baccy if he was to step out on the plateau trail with any vigor. Crean coughed, a normal morning waking hacking, as any man familiar with a pipe might have on rising. Scott must have been listening outside. He stuck his head inside the door and said, *"You've got a nasty cough, Crean, you must be careful with a cold like that"*. There was more to these words than concern for his health, and Crean knew it.

"I understand a song half-sung, Sir!" Scott laughed, but all the same the seaman knew what was up, and had it confirmed a moment later. Crean got his orders to turn back, with Lashly and Lt. Evans. Something, someone had changed the Owner's mind at this last minute, at this last reach, about the best way to assure success in the goal. The new idea was that if four could make the final dash, then five could do it faster, so much so that they would catch up the three-man support party on the way home just before they reached Corner Camp.

Lt. Bowers, went over to Scott's tent to join the Polar Party. So, this was they way it would be--five men to go on, three to return. Birdie would be without skis on the polar advance—would that not be a hindrance? There was nothing for it but to trust the Owner's wisdom and follow his orders, and trust that all would be for the best. There was a long parley in the second tent over things in general. Scott, confident of success, thanked them one and all for the generous way in which they had assisted in the final goal and assured them that he would indeed be sorry when they parted.

The thought that some were judged fitter—better—struck a blow that damaged a man's pride, here where he needed it most. Even so, there was something to be said for the fact that the Owner had confided, as Nelson had, that each man would do his duty, and that the right three men sent home now could amply fulfill the work of four. Of those three, two had manhauled a full 360 miles further than any other. If they were physically weaker now, it was through greater devotion to the goal on the outward march. Each had given his all, the decision had been made, the die cast, and now let events play out as they would.

It was a day of cold drift, as cold as any they'd yet encountered. Even so, they all made one good last outward march together, twelve more miles toward the Pole.

Chapter Nine

The Long Walk Home

South Polar Plateau.   January 4, 1912

So this would be the great parting.   Some would go forward, some return.   The fates of all who had struggled equally to gain this far advance would now fall out to different advantage.   There was no doubt about it at all; the South Pole was British now.   It was theirs for the taking.

Bowers could barely contain his excitement during his farewell breakfast in the tent with Crean, Lashly, and Lt. Evans.   The meal itself wasn't much, just the usual sledging fare heated over the hissing primus. The sound of the burner spoke for them; the words they shared were few. Words themselves could bear little weight or value in comparison to the great challenge they'd undertaken together to reach this place.   What, after all, could be said that was not already understood?   Sledging, like life before the mast, reveals the best and worst in every man who lives it. Strengths and weaknesses alike are exposed in the shared trials from which there is no escape.   Here, over time, the bonds of friendship are forged which will never be easily broken.

Then camp was struck.   The clatter of the tent-poles, the scrape of the canvas folding upon itself, the clink of the cooker laid into its carrying-case—each sound had a sudden, peculiar, final ring to it. The breaking-down took a while, longer perhaps that it should have to see to it that everything was well and properly divided. The change from two four-man teams meant that much of the depot supplies would have to be recast into three- and five-man units, with no mistakes in the division. They'd reached the place of final separation, ten thousand feet up on the plateau, and Scott was anxious to get on with it. With a hundred and forty-eight miles remaining to the Pole, from this point on it was a sure thing.

The immense dome of the sky, overreaching all, closes at all directions with the unbroken prospect of the stark and windswept plain. Eight men alone together breaking down and packing their gear, their little all, marked the center of this void. They were more than a long way from home, from succor and repletion. Their dark forms, stooped over the flattened tents, the last homestead they will share together, intensified the emptiness of this frozen desert.

The three men of the last supporting party came along on the first leg of the march south, helping with the Pole Party's sledge another five miles until Scott called a halt. There had to be a point, a place where no further help was needed, and each team must look to its own affairs. Here was the true farewell, the final goodbye. They shook hands all around, and spoke their few parting words--best wishes for success to the Pole, and for a safe and speedy return home. One by one, Crean made his last farewell with each. Titus Oates, always the gentleman, albeit with a cavalryman's facility with language, had changed the sailor's view of what a soldier could become. Lieutenant Bowers--dear, happy chirpy Bowers, tireless faithful Birdie whose short legs and stout little frame had always taken on more than their share of any burden and could be counted on to see the Pole party to their destination and home again. Dr. Wilson, the steady hand guiding the higher purposes of two magnificent expeditions, now going forward to realize the greatest temporal goal as well. And Scott, his Captain. Years of constant companionship between the captain and his coxswain had engendered a friendship that transcended society's constraints. Scott was, like any man a mix of strengths and weaknesses; of his great courage and charisma there was never any doubt. Crean knew him, and loved him, better than any other man. They would meet again in a few months back at Cape Evans, and next year it would be off together onto a new ship.

For a few parting seconds Crean and Taff looked at each other, past the white patches, shredded skin, blistered lips, frosted whiskers, each into the other's eyes deeply as only true friends can look who know it will be some long time before they meet again. Whatever there was to say had been said, in actions if not words, over the course of years and shared experience.

Both men had a long way to go before they might meet up again. One would come home to acclaim, a conqueror; the other, his helpmate, to lesser glory. One would have four companions to share the terrors of his harrowing isolation, the other only two. One was weakened, injured, diminished—one was not. The flat white plain surrounding them could not contain the awesome consequence of this moment.

Crean possessed an emotional side that most times he concealed as well as any other man, but now deep within his breast the sob that he had so far manfully controlled refused to be beaten. It forced its way out, up and up, first one and then another, and more thick and fast until he gave up the struggle and wept openly and freely. It was not a show of weakness, and no man took it for such. In time the paroxysm subsided, and last handshakes and fond farewells were exchanged. Crean and Evans, the cobbos parted.

The last supporting party gave three cheers for their friends. There could be no more fitting, or more desolate, setting for this last farewell. Here the great cathedral spread under the vaulting dome of the sky, nave and transept 87 degrees 19 minutes south by 160 degrees and 40 minutes east. There was nothing against which the sound could echo and amplify. Instead, the wind flattened it and carried it away, rendered it pitifully weak against the vast emptiness of the plateau. They stood watching until their feet began to grow cold, then turned away homeward. The two teams went their separate ways, one into the great unknown, the other back along the long homeward trail, following their own footsteps across the featureless plain. North and south they walked, opposite ends of a straight line that grew in length with every step, a tenuous thread laid out along the meridian, a last communication that would be severed in time by wind and drift. From the top of a rise Crean could see ahead his party's own sledge in the distance, a black mark against a white backdrop that had no limit but the horizon. Turning, he saw that their companions had at last vanished from view.

Now they were three. There were, perhaps, no three men lonelier in all the world. The remoteness of their advanced position was exceeded by only that of the five who were now on their way to the Pole. But, in their suddenly diminished company, they felt their isolation yet more acutely. It drew them together, men and officer, encircled them and seemed to ease the proper distinctions of rank and class. Leaning into the harness, they knew already how much they would miss the cheerful companionship of their tentmate Birdie Bowers, ever-optimistic, ever-energetic, and the determined swing of his short and sturdy footsteps in the traces alongside.

The journey back to Hut Point and safety would be long one, a dreadfully extended haul on foot under any circumstances. Coupled with the outward march to this Godforsaken place, it would give them for a brief moment the distance record for the longest polar march ever done--1,300 miles for the round-trip give or take a few. It was not a record that brought much joy in the contemplation. Before long it would be exceeded by that of the Pole Party, who would also enjoy that other, dearer, record of having been the first men to stand on the South Pole of the Earth. Some were bound for glory, others for the muted praise that accrued to those who toiled in support.

Each man kept his innermost thoughts about the matter to himself. It would not do for Crean and Lashly to share too much with their officer; they were inwardly relieved that he kept an unaccustomed quiet to himself. Each man had known, from the day he'd signed on with the expedition, that some would get the Pole, but most would not. Odds were for any man he'd be among the latter, his part to promote the goal, but not to gain it. Each admitted, though only to himself, that it was a heavy blow to be turned away after having come so far. And each man knew in his bones how tired he was, how dauntingly far from home, how immeasurably greater the work remaining to those who'd gone onward.

The worst of it was that being chosen for the return party meant that these three men, collectively and individually, had been tried and found wanting. After all this effort, nothing could erase the sting of that.

Certainly it was not unexpected.   It had long seemed a sure bet that all the men in Scott's tent would continue onward, that the choice had been made miles, perhaps months, before.   Even so, hadn't they watched Oates, gallant soldier that he was, hobbling along to keep up with the others in the march despite the lame gait brought on by an old war-wound?   Wasn't that a nasty cut on P.O. Evans' hand?   Would that have any chance to heal, weakened as its owner was by frost and fatigue?   Might not one of these three returning have gone on in the stead of one of them?

And might not Scott have given them a fourth man for their team? If five men could travel faster and stronger than three, then by the same reasoning three men must travel slower, and carry their burden more heavily.   The weight of a tent and all the necessary gear for the trail was the same for three men as it was for four, but the motive power was far less.   True, the homeward trail was well broken by their outward tracks, the way downhill at best and level at worst--certainly an easier slog than that to this point, uphill with full loads.   Well, the choice was made for good or ill, and as the sailor says, *Growl ye may, but go ye must.*   These three men, tempered by their long baptism by ice, would be the ones to pull through, no matter how long and difficult the road.

Taking up their load with a will, they made thirteen miles to the good before camping for their first night on the homeward trail.   They had no sledgemeter to record the distances traveled.   A screw had fallen out on the way up the Beardmore, and the useless wheel and carriage had been left by the wayside.   Now they had only their own dead reckoning and what remained of the visible marks of their own footsteps to log their transit.   Here on the plateau, with no landmarks of any kind to triangulate their progress, they would be dependent on their outward-bound cairns to show them where they were.

In all his thirty-four years Tom Crean had never felt so alone. True, he was in the company of two of the best seamen to be found on earth. Lieutenant Evans might have his shortcomings as an officer, but when it came to pitching in when he was most needed, and in sheer courage in the face of overwhelming odds, he had no equal. Lashly was like Crean himself when it came to doing what must be done with no fanfare and no complaint. These three, of any three, would win through. But the three of them were all alone in the world. Home, safety, a warm night's rest were an impossibly distant six hundred fifty miles away. All of a sudden it seemed as though the unequal division of the company was a huge mistake, and the burden of it must be borne by these three. No great matter now; these things are what they are.

The camp was eerily quiet that first night. Crean missed the chirruping good humor of his absent tentmate Birdie, and the reassuring presence of another tent in company here on the wide and windswept plain. Whatever misgivings he had over being thrust into the care of Lt. Evans for the long walk home, he kept to himself. With Lashly as shipmate, he knew the two of them would provide out of their common stock whatever lower deck grit and common sense might be required. Supper for three was a briefer effort. There didn't seem much to talk about, and after the cocoa they were soon bundled in their bags and fast asleep.

A stiff breeze straight from the South Pole sighed through the threadbare canvas and sifted into their dreams appointed until the hour to rise and face the day's work. Morning's *lash up and stow* came as cheerlessly as the evening had gone. This endless plain was as bad as the

Barrier for sapping the ardor out of a man's spirit. The eye searched in vain for some dark object, some shadow to break the white monotony of the trail ahead, but there was nothing. Snow-goggles worked well enough for the pullers, but the man who led the way needed better vision to pick out the indistinct humps of weathered snow-cairns in the distance. On the road after breakfast, Crean led the way, his eyes fully exposed to the bad light. By early afternoon the telltale stinging told him it was too late to stop the damage. By *camp-oh* the same light that for days had no effect blinded him like hot sand rubbed against his unprotected corneas and massaged in with ground pepper for good measure.

It would pass, his vision resolve itself after a few days' utter misery. He wouldn't be sleeping much; zinc tablets from the medicine kit gave but scant relief. He marched blind, overhearing snippets of talk about the lost trail, the suspected cairns and wished-for nunataks rising up ahead. while the others took the lead. Only the groaning of the sledge lashings and the whispering south wind broke the ghastly silence of the empty plain.

Evans and Lashly led him seventeen miles that second homeward day, and another sixteen and a half the next. Along the way they passed the remains of their old Three Degree Depot camp with four pair of skis sticking up out of the snow—one pair for each of them, and one for Lt. Bowers to pick up on his way home. Evans kept them going at a pace, anxious to reach the Upper Glacier Depot before the oil for the primus ran out. His voice trembled when he spoke of the miraged-up mountains far in the distance, broke when he saw the first nunataks rising like island peaks after too long a voyage at sea. Crean's eyes were well enough by then to make them out. It was awfully good to have something to steer for again. There was, after all, a world beyond this blasted plateau.

It was swept from sight by the blizzard coming down on the fourth morning of the homeward trek. The storm gave rise to second thoughts about the wisdom of plugging onward, but even with their remarkable mileage on the return so far, the three men agreed it best to kick off rather than lay up. It was a wise decision—that blizzard was with them three days. A wait for better weather could prove to be fatal. The sailors rigged the floorcloth as a sail on a mast and yard of bamboo, and with its aid in three days pulled fifty-four miles. When the trail disappeared from view and was lost for good, Evans' pocket compass pointed the way toward the head of the glacier, but it led them wide of their course. The wind was a help, but its sub-zero temperatures chilled their bodies thoroughly now that they were no longer warmed by the constant effort of manhauling. The descent became more difficult, the sledge harder to control as the glacier beneath them inclined into the upper reaches of the gorge. Even so they made seventeen and a half miles to the good, camping in a very rough place on the evening of January 12th. There would be some difficult travel in the morning.

They had reached the head of the icefalls found by Shackleton on his own return. Here the dammed-up ice of the plateau finds an outlet between two mighty ranges and begins to drop, tumbling and surging in slow motion waves like the upland rapids of a mountain stream. This torrent of ice, fractured by deep blue crevasses crossing in every direction, accelerates its descent, plunging abruptly into the upper reaches of the Beardmore Glacier. From the top there is no way through to be seen; a circuit around them would add days to the journey. Coyly beckoning, the smooth traveling-surface of the upper glacier lay in full view hundreds of feet below. Lt. Evans offered his men a choice: go straight into the icefall, or take the sensible, longer route and walk around in safety.

Crean was accustomed to his officers giving orders. Naval life was never intended to be a democracy where seamen could debate the wisdom of any course of action. The men didn't harbor much respect for a skipper who went for'rard too much. Still, out here the boundaries had become blurred; they were three, and in it together.

The discussion was short-lived. Time-saving won out; a sailor could count on himself to pull through, but he couldn't speed up the clock. They began the steep descent into an absolute wilderness of gigantic ice-blocks staggering against each other, splitting asunder and colliding with titanic force as they pitch into the sudden drop. It is a chaos of knife-edged crevasses, blue ice going black into the vanishing depths.

All the forenoon they worked their way into this maze, one man guiding as two hauled back on the sledge. Many times it took charge and escaped, skittering down the slope to capsize over some huge boulder of ice just short of a yawning crevasse. The sledge overran the men and fouled the traces; there were frequent falls, but no complaint. The party crept along, lost in a welter of dangers at every hand. They came at last to a brink over which they could not hope to control the sledge. If they were to go forward at all it would be on board as passengers on a runaway, to find whatever fate might deal them at the bottom of the slope. There was no going back.

Lt. Evans put the question to his companions. Crean replied at once, *"Well, Mr. Evans, you're the only officer, it's for you to decide."*

Lashly had a different take. *"Well, Mr. Evans, if Captain Scott was here, he'd never ask us to do a damn fool thing like that!"*

"Captain Scott isn't here, so jump on!" Evans threw himself face-downward across the sledge at the bow. Crean took the midships, and Lashly the stern. The men inched along toward the brink, grabbed on, and tipped the sledge into the drop, picking up speed until it was beyond any sort of control. It must have reached sixty miles per hour and yet by some miracle kept upright and on course, bumping mightily over unseen obstacles, clattering uncontrollably over hummocks of hard ice. Without warning it left the ice altogether and leapt into the air, catapulting clear over the blue depths of a yawning crevasse. Crean and Evans locked eyes in that brief airborne moment. *"What next!"*

A second later the sledge crashed into the soft snow beyond, rolling over and over with three men still hanging on until it came to a halt. Crean looked at his commanding officer. *"Mr. Evans, you're lucky!"* They all were. The sledge and its load were intact. There were no broken bones. A ski stick that had vanished into the abyss as they flew over was their only loss. There must have been more than luck at work when, after all this, they came ashore in familiar territory. By a divine miracle of coincidence, the sledge brought up all standing hard by an old lunch camp near the Upper Glacier Depot.

Shaken, they pitched the tent and gave themselves a biscuit and a soothing pannikin of tea, barely enough to sustain a man--before going on. In risking a descent of 1,500 feet in only half a day, they had saved themselves a good three days' marching. That night on retiring to their bags they felt like so many bruised pears, though no one cared to look too closely for the damage.

All three were well beaten about the body, but Crean and Lashly now felt a private, inner distress that didn't trouble their commander at all.

Even in the close quarters of three in a tent, and as alone in the world as any may ever be, a leader must maintain the isolation of command. In the inflexible hierarchy of the navy, the men are trained from their enlistment day to look to their officer for direction. To show weakness or indecision is to betray the faith his men have put into the whole structure of authority. Lt. Evans had always been a joker whose too-quick casual confidences served their purpose in the ship, but here in the wilderness these no longer were the hallmarks of boyish charm. They were cause for doubt. The two seamen would soon have to take on a responsibility for which their modest attainments in the service had left them poorly prepared.

Still, on the glacier they had come again into familiar territory and spotted the cheerful red flag of the Upper Glacier Depot halfway into the morning march. Taking their crampons and fair share of pemmican, biscuit, and oil, and leaving a note for Captain Scott to pick up on his return, they moved on. One more hundred miles down the glacier and another four hundred across the Barrier would see them home. The sun was bright in the sky. The descent from this point onward was more in the line of hauling back on the sledge and easing it down the hard blue ice slopes. That night in the tent the three men thought about their fellows elsewhere on the trail, and speculated on the arrival of the dogs at Hut Point.

What a blessing it was to be off the plateau with its everlasting breeze and deadly cold. Here the air outside registered a balmy plus-one degree. With clothes dry and the weather mild and promising, they slept in warm, well-fed luxury under the comforting green canopy of the tent and woke at five for the next march toward the Cloudmaker Depot.

Bright sunshine had given way to a low-lying cloud that filled the valley with a dense fog. The slope of the glacier drove their route far to the west where a pair of tributary glaciers poured into the Beardmore Glacier at grade, churning up a perfect nightmare of crevasses. These mazes are hard to see even in good light, easy enough to work into and the very devil to get out of. With every landmark hidden by the mist, a man steers by dead reckoning and the gut reaction to the trouble just in front of him. By the second day it was clear the party slipped into the trap.

Great tumbled blocks of ice the size of churches loomed through the floating crystals. Narrow passages ran between them; sagging bridges linked them overhead and underfoot. By noon the sun showed through, a sickly yellow globe hanging over the mist. Its stronger light was a help, but there was no height, no vantage from which to judge even the shortest of courses. The way back out was forever lost to them; they had only to stumble onward, picking out a path as they went and hoping for the best as they worked their way deeper into the labyrinth. Enormous chasms, deep enough to swallow whole the biggest ship afloat, appeared abruptly alongside the sunken lids over which the only possible path must inevitably go.

Exhausted and overwhelmed, the three men sought out a ledge barely wide enough to raise the tent and brew a cooker of tea. Inside, they shared a biscuit or two in silence. There was nothing to be said, no plan but to press on. Crean had a smoke, and then they were on their way. For hours they struggled forward, using the sledge as a bridge across the narrower crevasses, creeping along the ridges between the wider ones falling away at either hand, at times lifting its 400 pound weight over some obstacle. The crevasses seemed to grow wider and deeper as they went, forcing a new line of travel across the intended route. There could be no progress this way. Somewhere ahead there *must* be an end to it all, one way or another.

At midday the mist began to clear. The sun broke through, showing a bright halo in the floating ice crystals, but the light revealed only a broken landscape with no way out. The three men came to a decisive halt at the brink of yet another yawning chasm. A narrow snow bridge, sunken down in the middle like a saddle, led to the other side. The top along its length was a knifelike ridge, an inverted "V," dropping away on either side into the black abyss, so narrow that the sledge runners would not bear. The sledge would have to be dragged along the top balanced on its load, inch by inch.

Lashly went first, with the alpine rope tied about his waist, straddling the bridge's swaybacked spine as he would a horse and shuffling his way along not daring to look into the awful void that lay at either hand. Under the weight of this one man, the bridge held. The rope was barely long enough to give him scope to climb up the snow-bank that rose at the opposite end. Gaining its slight summit, he turned toward his companions. Across the gulf, they could see his face gone white with fear. Now it was their turn. They wasted no time.

Crean and Lt. Evans sat face to face astride the bridge, with the sledge between them, its runners just resting on the snow on either side. The blue depths of the chasm dropped away beneath their feet. The slightest shift of balance, or the collapse of the bridge with two men and a heavy sledge on it, would doom them all. Crean dug his heels into the sides of the bridge like a cavalryman, sending a shower of ice-crystals rattling into the bottomless pit. They gazed steadfastly into each other's eyes—neither dared look down or about into the horrible gulf that fell away just below their straddling legs.

If a man's face can be read like a page, if the lines and scratches convey some deeper insight into the depth of the book, then Evans' face to Crean, and Crean's to his, told a shared tale that none other would every fully understand. Here, locked eye-to-eye, the universe closed about them. No thought intruded. Those would come later, in some leisure moment, some calm recollection far removed from here, in a place where life and future again have meaning. Here, on this bridge, it was *"One, two, three, heave!"* again and again, and nothing more until the relative safety of the far side was won. The images cast here, and the bond forged in this shared ordeal, would last in memory a lifetime.

With every launch the sledge drove forward another. Lashly, waiting on the far side, dug himself another inch into his meager toehold. When they were close enough he reached down, took Evans by the collar, and on the count hauled away. Digging their crampons into the slippery slope, they were up beside him in an instant. Once anchored there, the three desperate men with the last of their strength pulled the sledge up the uneven ice. It slipped sideways and capsized. Their precious sledge lay on its side, poised for a final plunge into the blue-black depths of the glacier, and on it everything necessary to live even one more night. Here is where long years of navy training and discipline proved their worth. One slip, one false move, and the sledge and with it all their hopes would go tumbling into the void. There was no panic—only a quickly laid plan, a few well-chosen moves, and the sledge was secured.

They took a moment to look around, but the view from the top of the rise was not encouraging. There was no way out of this maze. The three men sat wearily on she sledge: they were well and truly done in, and there was not a single ledge wide enough to hold the tent. They had worked all this day without food, saving their last bits until the starkest necessity drove them to eat. Evans stood and said, *"I am going to look for a way out—we can't go on."* If nothing else, he must find a camping-place where they could recover some of their strength to look for a way clear.

Crean and Lashly sat together on the sledge, watching their Lieutenant disappear into the tumbled wilderness, idly wondering if they'd ever see their officer again, or home. From time to time Evans came briefly into view as he wound his way among the crevasses, then disappeared again. How frail and insignificant he looked, their only hope in the immensity of the wilderness. They listened for a shout, a call. Silence. He might not come back. Three men together had barely a chance of winning through; two men--well, they'd give it their all, and hope for the best.

Evans returned after an hour, bearing good news. There were some rough patches yet to cross, but they had made it to the bottom of the icefall. Threading along the path he'd found, they emerged that afternoon onto the smooth ice of the glacier and made camp to have a proper rest, and perhaps share a joke or two. Lashly had been hoarding oddments of food from their regular ration for just such a time, and produced a modest supper. Here they ate the last of their biscuit, and everything else but a little tea and sugar. No matter that the food was gone, they were within an easy downhill march of the Middle Glacier Depot. Arrived there, they camped again and had another meal, this time a full one. Replete, relieved, the three men crawled into their reindeer fur bags and were quickly sound asleep.

Lt. Evans allowed his men a blessed lie-in the next morning. They needed the rest—they all did—after the harrowing passage through the lower falls of the glacier. One long sleep was all that could be spared. Weary or no, they would find no leisure, no free moment to relax their overstrained muscles or compose the thoughts that spun uncontrolled through their minds. Evans was worn out, and his eyes had gone entirely snowblind from his anxious casting about for a route through the crevasses. It was his turn to be led.

Still, it was good to be in familiar territory again. The seamen rearranged the depot, taking just enough provision to see them through to the next at Lower Glacier Depot near the Gateway. Lashly penciled a note for Scott, but didn't say much in it about their difficulties above the Cloudmaker. The captain would have had his own troubles coming through; better, they thought, to spare him the worry. Lashly led off, calling out the course and landmarks to Evans pulling behind him. They camped early on account of Evans' suffering and for the same reason made a late start in the morning. Even so, a good day's pulling saw them past crevasses with collapsed bridges, bridges that their old tracks showed they had safely crossed on the outward journey. Determined to make a better show than yesterday's march, they covered twenty miles on ski and reached the Lower Glacier Depot at the end of the march a half-day ahead of schedule.

There was good reason to be pleased with their results thus far. Three men had improved on the work allotted to four, and stood every chance of making it home in very good time. Evans seemed to be recovering, and Tom Crean returned to his steady cheerful self, singing as he shoveled snow onto the valence of the tent. The words, the lovely melody, reminded them all of why they must return:

--I'll wait for the wild rose that's waiting for me
In the place where the dark Mourne sweeps down to the sea.--

Lashly, inside, enjoyed the concert as he pumped the primus into roaring life and stirred the bubbling hoosh. With their troubles behind them and a level easy trail just ahead, there was every reason to be cheerful. No one minded much the struggle to get this far. *"It is all,"* as Crean was fond of saying, *"for the good of Science."*

They were camped that night at the very foot of the glacier, a day's march away from the pitiful remains of Shambles Camp where, for all its grim associations in memory, a feast of pony meat lay buried. The deep snow that had trapped them there had been blown and shaped and hardened, ablated by the constant wind flowing down the glacier from the plateau. Three weeks had passed since they left the Polar Party to their advance on the plateau. By now those five had made their goal and were well along on the homeward trail, perhaps even into the head of the glacier itself.

The Barrier now so close at hand had somehow the feel of home; it was the great back yard of the *Discovery* Hut. True, the 400 miles that still lay between the three men and ultimate safety was daunting, but the old familiar Barrier promised a straightforward and level road, and more clement weather than the stiff plateau wind that must be even now battering away at Scott's party.

They made a good start in the morning, rounding the corner of the Granite Pillars and going up the snow ramp between Mt. Hope and the mainland. Mounting the crest, Crean saw for the first time the inviting flat plain of the Barrier and let out a whoop loud enough to wake the ponies from their graves in the snow. Now the snow sloped gently down and the sledge moved easily under the effort of just one man. The Great Ice Barrier spread away before, deep waves from the Beardmore's inflow settling down into ripples to level at last in the vanishing white plain. They were off the glacier; the hard way now lay behind, and a long straight road before.

Such elation would not last long. In camp that night, Lt. Evans complained for the first time of stiffness at the backs of his knees. Any sailor worth his salt knows this is one of the first signs of scurvy. Crean and Lashly had noted their officer's general decline in recent weeks, and now began to secretly examine his gums as he spoke, looking for the telltale swelling and discoloration there. For the time, they kept their concern between themselves.

Once on the Barrier they again made fair distances, aided by a southerly wind that filled the floorcloth sail and pulled the sledge along with only one man to guide it, the others walking easily alongside. The temperature had risen with the wind; it was really too hot, to the point where anyone could march wearing nothing at all. With temperatures of 34 and 36 degrees, what should have fallen as snow came down as rain--uncomfortable, yes, but nothing to stop them now. Looseness of the bowels was beginning to afflict the lieutenant, interrupting the march along the homeward track. Lashly doctored him with chalk and opium and a little brandy from the medicine chest. Evans was clearly weakening, complaining daily of stiffness in his legs, of his skin there turning black and blue.

The effects of scurvy as it ravages the body include a weakness and lassitude that render a man helpless, and a swelling in the joints that will cripple a man before it kills him. The skin turns all colors, visible even under the almost-black of sunburnt faces; teeth fall from their sockets. The cause was supposed to be a lack of fresh food in the diet. That had certainly been the case for all of them, having been away from Cape Evans and the surfeit of seal meat there, for over three months.

The two sailors now made clear to Evans what they had long suspected; their words confirmed his own suspicions. This bad news was coupled with a shortage of oil in the tins uncovered at the Mid-Barrier Depot. They could be sure that none of the previous returning parties would have taken more than their share. Faced with this unexpected deficit of fuel, they were finding themselves in a tight corner hundreds of miles from home with an ailing companion who was growing steadily weaker. Taking the barest minimum of oil for their own needs, they left the rest for the Polar Party and headed out again.

Evans' condition and the pain it brought grew worse daily, but he was still pulling—barely--in his harness. He suffered his agony in silence, keeping up a cheery front for the benefit of his tentmates. By now he was passing large amounts of blood daily. Even so, they had been making good mileages—16, 14, 13, 13—but these too began to diminish. Lashly and Evans had been out manhauling one hundred days. One the morning Lashly engaged in one of his own peculiar rituals of personal hygiene by turning his shirt inside out. Since each of his two shirts, under and outer, had two sides, he might by carefully counting the days change the inner side for the outer of each at intervals and so have a clean shirt to wear against his skin.

On the morning of February 3, still well south of the plenty that lay ahead at One Ton Depot, Evans was barely able to stand without help.

Crean and Lashly lifted him to his feet and strapped his feet into the ski. Trailing behind the others in the traces, he was at least able to advise Lashly in the lead when he veered off-course. They were well out on the Barrier, out of sight of land even when the haze lifted. When it settled and stayed, the bad light was enough to make man raving mad. The dim remnants of sledge tracks underfoot disappeared entirely to weary eyes, the sun and sky were nowhere to be seen; all was one enveloping white haze where *far* and *near*, *left* and *right*, had no meaning. Crean could tell by the feel of the sastrugi beneath his skis which way they trended, and judge from this and the breeze at his back which direction ought to be north. All was guesswork and dead reckoning, and it was always a relief when an old cairn from the outward march hove into view. The south wind was a help, but even so their daily distances were not enough to assure a safe arrival for all three, with still 180 miles—only two more Sundays--to Hut Point.

Mt. Hooper, that magnificent snow cairn built up by Evans and his team on the way out, still stood, a huge beacon rising out of the white plain to welcome all returning travelers. The air had warmed to an oppressive 36 degrees, the soft snow softened more by an unexpected rainfall. Everything was wet, and the snow stuck to ski and sledgerunner alike. Before leaving they left another note there for Scott following them on the homeward trail, probably now somewhere in the middle reaches of the Beardmore Glacier. In composing this note they all agreed it was the wiser course to avoid worrying their captain about his Lieutenant's rapidly failing condition. Better not to mention that he needed help even getting into the tent. Heading north from Mt. Hooper, they began to look out for the bold headland of Minna Bluff to rise ahead, for a hopeful sign that the journey's end lay within reach. The sun continued bright and hot, and the sweat poured off their faces, working in behind the green-tinted snow goggles to sting their weary eyes.

They made One Ton Depot, the last major port of call before Hut Point, in the late afternoon of February 9. *"Oh what a Godsend to have a change of food"*--a good feed at last of oatmeal with a surplus of fuel over which to stir their hooshes to a proper boiling. They loaded the sledge with nine days' provisions, no more. Only Crean and Lashly were pulling at all now, *"in the best of health"* as Lashly wrote in his diary, though long months afield had worn them down as well.

By this time Evans was walking slowly alongside the sledge, silent in his pain, alone in his thoughts. He required help to attend to the simplest of matters, but he never failed to put on a cheerful face. As their own pace slowed, the certainty grew in them that the five-man Pole Party, now homeward bound, must be steadily gaining on them. Crean was continually looking over his shoulder, expecting to see them in the distance at any time, hoping for aid in getting his officer safely home. Evans did his best to keep up—Lashly thought him the very essence of a brick--and vowed to do so until the very end, but all knew he would have to ride on the sledge before long. In the long marches they were still pulling in eleven miles, but it was a struggle for two men. Eleven miles a day might not get them home in time.

Two days later they built a snow cairn and cached all the spare gear and Lashly's rocks, brought all this distance from the glacier for "the good of science." These could be fetched home later, after spring had come. The day's run was still eleven miles, hard-fought every inch of it, with bad light the whole way. They might have gone more—in these straits, still ninety-nine miles from safety, every inch now might mean the difference between stranding and survival--but a blizzard forced them to camp.

In the morning just before departing for the north, Lashly took a moment to change his socks. The moment lasted just a bit too long, and before his foot was well-covered again it was frostbitten. They were all three too deep into it to stand on rank or sympathy for an invalid. Evans took the frozen foot up under his shirt against his stomach and in a few minutes restored the circulation. Each of the three was prepared to make whatever sacrifice might be necessary.

On February 12 the smoking summit of Mt. Erebus appeared above the horizon ahead. This image gave hope to all—at the foot of that mountain now in view lay home, the warm inviting huts at Cape Evans and Hut Point, all the food one could eat, soft beds, a change in company and above all else, safety. The image did not last; its encouragement was not enough to keep Evans from fainting more than once, to be revived with difficulty by a drop of brandy.

The following day Evans could not go on. He could not go on. He begged his two companions to save themselves and leave him to his fate then he ordered them, but they would hear nothing of it. *--If you are to go out Sir, then we'll all go out together.--* It might be mutiny, but Crean and Lashly were determined: *"We shall stand by him to the end, so we are the masters today."* After a council of war they concluded to drop by the wayside everything they could possibly get along without, and go on with only the tent, sleeping bags, cooker, and what little food and oil was left. They would carry Lt. Evans on the sledge, and win through all three, or not at all.

He was so weak by this point that he could do nothing for the tent, or for himself. It added hours to the day's work, to break down the tent around him and get him ready to lie on the sledge, but it was impossible for him to stand. The slightest movement put their leader into extremes of agony—he never yelled out, but Crean could hear the grinding of his teeth from the pain. Longer hours on the march gave some progress, but at a pitiful rate even with the help of the sail. During the heavy drag of February 16 Castle Rock and Observation Hill came occasionally into view. Closer to home, they were looking for relief from the dog teams. All hopes were raised when they saw what they thought was the dog tent, but it was only an old biscuit tin stuck on the top of an outward cairn. There would be no dogs. They would have to make it in under their own steam.

What a pleasant surprise it was to see the last abandoned motor announcing Corner Camp just ahead. Crean and Lashly uncovered Lt. Evans on the sledge to let him have a look. They picked up some biscuit at the motor camp, but that was all. On half-rations they might get four more days to win through to the *Discovery* Hut. With lower temperatures all the time and Evans so weak, they were almost afraid to go to sleep that night for fear he'd freeze.

He wasn't frozen when they awoke the next morning, but he was so weak as to be totally helpless and when Lashly tried to move him he fainted dead away. Crean saw the collapse and thought he had died outright. It was all too much--they'd come so far together, and faced so many hardships, to have it come to this. He leaned over his fallen comrade, and again on the trail he gave himself over to weeping. His hot tears unrestrained ran off his cheeks to splash on Evans' face. The officer's eyes slowly opened, focused on Crean's face so near to his own, the familiar lined and leathered countenance of one who never gave up. There were still a few drops of brandy in the medicine chest, enough to bring him around one last time, but that was all.

Clearly Evans could not be moved again. They'd come to the end of their food; one more day's oil remained. They'd made the long journey, advanced the Pole Party to within striking distance of the goal and returned thus far, only to be waylaid by misfortune and stranded hopelessly on another Godforsaken ice plain.

Crean and Lashly stood outside the tent and talked over what to do next. Lashly was the better nursemaid, Crean the man who could least bear the thought of sitting still and helpless. They brought the plan to their Lieutenant, and the three of them decided what to do next.

The Discovery hut was only thirty miles farther on. Someone might be waiting there, ready with the dog teams to come out to meet the Polar parties surely close at hand on their homeward journey, to help them in. Just as likely, the Hut might be empty, the relief parties waiting at Cape Evans farther north, assured by recent reports that the advance parties were going strong, and could make it home on their own.

The reports were wrong. Out on the Barrier, the Last Supporting Party in their diminishing marches knew the truth of the matter—the whole long walk, thirteen hundred miles of it to the plateau and back, was more than any man could bear.

Although it was risky for one man to set out alone on this last thirty miles, his odds were better than the certain death that would come to all three men by remaining in camp. Bereft of strength after long months on the trail, they had reached the limit of their common endurance. Barely a crumb of food remained for them, and only the merest glimmer of oil for the lamp. Of the three, one was almost dead from scurvy, unable to walk another inch. Left alone in the tent, he would surely, and quickly, die. The other two were almost equal in their waning strength, diminished as it was. Together they might have made it in, but neither would agree to leave the third behind alone to die.

Now, of the three, one man must go forward to get what help there may be, or die trying. For Crean and Lashly, it had mattered little who drew the short straw, and who the long—who died on the trail and who in the tent with Lieutenant Evans. Thirty more miles to the hut wanted more strength than either of them could muster. Still, no seaman would, or could, forget Nelson's admonition: *Do the best you can with what you've got.* One man would go forward and bring back aid or die in the attempt.

Crean drew the short straw. He made his farewells—they might well have been his last—to Bill Lashly the stouthearted stoker, and Lieutenant Evans, too sick to come to the tent's door to wave good-bye. Two sticks of chocolate and two biscuits in his pocket, that was all he took. Whether or not it was enough he would find out, but it mattered little. There was not another ounce of food to be taken for the journey.

He stopped, as he supposed, at the halfway point. Fifteen miles, on, fifteen more to go. The chocolate in his outer pocket was frozen hard as a brick, broke up like sand in his parched mouth. It was the last food in his pocket, the last thing he might ever eat. He sat down on the snow to rest his legs.

Funny the thoughts that enter unbidden into a man's head, like the words of a trollop shouted in passing. It would be easy for him, to throw it all over, to lie down and rest. It had been a long time now since he let himself feel the comfort of a downy bed, since dreams of any kind but hunger's nightmares had softened a night's passing. But easy has no place here, it makes no sense, has no allure. He heard the voice of his captain, or perhaps it was the Barrier wind. *--Crean!--* it said--*We've made the Pole! We're coming along behind you, on the trail you've broke for us. Don't fail us now.--* The sailor stood, looked back at the long straight line of his shadowed footsteps leading back to the tent, then forward at the empty snow-covered plain ahead. The well marked road on the level ice ahead had at its end the *Discovery* Hut and in it the promise of survival, almost within reach.

If he weakened and fell short on this final stretch, if he stopped to rest a moment and fell asleep, if a blizzard closed over him and blotted out the light one final fatal time, then so be it. Who was he to challenge God's will? But it was Crean's will now, and one foot in front of the other with only another fifteen miles left to go. What were they to the thirteen hundred out-and-back that lay behind? No one walked beside him, but he was not alone. Two companions waited in the tent pitched on the Barrier ice fifteen miles back.

Five hours of steady going later, he passed Safety Camp. By twelve-thirty Monday morning he was growing tired and cold, but he was off the Barrier and onto the sea-ice. Behind, the weather was beginning to come on thick. No time to slow up now. He headed for the Gap, but with no rope, no help, and precious little strength for climbing, there was no getting up over the ice-foot. Better to head out around Cape Armitage while he still could. The wind and snow was really beginning to come on now. He felt rather than saw the slush he was walking into—better to try again to scout out another way up and over the Gap, or he'd never get in. This he managed—barely—and through rifts in the ragged drift he made out the Hut in the distance. There was no sign of life. There were no sledges or dogs in sight. The place might well be cold and empty, but it lay just ahead. He sat down under the lee of Observation Hill and had the last of his biscuit with a bit of ice. A few more steps and he was at the door.

Atkinson and Dmitri were warming themselves by the blubber fire inside, listening to the rising wind and glad they were safe and secure when it looked to be a long hard blow abrewing. Outside the dogs began their infernal howl. There was a sound at the door, a rhythmic insistent rapping unlike the occasional rattling of wind-blown gravel against the painted boards. Crean's knock at that wooden door took them by surprise—the supporting party was not unexpected, but anyone on the trail would surely be holed up in his tent for a blow like this. Flinging open the door, they found their old friend and companion standing outside, covered with new-blown snow, thin and ragged and barely recognizable, so brown was his face, so bleached-white his hair. --*Crean!*-- They swung the door wide and ushered him in.

The dim smoky depths of the hut seemed to him brighter and more luxurious than Buckingham Palace. Inside was real warmth and plenty, and security such as he'd almost thought he'd never again enjoy. For three and a half months, the rustling green walls of the tent had been his only home, a damp half-frozen bag his bed, a pannikin of hoosh his daily bread. Outside the wind kicked up fiercely, battering at the wooden walls of the hut, but sparing the weary traveler home from the trail.

They helped him out of his tattered overclothes, sat him in a chair and started out his revival with a tot of brandy and a pipe--God Almighty, the pipe! Then the words fell out; the story he had to tell outdid any the good doctor had ever heard. There would be plenty of time to hear it all. No sooner was he safely inside than the storm buried the Hut in a whirl of drift. Despite the desperate situation of Evans and Lashly out on the Barrier, there would be no going out to save them until this blizzard had died away. Crean had done all that a man could do. It was sleep he craved, sleep in a fur bag that was both dry and warm, in the shelter of rigid walls made of wood and not threadbare canvas flapping in the wind.

Alternately, the big Irishman ate and talked and slept, and ate and slept again. The long journey from 87 degrees had extracted from him a heavy toll, and days would pass before anything like his former strength returned. To Atkinson—Dmitri knew no English—he told the story: how Scott had at the last added Bowers to his party, leaving the three to return on their own; how they'd fought their way tooth and nail through the crevasses at the Cloudmaker and made their way ever more slowly north as one of them gradually sickened.

Atkinson had stories of his own, of the return of his own party from the head of glacier, of the arrival of the ship and the landing of the mules at Cape Evans, seasoned with news of the world. All day and night until the next morning, the blizzard surged around the hut, where the three men drew close to the blubber stove and worried over the fate of the two still out on the Barrier. By afternoon the storm had abated enough for the doctor and Dmitri to make a start with the dogs, leaving Crean—who wished to go but was ordered to stay behind—alone in the hut. Weakened, he lay long hours dozing in his reindeer sleeping bag, waking only to enjoy a long pipe in the comfort of the hut's enfolding walls. Outside, the weather closed again. The old hut creaked and wracked fearfully in the blizzard, shaking like an old tent, but it held.

On the afternoon of the 22nd, Crean heard the dogs in the distance coming in over the sea ice from Cape Armitage.   As they drew nearer, he stepped outside to have a look.   He could see that each sledge carried a load, a man.   Were they still alive?   It had been three more days of starvation for Lashly and Lt. Evans out on the Barrier, three more days with no fuel to keep away the cold.

The sledges came to a halt in front of the hut.   Lashly rose unsteadily to his feet.   Dmitri and Atkinson lifted the Lieutenant, softly moaning, onto a makeshift litter.   Yes, they were alive.   But barely. They would need time to recover before moving on, but Crean was going home. Their terrible ordeal was over, and the success of the great endeavor assured.   After a brief reunion in the relative comfort of the *Discovery* Hut and a short rest for the dogs, Crean and Dmimtri were off for Cape Evans.

Chapter Ten

Another Winter

Cape Evans. February 22, 1912

With a rush and a whirl and a barking of dogs they were off, down over the tide-crack and away over the sea-ice north toward the Glacier Tongue, Tent Island, and the Hut at Cape Evans beyond. Crean, lashed into place on the sledge like a load of so much gear, settled into his fast-moving litter to enjoy the ride as the dogs fairly flew along. It had been nearly five months since he'd set out on this trail with Bones' leather bridle in his grip. The difference between that slow deliberate walking pace and this seemingly effortless glide was unmistakable.

With nothing but his rapidly changing view of the countryside to occupy his attention, he reflected uncomfortably on the contrast. If Amundsen had managed his dogs well, then perhaps he'd also managed to bag the pole by another route, and if today was any example, run away with it. But then his dogs would most likely never have been able to handle the convoluted trail up and down any glacier. Dogs were good for the level ice of the Barrier, but not much more. The sledge skittered and bumped rapidly along the uneven surface, at times nearly toppling its convalescent passenger out of his makeshift ambulance. Running alongside, Dmitri kept up a constant chatter of Russian course corrections understood only by the dogs.

They pulled up to the hut at Cape Evans as the shore party there finished their lunch. Everyone came out and crowded around to welcome their prodigal brother home. The reunion with Cherry was all too brief. It was imperative to get the dogs back to Lashly and Lt. Evans at Hut Point immediately, and then on out over the Barrier to help bring in the returning Pole party. By two o'clock, Cherry and Silas Wright had the sledge reloaded with fresh food and other supplies, and were on their way. The rest of the men crowded around to hear Crean's news.

He had much to say of the climb to the top of the Beardmore. Everyone wanted to hear all the details—how the men faced the crevasses and the sudden drops, the pitch of hunger that racked every man on that long climb, the last Christmas out on the plateau. The bitter cold, the final parting and the Polar party vanishing into the white distance, well advanced but not as fit as they might be. His audience sat spellbound for the long thrilling tale of the descent down the glacier and into the maelstrom of the icefall, the slow withering of Lt. Evans, his own last-ditch shot at reaching the *Discovery* hut before all was lost. There was no boasting to it—a plain recounting of the facts made a yarn that few could equal.

But first, a feed. The new cook Archer knew what was wanted: fresh yeasty bread right from the oven, dripping with melted New Zealand butter; seal steaks fried up and served hot with gravy; coffee by the gallon, rich with frozen cream. All the tobacco a man might need to keep his pipe filled and aglow, and a cloud of blue smoke drifting about his head to soften the memories of the terrible march home. Hunger would trouble him no more, not in this season. Oh what a delight it was, to hear unfamiliar voices and new yarns.

And finally, of course, there was the rapturous, transforming luxury of a hot bath in the makeshift canvas washtub. The skin beneath his underclothing had not seen the light of day, or even more than the most cursory of examinations within the green-tinted shelter of the tent, for many months. The sweaty, greasy fabric, dirty beyond imagining, had left almost nothing of its residue on his flesh showing white, almost deathly pale in the too-harsh light of the hut's acetylene lamps. A brisk toweling, a fresh change of clothes, a soft mattress on his old familiar bedsprings. It was all almost too much to bear; too clean, too civilized, too close. In time he'd get used to it.

After months of camp life it was good to be back in the shelter of a real house, with a real coal stove and well-insulated walls keeping the warmth inside and the cold without. Things had changed considerably around Cape Evans. The *Terra Nova* had arrived as expected earlier in February and landed another season's supplies in a week of frantic unloading, and gone on about her other business. She had left behind sustenance for the body--butter and cheese, mutton, potatoes and onions fresh from the green hills of New Zealand—and newspapers only a month old for the mind. There were new durable goods of all kinds--woolens and furs, oil and patent fuel for the stoves, lumber for an annex across the porch and for rebuilding the stables to house the most exotic freight of all. The Indian government had kindly donated seven mules, sturdy and well-trained, to replace the ponies sacrificed along the trail. Lashly would manage their care and feeding until Oates returned from the Pole. *"Some fine beasts,"* he said, but not likely to improve upon the slow

229

performance of their Siberian counterparts.

The ship was gone from Cape Evans by the time Crean arrived there, off on her assignments to pick up the field parties scattered about the cold shores of the Ross Sea. There would be one more call at the *Discovery* hut to recover Lt. Evans. With all her human cargo safely aboard, she would head north for New Zealand to winter there. As for the Southern Party, they had certainly made the Pole and should be coming in before long, but the ship could not wait. There was another season's valuable work to be done here before abandoning Cape Evans altogether.

Only a handful of men remained to populate Cape Evans. New sounds emerged from the unaccustomed quiet of the nearly empty hut--the ticking of time recorders from the physicists' corner, the bubbling acetylene generator, the whistling of the wind past the cookstove ventilator. Crean would be off-watch for a time to recover from the lingering effects of his long journey to the plateau and back. A man could get his work done, or take his leisure, without knocking into someone every minute. No one would disturb him as he lay back on the creaking bedsprings to open up his letters from Ireland. He read slowly, savoring each word, each bit of news, each reassuring confidence. What luxury it was to read over and read again the familiar handwriting telling of the dear ones and the warmly remembered scenes of home.

Here was a special note from an old and trusted friend, to which he must reply before the *Terra Nova* sailed away for warmer shores. *"Dear Sir,"* he wrote in his awkwardly formal manner. In a few brief and understated words Crean related a bit of his long journey toward the Pole, and his desperate return. *". . . If anyone has earned fame it is your own County Kerryman. . .It fell to my lot to do the 30 miles for help, and only a couple of Biscuits and a stick of chocolate to do it. Well sir, I was very weak when I reached the hut."* With Scott still on the trail, Crean claimed only a fine record for the supporting party, and left the triumph of discovery for his captain.

He had something else on his mind, a matter that had more to do with his home in Ireland than his life in the Antarctic. Before leaving home he had entrusted James Kennedy with a personal mission, to speak with the father of a certain Miss Hanna V., to tell the old man about the sailor's intentions, how he'd planned to come home with his pay from the expedition to ask her hand in marriage. Kennedy's letter made it clear that the answer was favorable, if not absolutely assured.

It would be another year before Crean would be home to make his proposal to her in person. He could only offer his thanks, and hope for the best. *". . . any how I am glad I am in the bidding for her now and. with the help of God we shall have a time at the wedding. please God."* Now he might rightfully dream of a bright future with her on his return to Ireland, a hero in her eyes if not the world's.

Already the autumn blizzards had begun with a dreary regularity, blowing up with little warning and dumping deep drifts of snow in the lee of everything standing. The black beach was buried early, and would never again be seen by these men. The ship, having successfully retrieved the geologists from the west side of the sound, stayed in the neighborhood a few days hoping to bring back news of Scott's victory at the Pole to an admiring world. Lieutenant Evans, taken aboard from Hut Point, was already showing signs of recovering from the scurvy under a regimen of fresh seal meat and bottled fruits.

When the weather cleared on February 29th the final loads were lightered ashore and she was on her way, leaving Silas Wright temporarily in charge of eight men--Crean, Lashly, Williamson, Hooper and Archer in the messdeck; Debenham, Nelson, and Gran rattling around in the nearly empty wardroom. It would be much quieter in the hut now with only eight in residence. There were two newcomers just arrived in the *Terra Nova*. Bill Archer was the new cook, taking over for Clissold, who'd never quite recovered from the fall he'd taken while ponting on the stranded Castle berg. Archer tended to take life as one great joke, a trait in high demand for polar explorers. The other was a familiar face--Tom Williamson from Mess Number One aboard *Discovery*, was back for another go at Antarctic exploring, replacing the Irishman Forde whose frostbitten hand had never really healed. There was something about the ice, the pull of the south, that seemed to draw some men back again despite the hardship and privation they'd be sure to face there. Crean hardly knew himself what it was that had brought him here and driven him to the very end of the earth, and very nearly the end of his life.

With Cherry, Dr. Atkinson, Dmitri, and Keohane away at Hut Point to keep a lookout for the incoming Pole Party, there was plenty of room to move about the hut now, to put one's feet up without getting them tripped over. With fewer pipes and sweating, breathing men, the air inside the hut was clearer, cooler, and quieter. There were no thunderous cags from the wardroom to disturb the peace, and barely enough hands to get up a game of whist or poker. Most of the singers, and all of the musicians had departed.

In the weeks that followed new arrangements of the duties of scientific chores, housework, and animal husbandry evolved, and new routines fell into place. The seamen's natural talents landed them the considerable job of overhauling all of the battered—and it was *all* battered—sledging kit. Lashly, by Scott's orders left in charge of the newly arrived Indian mules, assigned one each to everyone but the cook and the commander. Mules were not like horses. They were smarter, for one thing, and used their wits to better effect to manipulate and harass their handlers. Rani—quite a wicked one, and a trial to her master--became Crean's charge. Though not much to look at, she was certainly better built than wretched old Bones, altogether healthier and more spirited, apparently more intelligent, and certainly better trained. Given these advantages, her thinner coat and capricious temperament were trifles to be dealt with until Oates came home to take over her care. There was no firm ice in the South Bay; all the exercise the mules and their trainers could get must be confined to the beach and the Ramp up behind the hut. Pacing along that stretch of windblown snow with Rani in early March, Crean kept his eyes directed toward the *Discovery* Hut twelve miles away over the water, looking for a signal, a sign.

There were few worries as to the fate of the Pole Party. After all, there were five of them, and the going would be faster and easier. They could on almost any day come marching in, the Pole in hand, the accolades just beginning. Somewhere across the Sound Campbell's Northern Party might also be momentarily stranded, signaling their presence in the neighborhood with flares. A night watch was established on the tenth of March; during the coming winter the men would join their officers in taking a turn at it. Along with the lookout for the returning field parties, there were other familiar rituals: weather recorders to tend and clear; aurora, cloud patterns and the intermittent rumblings of Erebus to record; a fire to keep alight in the range; a pipe for the small hours after toast and sardines. There would be a great deal of weather to watch. The incidence of blizzards, the velocity of hurricanes, the number of white-out days—there was more of everything this second winter. At Cape Evans the men, secure in their winter quarters, remained always aware of the plight of their comrades in the field.

Scott and his men were expected to pull into Hut Point sometime in March. Atkinson and his small band were already posted out there to greet them, and set off flares alerting Cape Evans of their arrival. The signal was arranged to be two flares fired between ten and midnight, on each of two successive nights. Then the sky would be dark enough to show the light, even in the low overcast that sometimes haunted the camps. Each man stood his signal-watch in turn, waiting outside the whole two hours, pacing the slope of Wind Vane Hill away from the disrupting glare of the hut's three windows. In the still dark calm, only the crackling cold snow beneath Crean's finnesko and the occasional muffled shout from inside the hut, broke into the Antarctic quiet. The light of a yellow moon shone pale over Erebus, the brightest stars glittered in the cold half-light of midnight, but no flares showed above the distant outline of the Glacier Tongue. On other nights, fog- and drift-ridden, when the flares could not possibly be seen, Crean kept the watch according to his orders and his sure faith in the success of the Polar Party.

The connecting telephone wire had long since gone out with the ice. Other than the flares, there would be no communication between the two camps. There was no way of knowing if Cherry and Dmitri with the dogs had made it all the way out to One Ton Camp with supplies to replenish the depot, or what they might have found there. Autumn on the Barrier can be brutally cold.

In middle of March Crean celebrated St. Patrick's Day by taking a long walk on the ice with Gran and the two new men. The sandlike snow crunching beneath his bootheels made him think of the polar party struggling with the sledge over just such a surface, absolutely resistant to any glide. That evening there were bottles of beer uncorked in honor of the day, toasts to the expedition, and to absent friends. It was Oates' birthday; they all hoped he was alive and well and observing the day if not in comfort, then at least in good companionship. If Scott had maintained Shackleton's mileages, he must be getting near to Hut Point by now. With no clear communication between the two huts until South Bay froze over to the Glacier Tongue, it was hard to know for sure. It did freeze once, but a gale from the south immediately blew all the ice away. If the ship had not succeeded in picking up the Northern Party on her way back to New Zealand, then those men too were stranded out for the bitter autumn weather, and perhaps for the winter just coming on.

The end of March came and went without word or sign of the missing explorers returning from the Pole. The evening watch for signal flares from Hut Point had become almost unbearable, but no one was willing yet to think that they would not ever show against the deepening night. As the autumn weather closed ever more heavily down, a hard truth began to dawn and slowly become more fully obvious: they would not return. The wind flowed off the Barrier without letup, driving the gritty snow before it and freezing every ill-attended bit of exposed flesh in an instant. Still a regular watch toward the south continued, a sharp lookout for flares over Hut Point, but there was no sign of the Pole Party's return.

All the same, life must and will go on. Looking for a bit of adventure, Gran harnessed up the dogs to give them a workout and set off on a lark with Crean and Archer on the sledge. The passengers got more than they'd bargained for. Gran lost control and jumped, abandoning the dogs, the sledge, and its cargo to their fates. No bones were broken in the tumble over the ice-foot, but it was a long time before the Irishman would put his life in the hands of a Norwegian again. In a few days the ice in the Bay was sound enough for him to hike out to Little Razorback Island, and plan a trip to Hut Point to see if there was anything to be done, but another roaring southerly blizzard smashed the ice up and drove it north out into the Ross Sea.

Some continued to voice the wistful optimism that there might be survivors. Gran held forth an expected return on Easter Sunday. Crean knew better. On 10 April a shout raised up, *"The polar party's coming!"* Gran dashed back into the hut and set up the National Anthem on the gramophone to welcome his captain home, but the men at the door--bearded, coated with ice, dirty as sweeps--were Atkinson, Keohane and Dmitri. Home from their long sojourn at Hut Point, they confirmed the worst news. It was clear to everyone now; all hope for the Pole Party must be given over. Scott the commander, Uncle Bill the heart and soul, Birdie the optimist, Oates the steadfast soldier—all were gone now, and would not return alive. The worst of it was Taff Evans--the best friend a man could ever have--was lying out somewhere, cold as the ice, never again to breathe, laugh, hand, reef, steer. . . The image was unbearable; better, thought Crean, that his shipmate should have fallen into a crevasse far up at the icefalls, and be quickly done. That was way of the sea: you meet as strangers, go through hardship and danger and grow to like each other; the voyage ends, and it's --*So long, mate--;* one goes east, one goes west, and all that's left is a memory.

Dr. Atkinson was senior in rank and now in command of the shore station. He called them together to tell them what had been tried, and what he proposed to do. As far as Scott was concerned, all agreed that all that could be done, had been done. The Polar Party were most certainly all dead now, wherever they might be. Campbell and the Northern Party were also still out in the field, hopefully well along on their way home from Evans Coves on the western shore. They might still be alive, stranded on that western shore if the Terra Nova had not picked them up as she made her way north. Atkinson proposed a relief mission to try and reach them with three men, across to Butter Point and points north towards Wood Bay. Gran and Dmitri went along as far as Hut Point to fetch in Cherry, who'd been left there alone to recover from his ordeal on the Barrier in the last search south. Crean, in charge of sledging stores and equipment, remained at Cape Evans.

Almost empty now, the hut was quieter than ever and would remain so for weeks. The rickety clatter of the sewing machine was not enough to fill the empty hall. It was a lonelier place, haunted by worries for the rescuers enduring the harrowing winds of the polar autumn, and memories of those already succumbed. When the wind stopped blowing for a spell and a calm fell over the place, Crean could almost hear Taff's booming laugh, his outrageous yarns. Mourning would not bring back the dead. On still calm nights, he climbed the ramp and looked over toward Hut Point, but there was nothing to be seen but the moonlight reflecting blue off the open water of the sound, and a thin column of smoke rising from the chimney of the hut below. The year's slow turning round had brought the dark night back. The sun set for good on April 23, and the darkness

237

wrapped itself around the camp like a blanket to keep away the cold and emptiness outside.

The relief party returned empty-handed, driven back by extremes of cold that no one could be expected to long survive. They could only hope that Campbell's men had made their rendezvous with the ship and gone north with her to New Zealand. By May 1, with Cherry home at last, the outpost at Hut Point was abandoned for the winter; all thirteen remaining of the shore party were now reunited at Cape Evans. There had been no sign of the Northern Party. The need for scientific observation from this most remote weather and magnetic station continued unabated. Nearly the same amount of work would be expected of these remaining men as had been required of the twenty-six who'd taken on this job a year before. The lecture series was reinstituted, although this winter mercifully once a week. Debenham's address reported the presence of marine and plant fossils in some of the rock specimens brought back from the glacier by the first returning party. This news was received with great jubilation—the expedition had always been after the twin goals of science and discovery, and here was another milestone for the scientific side.

A billiard tournament was got up and held sway for months, the clack-clacking of the balls crossing into the messsdeck. Everyone but Lashly joined in. He was still the odd man out, that Lashly--as dependable as rain in Kerry in the summertime, but he was quiet and reserved, and kept to himself. The artificial separation between the men and their officers had less significance this season—traffic, words, and genial camaraderie flowed much more readily through the hut now. This was a tribute to Atkinson's relaxed, civilian style of leadership, where all the men were nearly equals. There was no need to maintain a fiction of separation between the messdeck and the wardroom. What social divisions remained were a matter of personal choice. For the sailors, the messdeck would remain their inviolate domain. Outside, the gale rose to a record 112 miles per hour and blew out the ice on May 4. The wind died and came up again with a clockwork regularity that defied all previous experience, rattling stones from the Ramp over the roof like a hard, hard rain.

On May 9 the final round of the first billiard tournament had Crean and Keohane facing off, each baiting the other in words as much above the green as strategy upon it. Tom Crean emerged victorious, his prize a bottle of beer. Keohane was officially designated Jonah and given a tin medal to wear round his neck, with orders to declare at lunch a week hence, *"I am Jonah!"* As if in answer, the hut rocked and creaked under the blows of the hard squalls from the southwest. The young ice in South Bay, newly formed and yet tender, blew out again. It would freeze over again before long, and by spring would be strong enough to carry the weights of men and mules and sledges.

These would all need a refit before the spring campaign. Antarctic winters were the time for making and mending all manner of sledging gear: new beckets for the finneskoes, bands and eyesplices for the sledging harness, new solder joints for the remaining primus burners. A question always stood unanswered: was there some flaw in the equipment, some failure of the sailor's work that had led to the disaster? There would have to be another expedition south in the spring to clear up the story.

On June 14 Atkinson called the party together to discuss plans for the coming year. Crean and Lashly were the old hands at this now, well respected for their experience, included in his councils. To all the men he posed the question: should they use their resources to go north in relief of Campbell and his men, who if they were still alive would be desperately in need of deliverance, or south in search of the remains of the Pole Party? They were now most certainly dead, but the record of their accomplishment would surely be with them. Was it not owed to the families of these brave men, to the Expedition, to England herself, to know that their noble sons had met their goal?

The decision was unanimous: go south in the spring, and leave Campbell and his men, if they had not previously embarked on the *Terra Nova*, to make the best of their way home. Once the debate was ended and the decision rendered, once the men had faced up to the loss of the Polar Party and all that it had stood for, the atmosphere in the hut was decidedly different. The place was certainly colder—there were fewer bodies to contribute their animal heat to the warmth of the air inside--but the darkness outside seemed to throw up a protecting wall around those within. The men went about their work quietly, venturing out when the blizzards permitted to the stables, the weather screens. Crean's return from the fishing-hole in the ice with an unexpected load of twenty-five fish broke the stillness and woke the laggards with a cheer.

Thirteen was a good number for a group so isolated in their endeavors. With a common sense of duty they acted as one to anything required of them by the Expedition. No cliques were formed. New friendships arose between the men to fill the void created in each, for each had lost a dear friend and respected leader. Taff, Birdie, Soldier, Uncle Bill, Owner.

There was no end to the work to be done; if anything, it had multiplied. Idle talk again filled the smoky air in the messdeck, tales of late adventures told straight, requiring no embellishment. At the close of the workday, dinner—sturdy polar fare heavy in seal meat, muscle and liver—was followed by more talk, games of various sorts (though neither chess nor cards came into fashion this season) including ping-pong, which ran a tournament of its own for months. The acetylene plant was shut down earlier in the evening now, to spin out the modest supply of carbide throughout the long winter night. Candles were also in short supply and soon extinguished, leaving the hut in darkness but for the flickering yellow glow cast by for the watchman's lamp.

No soft vespers came from the gramophone this year. Taff Evans' bedstead had been taken by the new man, Tom Williamson, well-suited to the extremes of polar isolation, and well-liked for his enduring sense of humor. "The Tenements" in the wardroom had given up two of their number to the Pole and another had returned to the world. The empty bunks, sad reminders, were now given over to storage. Cherry's typewriter could still be heard clattering away behind the curtain of the editorial office of the *South Polar Times*, but his artist, poet, and illustrator was gone. No one touched the cubicle left vacant by Scott and Wilson until Hooper at last cleared it out much later in the season.

An air of somber melancholy filled the hut this second season, but Midwinter's Day 1912 would not be allowed to pass without a celebration. Birdie's bamboo-and-penguin-feather Christmas tree was still around, somewhat knocked about a year later. Crean and Williamson worked in secret to restore it to its former glory for another appearance, this time bowed down with decorations, tinsel and electric lights. The hut, gaily decorated for the occasion was draped with streamers and paper chains, and a large white ensign hung from the ceiling. The single copy of the *South Polar Times*, published after lunch, was passed from hand to hand throughout the afternoon. The dinner menu was printed on card cut in the shape of a penguin; from the galley Archer produced seal roast and rissole, soups, breads, candies, ice cream. After dinner, after the toasts, Gran emerged from the darkroom in a baggy white, big-buttoned clown costume, with presents for everyone. There was a show of Debenham's magic-lantern slides, and the evening ended with a sing-song at once uproarious and wistful in thoughts of home.

This marking of the passage of half-a-winter in the Antarctic, with the midnight gone by and the wee hours at hand, was Tom Crean's fourth. This world was starting to feel more home than home to him. Slowly the dim twilight grew each day brighter, longer. South Bay had finally frozen permanently over, though the blizzards still howled up relentlessly from the south.

In late July the smoke rising from Mt. Erebus was properly lit by the sun for the first time, the plume of it glowing rose and gold as it floated away to the north, softly illuminating the snow-covered roof of the hut. This was the quiet promise of spring, of new life to fill the barren shores, of the end of one service and the start of the next. The mere sight of it was enough to quicken a man's pulse, to fill his heart with hope.

One day after the official return of the sun Atkinson laid out his plans for the coming season. A search party would head south provisioned for the top of the Beardmore, should the search extend so far. There were to be no advance depots laid. The hut became a hive of industry in preparation for the march. Crean celebrated his thirty-fifth birthday. A party followed, more for the genuine feeling of spring in the air; all felt the release, and carried on like schoolboys let loose on holiday, dancing and singing with more than the usual abandon.

Throughout the winter each man had exercised his assigned mule on the snow about Cape Evans. With the coming of spring these jaunts became longer and more energetic. The animals were much wiser than the ponies had been when it came to outwitting their men to make an escape. Rani, sensing a moment's inattention from her master, would break free and take off over the ice with Crean tearing over the sastrugi in pursuit. It was all a game with her; she knew there would be no place for her to go in the end but back to the stable.

With the coming of daylight minor sorties were made, mostly with the dogs, to carry supplies over to Hut Point in preparation for the search journey. Crean went there himself in an uneventful overnight with the mules, while Atkinson and Meares ran a cache of dog and mule food out past Corner Camp. The allure of sledging, of the manly and invigorating life on the veldt, had fallen away. The second season's work loomed--three months of it--glumly ahead like a marriage with all the passion run out. By October 28 all was as ready as it would get for the final push south, to seek out the fate of their lost companions.

Chapter Eleven

The Search

Cape Evans.   October 29, 1912

All winter long the word *disaster* hung around just outside in the darkness, the word that everyone knew and felt but could neither consider nor say.   *Accident* came more easily, with its implication of the unforeseen and unavoidable--a collapsed snow bridge, a sudden oblivion along the trail, a quick death.   The story of the expedition, its ambitions and results, would not be fully told without some proofs, some evidence of their success or failure at the Pole.   When the time came to write that story for the world to hear, Cherry would do it best.   He of all the explorers felt the tragedy most keenly.

Every departure of the expedition since London's riotous farewell had been an occasion for celebration, but there was no great fanfare as the mule party set out from Cape Evans on 29 October.   There was no joy in the start of *this* journey; its best conceivable end would find the corpses of the gallant Polar explorers with their records confirming the discovery. The recovery of the bodies and the records would be a sad triumph indeed. Worse, there might be no remains and no records, only a vanished trail of footsteps and a vague foreboding that the business might have gone unfinished, the sacrifice made in vain. With all but two hitting the trail—Archer and Debenham alone were staying behind to tend to maintain the meteorological recorders and meet the ship on her return—there could be no great sendoff party anyway.

Everyone was sure that the Pole had been conquered and all the new land between explored and described. Like true naval tars, they stepped out smartly at 7:30 that fine spring morning. Wright, the only real navigator in the party, led off on foot to lay the course. He was followed by seven men leading seven mules.

Rani was at the peak of her form, as well fed and trained as it was possible to keep her through the heart of the Antarctic night. She was one of the stronger mules and quite the wickedest one to her master, though at times it seemed the other way around. It was good to finally have an animal, even if only a mule, that was up to the task at hand. Crean was not going to let himself become attached to this one; it would only make the parting, when it would most assuredly come, that much the harder. Mules were smart; she must have heard Crean's flattery that her role in this expedition was one of great import. The sledge behind her moved lightly over the snow. The full loads were out at Corner Camp, waiting for their arrival.

Lashly had charge of Pyaree as well as responsibility for the unit of mules as a whole, but there was much he didn't know. Abdullah, Sahib, Gulab, Begum, and Lal Khan made up the rest of the herd, led by Hooper, Nelson, Williamson, Keohane, and Gran. The rambling cavalcade pulled up to the *Discovery* Hut later the same day, and spent the night catching up on news with the dog drivers already waiting there. Supper was seal-meat fried over a blubber fire filling the place with greasy black smoke, just like old times.

They set off over the sea ice around Cape Armitage in the evening of the next day, starting out the old routine of night marching to make use of the firmer surface. Sahib went into the tide crack going up on the Barrier. After a struggle a bight was taken about her hindquarters, and she was hauled to safety only a little damaged from the incident. At the end of the night's march they camped well-in from Safety Camp. Tryggve Gran was cook for the week in Crean's tent. He couldn't be blamed for his countryman's underhanded attempt to steal the prize from the British. He was certainly willing to pull his share and more, and brought a boyish vigor to everything he set his hand to.

Now that they were well out on the trail Crean could see what the Indian mules were made of. A mule resembled a Manchurian pony the way a schooner resembled a barge. They were taller, handsomer, stronger, smarter—an improvement in every way but the last. They even made a better job of it sailing into the wind, but they had one shortcoming he could see would be their downfall. Strong but not stout, they just weren't built for ice work. Their legs were long and thin, their coats sleek and shining with none of the thick wool of their far northern counterparts to protect them from the cold.

Miserable in it, they went off their feed almost immediately. With no real horseman in the crew--Lashly was an engineer, not a farmer--no one realized just yet that the diets of mules and ponies were not the same. The fodder in hand would not be suitable, and there was no substitute. No one realized that the subtropical mules, unlike their counterparts from the frozen steppes, had to be taught to eat snow for their water. They were already becoming dehydrated, though it wasn't immediately apparent to the men. The minute a halt for the day was called, the short hair of their hides grew hoary and long icicles flecked with blood grew from their nostrils. The fourth day of the march was given over to rest--not for the men, who'd exerted themselves but little on the trail—but for the animals whose vaunted strength was already beginning to wane.

The whole enterprise had become even more depressing. Gone was that old hunger for the untamed wilds of the wide open plain, for the undiscovered new land just beyond the horizon, the new adventure about to happen. None of these lay in the offing. Instead, the future held an end that no one wanted to see realized, even though each man knew in his heart how things must inevitably play out. The very best to be hoped for was that sooner or later they must come upon the tent. It would break Crean's heart to come upon his oldest, dearest friend's remains cold and hard as the ice beneath his feet, the hearty laugh and every-ready jokes silenced, the quick mind and brawny vigor wasted away to nothing, stilled forever. It would be harder still to come across no sign at all, and have to go home empty-handed never knowing whether those five brave Englishmen, steady and true, had reached the goal. Time and effort would find out an answer either way, with nothing left but a cold and cheerless return march to bring the searchers home.

Every evening it was pack up and go, with the mules roped together again for the march, twelve feet between. It was a dreary march, made even more so by the realization that here in the vicinity of Corner Camp the Barrier temperatures were always at their lowest, reaching into the minus-forties even with the feeble warmth of the midnight sun. South of the corner, as expected, thick snow and headwind came on in a fury.

Frostbites sprouted like white spring blossoms on the men's faces. The mules, still not eating well, were clearly breaking down. Crean saved a biscuit from his breakfast each morning and slipped it to his Rani on the march. The dog party, having stayed behind at Hut Point to let the others get some little way ahead, caught up on November 5 running in with their customary ease.

With the mules faring so badly, the following day was declared another day of rest. Lashly concocted a warm mash for the mules in hopes of reviving them, but this too was not well-received by his charges. If Rani would not eat, then she would not eat; these animals had clearly earned their reputation for perversity. The frequent days in camp meant the sleeping bags were lately seeing much use. Crean's patient stitchery in mending them over the winter held perfectly; it was the rotten hides already worn out from two hard seasons' use that simply ripped asunder in new places. Looking inside his, Wright saw daylight in thirty-odd places; it was fairly breezy in there, he reported—"*one hoop*".

After the lay-up, the slow cortege continued. General opinion had it that the Pole Party must have met with some mishap on the glacier. It came as a shock when Atkinson spied what he took for a tent sticking up above the general level of the Barrier. It couldn't be the tent, not so far north, so close to home. He headed off to the right alone to have a look, but it proved to be nothing at all, a trick of the light. They came later upon Bluff Depot from the previous season; it had traveled with the Barrier's slow movement some nine hundred yards to the north in the intervening months.

In the recent calm, the bright sun became almost warm. The surface of the snow sparkled and glittered with refracted light, as though a trove of precious stones—rubies, emeralds, sapphires—had been sprinkled over the trail ahead. The sky, at least on clearer days, always gave something to amuse the eye. Stunning cloud-effects, deep black to the west shading to long lines of gray and yellow around the sun like a halo, accented an orange glow bright along the horizon. With the measured progress over the Barrier a man might have had a chance to enjoy the sights, were it not so infernally cold.

The mules wore blinkers to save their eyes for another day. Declining to take their full ration, they had instead taken up chewing on any rope within reach. Perverse though their eating habits might be, their intelligence was not to be underestimated. A few had learned to trip the toggles on their tethers, and so set themselves free to wander away from the camp while their handlers were asleep. Rani was too smart to leave vicinity of the tents entirely, just a mile or so in a game of catch-me-if-you-can. The exercise was one quick way to warm up after a long night's shiver in the doubtful comfort of the balding reindeer bag.

Thirteen days out from Cape Evans, the search party pushed on into the teeth of a ferocious wind until they arrived at One Ton Depot. The blizzards and gales of the winter had built up long drifts behind it, streaming to the north. Deep within the mound of stores left behind by Cherry and Dmitri, they came upon an alarming circumstance. The oil for the primus stoves had leaked past the seals in the bungs and spread through the stacked snow. It had saturated the biscuit and pemmican left there; little remained that was fit to eat, not even for starving men digging it out with the last of their strength. Perhaps it was best that Scott's men had perished elsewhere, in some quicker, more humane manner. With only that small bit of hope to cheer them, the search party camped for the night, awaiting better weather for the morning. The proof would be found somewhere farther out on the Barrier, or up the glacier toward the plateau.

Near midday on the first march south of One Ton Depot, Wright's sharp eyes spotted something unusual in the distance. Out here on the snow plain where distances can be so deceptive, a dark spot in the distance had caught his attention. Crean saw it next. In earlier, happier days it might have been a man or a dog in the distance. Today it could be an abandoned petrol tin or another bit of discarded gear, or a ragged flag from a marker cairn that had survived the winter.

Wright bore away to the right for a closer look. Glancing over at him occasionally, Crean was surprised to see him waving in the distance. A shock ran through the party. This could mean nothing else. They turned off the trail, and so did the dogs just coming up behind. Wright came out to meet them, and called halt, a few hundred yards from the spot. *"It is the tent."*

It had been pitched near an old cairn, and was nearly drifted over. Only six inches of the green canvas of the ventilator, and the bamboos which had kept it upright through the winter, showed above the plain. These were enough to mark the awful spot and tell the tale of what lay below. *"We know at least some of our comrades are sleeping."*

Strong hands took up the shovels to dig down into the barrier snow. Four feet of it had settled over the tent during the winter. It had been well-pitched—Scott's tents always were. Within, everything would be neat and shipshape. Tender hands brushed away the rime from the threadbare green canvas. No one spoke. Words here seemed out of place.

It was Crean who unlashed the door. He knew before looking inside what he would surely find there: the Captain, so staunch and so brave, who would go any distance, as far or farther than any of his companions, before he would ever--as he surely must--succumb. Dr. Wilson, brave, true-hearted Uncle Bill, as strong as his Captain in body, and stronger yet in spirit. Dear, sweet Birdie, to whom no obstacle but this one was insurmountable. They were peacefully nestled in their fur bags, as though they'd only gone to sleep, all except Captain Scott, whose cold dead hands rested gently on the shoulders of his companion. A spirit lamp fashioned from an empty tin and a bit of finnesko lacing had provided the last light to enter his eyes. The others were missing. Taff Evans, Oates—gone. This was the sad end and object of it all.

Atkinson took the sledging diaries, the notes and letters found, back to the solitude of his own tent pitched some little way off from Scott's last encampment. There he read just enough to tell the tale. The dream of being the first to plant the flag at the South Pole of the earth was not to be fulfilled. Scott's words told the story of a grueling march over the plateau from that far-off place where Crean, Lashly, and Evans had been the last to see these men alive--bound for glory, full of hope.

Back in the blazing sunlight, he read aloud to his men from the worn, grimy pages of Scott's last diary:

"The Pole. Yes, but under very different circumstances from those expected. We have had a horrible day--- The Norwegians have forestalled us and are first at the Pole. It is a terrible disappointment, and I am very sorry for my loyal companions. . . .All the day dreams must go; it will be a wearisome return.".

The men stood around the tent, silent in the stiff breeze. Gran stood a little way off. The wind picked up the leader's words and carried them away, scattered them through the limitless spaces of the frozen wasteland.

Crean broke the silence. *"Mr. Gran, Sir, permit me to congratulate you. Our people found the Norwegian flag when they came to the South Pole."* His tears ran freely; there was nothing more he could say.

Scott's painfully written words said more. They related the gradual sickening and failing of Taff Evans, once the strongest and most resourceful of the lot. He--the first--succumbed to the long season of exposure and want. Crean himself, out on the plateau, had been just as eager as these brave men to go on, to test himself and the dreams that had led him to that place. Only the Owner's whim had put him in the last returning party. One never knows, on saying goodbye, when or whether one will see his friends again. Strength and will may in the end be not enough to see the job through.

Oates had fallen next, his poor lame foot frostbitten and then frozen into a lifeless appendage fit only to carry him to his end, in one brave self-sacrifice to save his companions. The three remaining struggled against their mounting hardships through the bitter weeks of early March, coming at last to rest here a scant eleven miles from the plenty at One Ton Depot--their food, their fuel, their lives spent. Deeply buried in the snow near the tent, the sledge still carried a few odds and ends, and thirty-five pounds of geological specimens Wilson had taken from the glacial moraines. This was a huge weight for these exhausted men, more than the food and fuel they hauled at the last, a testament to their devotion to science.

It seemed as though Atkinson read aloud for hours. His voice made each word of the story, the tales of courage and resignation and endurance, ring true into the heart of every man. The diaries, the records, the chronometers and specimens, all were recovered and loaded onto the sledges for the return to Cape Evans.

Crean entered the tent one last time. He had lost the truest of friends, the seaman with whom he had shared unnumbered days in the South and the Captain who had kept him a close and trusted companion for eight years. All gone, having found their earthly reward and gone on to seek a greater one. He knelt inside the tent and kissed the yellow, frostbitten cheek of Captain Scott. There were no more tears in his eyes, the sorrow in his heart already transforming to a peaceful recognition. Ambition, pride, endeavor, the thrust and surge of the human heart must for all of us come to a final close, and for some that end comes in pursuit of a noble truth. He pulled the head-flap of the sleeping-bag up over the face of his captain.

Five men gathered around the perimeter of the tent and scraped away the last of the snow valance so carefully placed by Scott and his men as the blizzard closed over them eight months before. Strong hands gripped the poles beneath the valance, and with the greatest care eased them out so that the folds of canvas might settle over the still forms beneath it.

The great dome of the southern sky arched overhead, a solemn chancel built by no earthly hands. Atkinson read the burial service, the familiar prayer. *--Grant to us your servants so to follow in faith where you have led the way, that we may at length fall asleep peacefully in you and wake up in your likeness, for your tender mercies' sake,* *amen.--* All the men gathered round, their caps in their hands, repeated: *--Amen.--* The searching wind carried their words away north.

Each took the shovel and dug out one scoop of pristine snow and laid it gently on the mound of folded canvas. Before long the green fabric was covered, the sepulchre it once marked with color restored to the universal white of the Great Barrier. The men continued, each in turn, adding more snow to the mound, building it higher and higher, the greatest--the only--earthly monument within their power to build. By the end of an hour, it stood twelve feet above the Barrier, a magnificent cairn, a tomb that kings must envy. Gran lashed together a cross of his own skis and planted it in the summit. He would wear Scott's skis on the trail back to Cape Evans, ensuring that in this small way the captain's footsteps might be said to have made the entire march to the pole and home.

Eleven men sang out one final, mournful hymn, as whirling snow drove up from the south to lay a new mantle of white over the dead. A sledge was stuck upright in the snow beside. Atkinson composed a note, a requiem:

"This Cross and Cairn are erected over the bodies of Captain Scott, Dr. Wilson, Lt. Bowers. A slight token to perpetuate their gallant and successful attempt to reach the Pole. Also to commemorate their two gallant comrades, Captain Oates and Seaman Evans. The Lord gave and the Lord taketh away."

Tom Crean signed his own name beneath the others', the pencil making its careful scrawl across the paper, to be left pinned to crossed skis and a towering snow cairn until the searching wind should obliterate all these transient marks. Before the notes of the last hymn had died away, a light crusting of snow was already clinging to the upright cross.

255

The mules, for all the promise of their initial vigor and training, had reached the end of their usefulness many miles before the weakest of the ponies had. Gran's Lal Khan and Sahib were shot and most of the gear depoted, before the party set out on the next outward leg of their sad journey, to scout the trail southward for some sign of Captain Oates. Thirteen miles on, they came upon his sleeping bag, the theodolite, and a camera, all abandoned by the doomed southern party on their final homeward march. There was no sign of the lost and valiant Soldier.

The work of the search party was done. Plans for mapping the coast south of the Beardmore, for geologizing on the glacier, were abandoned in favor of a quick return. The fate of the Northern Party, still unknown, might hang in the balance. The dog drivers stayed behind to erect a cairn and a cross with a note: *"Hereabouts died a very gallant gentleman..."*

Stopping at Scott's last camp, they picked up the Southern Party's gear to carry it the rest of the way on the long walk home. The Barrier was not yet done with the explorers. Snow and wind persisted for days on end; the saving grace was that it blew now on Crean's back, and not his face. The mules were now a hindrance; without them dragging down the pace, sails might have been set to speed the travelers home. The dog teams came across some of the material Crean and Lashly had jettisoned in the fall during their desperate struggle to bring their Lieutenant home alive—some rocks from the glacier, a roll of Birdie's film. These would help to flesh out the story in the end.

The remaining mules were refusing their ration entirely now. Crean's Rani was steadily weakening. In contrast, the dogs, sensing the nearness of their home and the end of the Barrier, the world's coldest and most awful place, found renewed vigor. Ahead, black rock and white snow revealed the bleak outlines of Black and White Islands against with the lofty peaks of the Royal Society Range in the distance, surmounted by roiling dark cumulus clouds. It made a beautiful picture, with Observation Hill and Castle Rock the welcoming beacons of home. For all its stark grandeur, it was a view none in the search party ever cared to see again.

As they approached the *Discovery* hut, they could see figures moving out towards them over the ice. The silhouettes, seen black against the white snow in the distance, were easily identified. All but one was familiar. Seaman Williamson, well in the lead with Gulab, suddenly let loose with a shout. *"It's Lieutenant Campbell!"*

A shout of joy, a thunderous *hurrah!* shattered the Antarctic silence. Some happy news at last! The men rushed forward to hear the Northern Party's story. The five members of the Northern Party were all well, having survived the winter in a miserable ice-cave on Inaccessible Island. The tale of this ordeal would soon unfold in all its dreary detail around the smoky comfort of the hut's makeshift blubber stove. The *Terra Nova* had failed to make their rendezvous, so they concluded she had sunk and resolved to make the best of it for the winter. When springtime arrived they'd return overland in the spring to Butter Point on the west side of the Sound, thence homeward across the sea-ice to the shores of Ross Island.

After one more day on the trail the search party and all the remaining members of the expedition still in the South were at last reunited in the shelter of the walls of their good old Cape Evans hut.

The work of the expedition was complete. The Pole had been

reached; the geological and surveying work in the north and west was done; the penguin eggs brought in; magnetic and gravity series run; the changing weather and aurora logged daily for nearly two years. There were no more journeys of great importance to be made, though there would be time for a pleasant surveying jaunt to Cape Royds and a second-ever ascent of Mt. Erebus before the ship returned to pick them all up. Beyond these excursions there was little else to be done save pack up and await the appearance of the ship. Gran and some of Campbell's men took off to conquer the summit. Cherry and another band left for a few days' holiday to Shackleton's hut, leaving Crean and the handful of others to enjoy the relative peace and comfort at Cape Evans. In the shadows and the quiet there was room now for the remembered forms and voices of those now departed.

There was still mule-tending to be done. None of the mules had fared well—the contrast between their temperate Indian home and this cold and windswept waste was too much for their constitutions and the thin hair that covered their hides. Five finished the walk home; of those, Begum and Abdullah were so worn-out they had to be shot soon after their return. Crean's old Rani was among the survivors. Lodged again in the comfort of her stall, she thrived on the full feeding and daily exercise at the hands of her sailor. He knew, as she did not, how soon her end must come.

The breeding season for the gulls at the Skuary was in full swing and there were fresh eggs for all hands on the table every morning. Christmas this year was a very modest affair—the available provisions would not admit of a luxury meal—but Crean's, and everyone's thoughts were of home. Next year at this time, wherever any of them were, it would not be here.

The ship might show up almost any day now, and the idle men--they were all pretty much idlers now, except the cook--kept up a sharp lookout. New Year's 1913 for most of the men present was their third in the Antarctic. For Crean and Lashly, it was the fifth. A week later, Williamson's shout that he'd seen the mastheads of the ship beyond Cape Barne emptied the hut in a rush, but he was mistaken. There was nothing to be seen. For men with all their work done and time on their hands, the wait seems longer.

Football on the ice helped pass the time, as did long yarns spun in the warm clear air, or the close nights in the hut when the blizzard held forth. With no sign of the ship by mid-January, the time had come to consider that if she had indeed been lost, then the possibility of a third winter on the ice must be faced and the larder stocked accordingly. The prospect of nothing but seal meet and penguin was not enticing, but the slaughter was slated to begin January 18. A year already had passed since Crean had said goodbye one last tine to his old shipmate Taff Evans far out on the polar plateau.

That very day, the *Terra Nova* hove into view. When she was close in under the Cape, Lt. Evans, now recovered and in command, shouted through the loud hailer, *"Are you all well?"*

There was a moment of silence. Campbell shouted back, *"The party reached the Pole on 17 January, but perished on the way back."*

Another moment of silence followed, on board and on shore. *--Let go anchor.--*

First off the ship were the mail-bags, laden with a whole year's letters full of news from home, some of it by this time quite old. Some carried congratulations on the attainment of the Pole. All of it was innocent of any knowledge of the southern party's woeful end. There was another letter for Crean from James Kennedy. No news in it of Hannah; a girl wouldn't wait forever. Still he was looking forward to a return to active duty in the Navy, where the hardships and tragedy of polar exploration might fade into memory. He penned a quick note in response, to post from New Zealand when the *Terra Nova* landed. It didn't say much about the expedition or the fate of Scott's polar party. All of that news would come out in minute detail in all the papers long before any word from Crean would make it back to Ireland. *"I. will. tell. you all"* he wrote, *"when we will be having a quiet. tot. one evening. But I must say I have lost a. good. friend . . ."*

Twenty-eight hours later, everything going back—records, photographs, specimens, personal gear, the dogs—was loaded in the ship. The surviving mules kept their appointment with the bullet.

As soon as this sad chore was done the ship steamed over to Cape Royds to pick up some scientific material, then headed south through the rolling swell, bound for Hut Point. The shore party had pressed for a memorial to be erected on Observation Hill. Davies, the ship's carpenter, set to work immediately on a stout cross of Australian jarrah wood.

With the ship hooked to the fast ice some miles from Discovery Point, eight men walked toward the hut pulling a sledge laden with the cross. Halfway to the shore the slushy ice beneath Crean's feet gave way without warning, and he dropped into a pool to his armpits. Quick hands hauled him out. A few more steps, and he found another hole, this time almost dragging the sledge in with him. Soaked to the skin, half frozen, his legs refused to go another step. In minutes, he was naked in the scant shelter of the sledge and dressed again, the pile of his wet clothes already freezing solid where they lay.

They spent the night in the *Discovery* Hut, gathered one last time around the smoky fire in the blubber stove, somehow warmer for the shared memories of long-past hours there together, talking of what had been and what was yet to be. Bill Lashly was there, Atch and Cherry and Keohane; all had fought their way up the glacier, and then their way home from it. Cherry recorded the evening: *"You would not think Crean had had such a pair of duckings, to hear him talking so merrily tonight. . . ."*

In the morning they made the long climb up the windswept rubbly slopes of Observation Hill to its summit, bearing on their shoulders the wooden cross. There they anchored it in a base of heavy stones, to rise nine feet into the air, the deeply incised inscription facing south: *"To strive, to seek, to find, and not to yield".* They gave three cheers, and then one more, and scrambled down to the waiting ship.

The sea-ice was melting fast as they dodged the open pools lining the way back to the *Terra Nova*. When all were at last aboard, she set sail for Granite Harbor on the Victoria Land coast, to pick up a cache of geological specimens left there by the Western Party. Crean stood at the railing of the quarterdeck, looking backward on what had become another home to him, somehow warm and inviting for all its bitter tempests and the faded luster of its memories. The goal had been won; would there ever be a reason to return?

The broad white shoulder of Ross Island slowly diminished with every turn of *Terra Nova's* screw, and with it the slight marks of man, the little settlements clinging to its shores and all they'd come to mean. Farther away and growing farther lay the strange and dangerous works of ice--the Glacier Tongue, the Barrier, the Beardmore, the Pole. Some of the men looking southward across the water toward the desolate and deadly land they'd called home swore they'd never return. Tom Crean was not so sure.

Ahead lay the stormy gray surge of the Southern Ocean, and beyond the green land—not Ireland, not home, but near enough in scent and color—of New Zealand, new faces, new voices, news of the great world beyond. Crowds of bergs followed them north, to harass and bedevil the ship and remind her and all aboard that they were not yet beyond the reach of the wild Antarctic. Groping her way in the mist and half-light, the ship became lost in a maze of narrow channels. As much by luck as by seamanship, she found her way clear at the last moment, through "Hell's Gate," and into the open water where the ice was to be seen no more. The Southern Ocean had yet one more gale to throw at them; the ship tossed like a cork, and chaos reigned below decks.

Signs of approaching land, shorebirds and drifting kelp, began to appear with increasing regularity. The air grew distinctly warmer, fragrant with new aromas. The outline of South Island appeared through the haze after breakfast the morning of February 9, becoming clearer through the day as the ship steamed north along the shore toward her first port of call. The trees and meadows seemed to glow with yellows and greens fresh and new to eyes grown long accustomed to blacks and whites and the cold lavenders of unending sunsets.

It had been well over two years. The *Terra Nova* slipped into harbor at Oamaru under cover of darkness. A boat was put over, with Crean as coxswain, to row Pennell and Atkinson ashore, where they cabled England and the world the news of the Expedition's return. The seamen were given strict orders to answer no questions. *"We was chased, Sir,"* Crean reported, *"but they got nothing out of us."*

The ship held silence for twenty-four hours, as word of Captain Scott's fate spread round the world. On the morning of the 12th she steamed slowly past Lyttleton Heads, her white ensign at half-mast.

The expedition landed to find the Empire in mourning.

There followed more weeks in New Zealand, refitting the *Terra Nova* for the long passage home. The trip itself was unremarkable, though well seasoned with weeks of gales and storms that harried her across the Southern Ocean until at last she'd rounded the Horn and sailed northward into balmier waters that led inevitably to home.

She arrived in England in June 1913. Crean returned to active duty in the Navy, now promoted to Chief Petty Officer. The Navy had been his career, his life for so long there would be no changing it now. It was Tom Crean himself who had changed. He had seen the greater world in its physical and natural extremes, endured and triumphed where another man would have turned away, or given up. More than this, he had come to know in his heart that he was not alone. The men of the Royal Navy, and the men who chose the path of discovery, could be counted on to do the same.

Shore life at Chatham had no allure. Shackleton was getting up a new expedition to travel right across the Antarctic continent from one shore to the other, stopping at the South Pole along the way. He applied to the Navy for the loan of Crean's services in the endeavor.

On May 23, 1914, less than a year after his return from the south, Tom Crean was released to join the crew of the *Endurance*. He was on his way back to the ice.

The Men of Scott's *Terra Nova* Expedition to Discover the South Pole

Shore party, Officers

• Scott, Robert Falcon Commander, R.N. - Expedition leader (perished on return from the Pole)   "The Owner:
• Evans, Edward R.G.R. - Lieutenant, R.N. "Teddy Evans" (first year only; invalided home after his return from the South Polar Plateau)
• Atkinson, Edward L, R.N. - surgeon, parasitologist
• Bowers, Henry Robertson – Lieutenant (perished on return from the Pole) "Birdie"
• Oates, Lawrence , Capt. 6th Iniskilling Dragoons (perished on return from the Pole) "Titus," "Soldier"

Shore Party, Scientific Staff

• Wilson, Edward Adrian - chief of scientific staff and biologist (perished on return from the Pole) "Uncle Bill"
• Debenham, Frank – Geologist (first year only)
• Cherry-Garrard, Apsley   - Assistant zoologist "Cherry"
• Gran, Tryggve - ski expert
• Meares, Cecil H. - in charge of dogs (first year only)
• Day, Bernard C. - Motor engineer (first year only)
• Nelson, Edward W. – Biologist
• Ponting, Herbert G. - Camera artist (first year only)
• Simpson, George – Meteorologist (first year only)
• Taylor, T. Griffith – Geologist (first year only)
• Wright, Charles S. - Physicist

Shore Party, the Men

• Archer, W.W. - Chief steward, late R.N. (second year only)
• Clissold, Thomas - cook, late R.N. (first year only)
• Crean, Tom , petty officer, R.N.
• Evans, Edgar"Taff" - petty officer, R.N.(perished on return from the Pole)

- Forde, Robert - petty officer, R.N. (first year only)
- Geroff, Dimitri - Dog driver
- Hooper, F.J. - Steward, late R.N.   (first year only)
- Keohane, Patrick - petty officer, R.N.
- Lashley, William - chief stoker, R.N.
- Omelchenko, Anton – Groom   (first year only)
- Williamson, Thomas - petty officer, R.N.   (second year only)

Northern Party

- Campbell, Victor - Lieutenant, R.N.   "The Mate"
- Priestley, Raymond E.   Geologist
- Abbot, George - petty officer, R.N.
- Dickason, Harry - Able seaman, R.N.
- Browning, Frank V. - petty officer, 2nd class, R.N.

Ship's Party

The names of those brave men who remained on board to sail the *Terra Nova* from Cape Evans to New Zealand, the round-trip relief voyage in the spring of 1911, and the outward and homeward bound voyages, have not been included. here.

Appendix Two

Glossary of Antarctic and Ice Terms

Afterguard: On board *Terra Nova*, those of the ship and shore party who were not members of the messdeck. The afterguard included the ship's officers as well as the civilian scientists, artists, instructors, and adaptable helpers. Housed in the wardroom, they held official (in the case of the officers) or nominal (in the case of the civilians) authority over the men, and were always addressed by them as "sir."

Aurora: Auroras, also known as southern lights or aurorae (*singular:* aurora), are natural light displays in the sky, usually observed at night, particularly in the polar regions. At some times, they form "quiet arcs"; at others ("active aurora"), they evolve and change constantly.

Barque: (ship's sail plan): any vessel with a particular type of sail-plan comprising three (or more) masts, fore-and-aft sails on the aftermost mast and square sails on all other masts. The advantage of these rigs was that they needed smaller crews than a comparable full-rigged ship as there were fewer of the labor intensive square sails.

Barrier or *Great Ice Barrier*: An enormous sheet of floating ice as large as France that fills the area between Ross Island and the continent to the south. Its seaward face runs east from Cape Crozier to King Edward VII Land In a bluff hundreds of feet high. It stopped ships but provided a long level highway to the Beardmore Glacier.

Biscuit: Hardtack is a simple type of cracker or biscuit, made from flour, water, and sometimes salt. Inexpensive and long-lasting, it was and is used for sustenance in the absence of perishable foods, commonly during long sea voyages and polar exploration.

Black Gang: The stokers and engineers in charge of the firing and maintenance of the ship's steam engines.

Bluejacket: Any enlisted man on a naval ship.

Blizzard: A cold storm with winds of at least 35 miles per hour and temperatures below - 20°F. Little snow may actually fall during a blizzard, the high winds pick up snow from the ground and carry it around, visibility is often greatly reduced.

Blubber: a thick layer of fat found under the skin of all cetaceans (whales), pinnipeds (seals) and penguins. Rendered, it provides fuel for cooking and lighting, and may be consumed as food for humans.

Brash ice: Ice rubble, loose pieces of ice of various sizes from gravel sized to table sized. Originates from sea-ice that is breaking up or commonly as debris from calving ice bergs or ice bergs that break up as part of their ongoing erosion.

Cobbo: An obscure term used by Wilson to describe the special friendship between Crean and Taff Evans.

Cooker: A nesting set of cooking pots originally developed by the Norwegian explorer Fridtjof Nansen. It consists of an annular ring-shaped pot and an inner pot for melting ice into drinking water in the most fuel-efficient means devised.

Crevasse: A deep, usually vertical, crack or split in a *glacier*, as the brittle ice flows over a uneven surface beneath the ice. Crevasses, even wide ones, can easily become covered over by blown snow. These lids are not easy to see, and can give out without warning beneath a traveler. Over time these lids may fall away, leaving narrow bridges across the deep crevasses

Fast ice: Sea ice that forms in situ along the coastline and remains attached, although usually there is a crack at some edge to relieve tidal pressure.

Field: A sheet of floating ice generally of great thickness, and of too great extent to be seen over from a ship's masthead.

Finnesko: Boots made entirely from fur including the sole

Floe: A discrete piece of flat, floating sea ice separated from its neighbors by lanes of open water from a few inches to miles wide. Depending on age and local pack conditions, a floe's size may range from a couple dozen yards to miles in extent. Unlike an *icefield*, its extent can be distinguished from the ship's masthead.

Foc's'le: A spoken abbreviation of the word "forecastle" referring to the raised forward ("foc's'le head"), the space beneath the deck usually reserved for the messdeck or men's quarters. The foc's'le is in the bow of the ship forward (or "forrard") of the foremast, and is the exclusive domain of the men who work the ship. In the merchant service no officer goes there unless invited. The quarterdeck at the extreme after portion of the ship Is likewise reserved to the captain.

Frost Smoke: Mist rising from the seawater in the open lanes of the pack, when quite heavy and dense it obscures all the the most limited visibility.

Glacier: A river of ice, generally flowing down a valley, with rock walls at either side. Glaciers can be small valley glaciers, ice streams, or immense flows like the Beardmore at 120 miles long from its head at the South Polar Plateau (10,000 feet above sea level) to the Barrier, and up to twenty miles in width. When rapidly descending n altitude, the surface of a glacier is split into multitudes of deep *crevasses*.

Growler: Smaller chunk of floating ice, rising less than a yard above the surface of the sea.

Hand: One of the seamen who work the ship, ranging in status from "boy" or "green hand" through Ordinary Seaman (O. S.) and Able-bodied Seaman (A. B.) to Petty Officer (P. O.) the highest rank normally achieved by an enlisted man.

Harness: In manhauling, a broad canvas belt wrapped around the abdomen and supported from the shoulders by straps, to enable men to pull a sledge behind them while leaving the men's hands free.

Hummock: A mass of ice rising to a considerable height (up to 40) above the general level of a floe, and forming a part of it. Hummocks are originally raised by the pressure of floes grinding against each other from the action of wind, wave, current, and moving ice.

Hut: The term used to describe the permanent structures erected on the shores of Ross Island, to house the men wintering over in the Antarctic.

The huts at Cape Evans, Hut Point, and Cape Royds were large enough to comfortably house their intended inhabitants.

Hoosh: A single-pot stew, heated over the primus and served as hot and generously as possible under the trying circumstances of the trail. Made from pemmican (dried and powdered meat) and grains, it may also include meat, blubber, and any other edibles that may be at hand..

Ice-anchor: A part of ship's gear used in ice navigation, a stout iron hook or grapnel adapted to take hold upon ice. Also known as *ice hook*.

Iceberg: A large piece of floating ice that has calved, or broken off, a glacier or ice shelf. Icebergs can be vast, the size of islands or small countries.

Ice blink: A brightness on the horizon, showing in the clouds above it caused by reflection of sunlight from sea ice even in overcast conditions. Such a sight is often called an "ice sky". Occasionally it also reveals the presence of leads or lakes out of view over the horizon. Conversely, a darkness on the horizon when surrounded by ice denotes the presence of open water and is called a "water sky".

Ice Cap: A dome-shaped cover of perennial ice and snow, covering the summit area of a mountain mass so that no peaks emerge through. The South Polar Plateau on which the South Geographic Pole lies is an Ice Cap of continental dimension, at an average elevation of 10,000 feet above sea level. This ice cap is two miles thick.

Ice foot: A "shelf" of ice that forms around many Antarctic shores in the winter time. Often formed where sea-ice joins the land, as the tide rises and falls, a layer of ice is deposited which builds up. Once the sea ice blows out in the spring a distinct ledge several feet high is left behind that can be difficult to cross for men and animals.

Ice shelf: A large flat-topped sheet of ice that is attached to land along one side and floats in the sea. Formed where glaciers flowing from the highlands have reached sea level and kept flowing, they are fed from the landward side and eroded from the seaward side by the calving of icebergs and melting. The Great Ice Barrier is an ice shelf.

Ice tongue: A long, narrow, projection of glacier ice out from the coastline, similar in origin to an ice shelf, but usually formed where a valley glacier flows rapidly to the sea or a lake. Erebus Glacier Tongue lies like a narrow ridge across the sea-ice route between Cape Evans and Hut Point.

Jaeger: Refers to the German-made woolen gear used on the trail, including socks, sweaters or jumpers, and underwear
Lane (of Water): A narrow channel among the masses of ice, through which a boat or a ship may pass.

Lead: Another name for *lane*, a channel through the ice. A ship is said to "take the right lead" when she follows a channel conducting her into a more navigable sea, and vice versa.

Men: The term used by the officers of the ship, to refer to the sailors. By implication, anyone who is an officer cannot be one of "the men."

Mess: An eating place aboard a ship, and the group of men who live and eat together.

Nipped: The situation of a ship when forcibly pressed by ice on both sides.

Nunatak: An isolated peak of bedrock that sticks above the surface of an ice sheet. They are the peaks of hills and mountains standing above the ice sheet which flows around them.

Nutrition: Manhauling at high altitude in polar conditions is one of the most physically demanding efforts known. The caloric intake required to perform the work and maintain body heat is about 6,500 calories per day, an enormous amount of food. Scott recognized the need for high--energy foods but seriously underestimated the necessary caloric intake. His Summit Ration provided about 4,500 calories per day. The men were eating their full ration, and slowly starving themselves.

Owner: In naval vessels, the captain was sometimes informally referred to as "the Owner" of the ship, since he was in charge of every one and everything on the ship.

Pack ice: Often used interchangeably with sea ice. Pack ice is frozen sea that formed somewhere else and has floated to its present position carried by wind, tides and currents. It is broken up and of variable size and thickness, some pieces can be the size of a coffee table and about 1 thick, other pieces are larger than a tennis court and can be 30ft or more thick. Usually pack ice is in its second season. Open pack - when the pieces of ice don't touch; Closed pack - when the pieces of ice touch

Pancake ice: Pancake ice grows from thickened grease ice and resembles pancakes or lily pads. The edges of each piece is upturned because the plates bump into each other as they gently move around in the sea. Usually between about about a foot and 6 feet across.

Peggy: In every mess, one man was designated "peggy" (a rotating honor shared by all) to make or fetch the meals and clean up afterward.

Pemmican: Meat cured, pulverized, and mixed with fat, containing much nutriment in a small compass.

Petty Officer: The highest rank generally available to naval seamen regardless of their performance or ability. This is largely a function of class distinction in British society and naval hierarchy extant during Crean's service in the Royal Navy.

Port: To a sailor, the left side of his ship.

Primus: The Primus stove, a pressurized-burner kerosene (paraffin) stove, was a reliable and durable stove in everyday use, and it performed especially well under adverse conditions: it was the stove of choice for Shackleton's and Scott's expeditions to the South Pole.

Sallying (a ship): from the early days of polar exploration, causing the ship to roll by crew and passengers running from side to side to prevent adhesion of the ice around her.

Sastrugi: Irregular ridges of snow on a small scale (rarely more than 1 foot) that lie parallel to the direction of the wind. Sastrugi can make travel very awkward or difficult, they can be quite soft or as hard as ice.

Scapular: Brown or Small Scapular: A pair of small cloth squares joined by shoulder tapes worn under the clothing on the breast and back as a sacramental.   Crean was a faithful Catholic of the Carmellite Order and wore his scapular throughout all his Antarctic adventures, and indeed every day of his life.

Science: Polar expeditions were concerned with the accumulation and analysis of raw data in geology, meteorology, terrestrial magnetism, biology, glaciology, and other sciences.   The shore stations at Cape Evans and Hut Point included magnetic and weather huts.   The pursuit of science was paramount in Scott's expeditions, in part to secure financial backing but largely from his own personal interest.   The weight of the sledge pulled by the returning polar party included 35 pounds of rock specimens collected along the way.

Sea ice: A general term for any ice that forms from frozen seawater. Sea ice covers large parts of polar waters in the winter and melts back each summer.   Ice which covers an ocean or sea; includes mostly continuous pack ice, broken only by narrow open water "*leads*" or wider "polynas", and discrete ice floes.

Sledge: Man-hauled sledges were the traditional means of transport on British exploring expeditions to the Arctic and Antarctic regions in the 19th and early 20th centuries.   Made from wooden frames and runners bound with rawhide lashings to allow flexibility in transit over uneven ice, they are the principal means of transport in the Antarctic, whether pulled by men, dogs, ponies, or motors.

Starboard: To a sailor, the right side of his ship, or sledge.

Stream: A long and narrow, but generally continuous, collection of loose ice.

Tide crack: Any crack in sea ice that is caused by the rise and fall of the tide. As the tide rises so the area of the sea increases and a crack forms, as the tide falls, so the area decreases and the crack closes. Often form around offshore rocks, between the shore and sea-ice, around grounded ice bergs or even stretching for miles between islands.

Wardroom: On board a naval ship, the officer's quarters.   In the Dape Evans Hut, the area beyond the bulkhead of packing cases accessed through the messdeck.

White-out: A weather condition in which the horizon cannot be identified and there are no shadows. The clouds in the sky and the white snow on the ground blend - described as like walking along inside a ping-pong ball.   White out conditions are potentially dangerous because it is difficult to find a point of reference and it is very easy to walk over a cliff or fall down a crevasse in such conditions.

Water-sky: A dark appearance in the sky, indicating "clear water" in that direction, and forming a striking contrast with the "blink" over land or ice.

Appendix Three

Bibliography: Works consulted during the creation of this narrative

Published:

Bernacchi, Louis C.,

A Very Gallant Gentleman; Thornton Butterworth, London 1935

Cherry-Garrard, Apsley, *The Worst Journey in the World;* Picador, London, 1994

Debenham, Frank,

In the Antarctic—Stories of Scott's "Last Expedition"; Murray, London, 1952

        The Quiet Land—The Diaries of Frank Debenham; Bluntisham Books 1992

Dodge, Ernest S., The Polar Rosses—*John and James Clark Ross and Their Expeditions,*   Harper and Row, New York, 1973

Evans, Sir Edward R. G. R.,

South with Scott; Collins, London, 1954

Happy Adventurer; Wilfred Funk, New York, 1951

Green, Bill, *Water, Ice, and Stone—Science and Memory on theAntarctic Lakes*; Crown, New York, 1995

Gregor, G. C., *Swansea's Antarctic Explorer: Edger Evans, 1876-1912*; Swansea City   Council, 1995

Gurney, Alan, *Below the Convergence—Voyages toward Antarctica*

1699-1839; Norton, New York, 1997

Lambert, Katherine, *The Longest Winter: The incredible Survival of Captain Scott;s Lost Party,* Pimlico 2002 (later Smithsonian 2004)

Mason, Theodore K., *The South Pole Ponies;* Dodd, Mead & Co., New York 1979

Philbrick, Nathaniel, *Sea of Glory—America's Voyage of Discovery, the U. S. Exploring Expedition 1838-1842;* Viking, New York, 2003

Ponting, Herbert, *The Great White South:* Duckworth, London 1928

Scott, Robert F., *Scott's Last Expedition,* Smith Elder, London 1913

Seaver, George, *'Birdie' Bowers if the Antarctic;* Murray, London, 1938

Solomon, Susan, *The Coldest March—Scott's Fatal Antarctic Expedition;* Yale   University Press, New Haven 2001

Thomson. David, *Scott's Men*; Penguin Books, London, 1977

Wilson, Edward,
*Diary of the 'Terra Nova' Expedition to the Antarctic 1910-1912:*Blandford Press, London, 1972

Wright, Charles (Ed. Pat Wright and Colin Bull), *Silas: The Antarctic Diaries and Memoir of Charles S. Wright,* Ohio State University Press, Columbus 1993.

Unpublished:

Crean, Thomas, SPRI: Letters

Crean, Thomas: Kerry County Museum (Tralee):   Naval Service Record, Crean letters

Crean, Thomas: Kerry County Museum;   deposition describing the search (copy, no   date)

Lashly, William, SPRI;   Diary *Discovery* Expedition;

Letters *Discovery* Expedition

Letters *Terra Nova* Expedition

Diary, *Terra Nova* Expedition

Keohane, Patrick; Kerry County Museum: *Terra Nova Diary*

O'Brien, Gerard (grandson); interview April 28, 2008, Pasadena CA

O'Brien, Mary Crean (daughter); interview October 31, 2007 @ Tralee

Newspapers:

NY Times March 18, 1914:   Evans lecture honoring Peary; reference and quote attributed to TC:

"The following day Evans could not go on.   He begged his two companions to save themselves and leave him to his fate, and then he ordered them, but they would hear nothing of it.   This was the first and only time Crean ever defied an order.   *"If you are to go out Sir, then we'll all go out together."* "(quoted NT Times March 18,1914: ERGR Evans lecture honoring Peary)

Verse:

French, Percy, *"The Mountains of Mourne"*; 1896

Nelson, Edward A.; *"Outspan"* published in *The South Polar Times,* June 21, 1911 and quoted in *The Worst Journey in the World*

Notes:

"We knew at least some of our comrades were sleeping." [Keohane, quoted in The Coldest March p259]

A note about the author:

David Hirzel (info@terra-nova-press.com) was born in Philadelphia, raised in West Virginia, and landed in northern California by way of Florida. Since 2005 he has headed the Living History Program at San Francisco Maritime National Historical Park in San Francisco. His podcast audiodrama *Sailor On Ice* is available online at www.imaginationlane.net/tomcrean/. Published works include poetry, short stories, and several one-act play including *"Francis and Sophy"*, about the ill-starred romance between Captain Francis Crozier (of the 1845 Franklin expedition) and Sophy Cracroft. He writes from Sky Ranch overlooking the Pacific Ocean, and when not writing he is engaged in the business of green building design.

Made in the USA
Charleston, SC
09 October 2011